THE NEW KNITTING DICTIONARY

1000 STITCHES AND PATTERNS

HOW TO KNIT · TOOLS · YARNS
SYMBOLS · JACQUARD · CABLE
FINISHING

RHODA OCHSER GOLDBERG

CROWN PUBLISHERS, INC.
NEW YORK

This book is lovingly dedicated to my
first teacher, my friend, my Rose
without thorns, my mother

Copyright © 1984 by Rhoda Ochser Goldberg
All rights reserved. No part of this book may be
reproduced or transmitted in any form or by any means,
electronic or mechanical, including photocopying,
recording, or by any information storage and retrieval
system, without permission in writing from
the publisher.
Published by Crown Publishers, Inc., 225 Park Avenue South,
New York, New York 10003 and represented in Canada by the
Canadian MANDA Group
Manufactured in the United States of America
Library of Congress Cataloging-in-Publication Data
Goldberg, Rhoda Ochser.
    The new knitting dictionary.
    Includes index.
    1. Knitting—Handbooks, manuals, etc.   I. Title.
TT820.G66 1984   746.43′2   83-21033
ISBN 0-517-55114-4
Design by Lauren Dong
10 9 8 7

CONTENTS

ACKNOWLEDGMENTS

I gratefully acknowledge the help I received from my many friends and relatives, manufacturers and store owners, who knitted samples, corrected instructions, provided yarns, needles, accessories, and even lessons when my own expertise was lacking.

A special word of gratitude goes to the Suffolk County Chapter of the Embroiderers' Guild of America for allowing me to recruit the main group of knitters from the membership at large. I also thank "The Board" for quietly taking over my duties and giving me the help and encouragement that made this book possible.

I must thank a wonderful lady who started my love affair with a very special machine. She brought us together, taught me to use and appreciate its possibilities, and then had the faith and trust to allow me to evaluate it without her prior approval. Thank you, Helen Deckelman.

This list would be incomplete without a very big thank you to my friend and business partner, Marion Pakula, for giving me my wings and teaching me to fly.

Without Brandt Aymar, my editor, my mentor, this would not have been possible.

Rhoda Ochser Goldberg

Materials and supplies for making the samples were kindly provided by the following companies and stores:

Associated Knitting Machine Co., Inc., Fairfield, New Jersey
(Passap knitting machine and accessories)
Susan Bates, Chester, Connecticut
(knitting needles and accessories, yarns)
Brunswick Yarns, Pickens, South Carolina
(yarns and specialty yarns)
Bucilla Yarns, Secaucus, New Jersey
(yarns and specialty yarns)
Busy Bea, Commack, New York (yarns)
Dal-Craft, Inc., Tucker, Georgia
(Lo Ran magnetic boards and knitting organizer)
Déjà Vu Yarns, Commack, New York
(specialty yarns)
DMC, Elizabeth, New Jersey
(knitting and crochet Perle Coton)
Gemini Innovations Ltd., Huntington Station, New York
(specialty yarns)
Knitting Fever Inc., Roosevelt, New York
(knitting needles and accessories)

Knitting Store, East Northport, New York
(yarns)
Lion Brand Yarn Co., New York, New York
(knitting yarns)
Melrose Yarn Co., Inc., Brooklyn, New York
(yarns and specialty yarns)
Needlegraph, Dix Hills, New York
(graph paper and KnittingGraph paper)
Reynolds Yarns Inc., Hauppauge, New York
(yarns and specialty yarns)
Spinnerin Yarn Company, Inc., South Hackensack, New Jersey
(yarns)
Studio Needlecraft, Huntington Station, New York
(yarns and research material)
Ulltex, Inc., Cambridge, Massachusetts
(knitting and specialty yarns)

The Knitters

Naomi Anselm, Dix Hills, New York
Ann Bellvardo, Brentwood, New York
Florence Booy, Bayshore, New York
Bonnie Braun, Dix Hills, New York
Jean Marie Doelger, Central Islip, New York
Laurie Egger, New York, New York
Alan Goldberg, New York, New York
(photo assistant)
Jacqui Goldberg, Dix Hills, New York
(knitter and model)
Barbara Greenblatt, Dix Hills, New York
(knitter and hands model)
Esther Hinderstein, Sunrise, Florida
Isabelle Hitzig, Brightwaters, New York
Ross Kass, Syosset, New York (photo assistant)

Ruth Kass, Roslyn Heights, New York
Marion Lombardo, Dix Hills, New York
Anita Miller, Cliffside Park, New Jersey
Marianne Pletcher, Huntington, New York
Helen Rosa, Dix Hills, New York
Vivian Schotter, Smithtown, New York
Dorothy Smith, East Northport, New York
Dale Sokolow, Melville, New York
Anne Swenson, Lake Ronkonkoma, New York
Eileen Theobold, West Islip, New York
Sigrid Walther, Middle Island, New York
Kathleen Wolter, Wheatley Heights, New York

INTRODUCTION

Everyone can learn the art of knitting. Basically, it requires a ball of yarn, two needles, some instructions, and a little practice.

The basic techniques are described in this book, along with many of the alternate regional variations from around the world. Although methods and terminology may vary in instructions originating in the United States, England, or Europe, you will find that most of the basics are interchangeable and can be easily adapted to most of your knitting projects.

This book should be used as a reference guide. Look up the name of the technique (listed alphabetically) and you will find the description, alternate regional methods, and photographs or diagrams for each of these technical terms. There are also over 1000 stitches and patterns shown with complete instructions, for you to apply to any basic directions for knitting your own original creations.

Whether you are a beginner or an expert knitter, this is your knitting dictionary, your guide from A to Z.

The Basics

TOOLS AND ACCESSORIES

To learn to knit, you must have a pair of knitting needles and a ball of yarn. There are many other tools and accessories that make the work easier and more pleasurable. Each can simplify the procedures or steps in knitting.

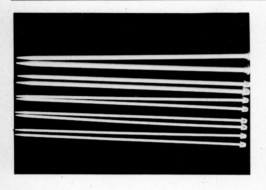

NEEDLES

A knitting needle is basically a rod made of steel, aluminum, wood, plastic, or ivory, with a point at one end and a knob or cap at the other. They are used in pairs and come in 10" and 14" lengths and many different diameters.

The diameter of the rod determines the size, or number, of the needle. The United States uses a sizing system in which the lowest number is the smallest-diameter needle. The English reverse the order, making the highest number the smallest diameter. European countries use metric measurements.

All these different systems may be found in the directions available to the average knitter. The following comparative chart of needle sizes will enable you to substitute one for another without altering the size of your knitted work.

Comparative Needle Size Chart

U.S.	00	0	1	2	3	4	5	6	7	8	9	10	10½	11	12	13	15
English	14	13	12	11	10	9	8	7	6	5	4	3	2	1	0	00	000
Metric	2	2¼	2½	3	3¼	3½	4	4½	5	5½	6	6½	7	7½	8	8½	9

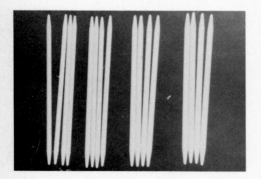

Double-Pointed Needles

Needles that are pointed on both ends are called double-pointed needles. They are available in 7" and 10" lengths and sold in sets of four or five. Double-pointed needles are used for round, or circular, knitting.

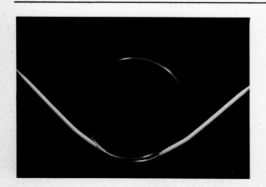

Circular Needles

The circular needle is a flexible plastic or metal wire with a rigid point at each end. It is used for round or seamless knitting and for pieces of flat knitting too large to fit on straight needles, such as an afghan.

Double-pointed and circular needles come in the same sizes as single-pointed needles.

Cable Needles

The cable needle is a short, double-pointed needle used for holding stitches to be knit out of order in cable and Aran knitting patterns. It may have a bend in the center of the needle, to help keep the stitches from slipping off when left in a waiting position. Instructions will call for a cable or double-pointed needle.

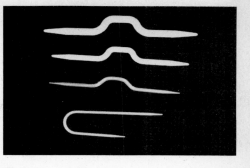

Stitch Holder

This is a bent needle, shaped like a safety pin with a dull point, used to hold stitches that are to be knit later.

ACCESSORIES

Graph Paper

Graph paper is used for charting designs. It is available in many sizes; most useful is the new KnittingGraph paper, with rectangles that are proportional to the knitted stitch, rather than square.

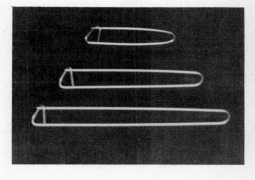

Knitting Counter

A complicated pattern or set of directions may require you to keep track of rows, stitches, increases, and decreases at the same time. This can be accomplished with a pad and pencil or a small plastic counter that slips onto the end of the needle. A printed plastic board is also available with holes and pegs to enable you to keep track of the many procedures done simultaneously in knitting.

Knitting Organizer or Bag

Any plastic or fabric bag can be used to store supplies and keep the knitting clean. The organizer shown in the photo holds needles and accessories in separate compartments for easy access.

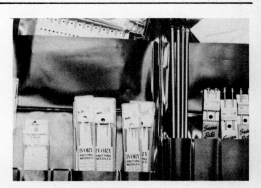

Magnetic Board

This is a most useful aid for the knitter who works with charts or complicated instructions. These boards are available in many sizes, including one that fits the pages of this book exactly.

Markers

A marker can be a piece of contrasting-color yarn tied around the needle or a small plastic ring slipped onto the needle. Markers are especially useful in circular knitting, to keep track of the end of the row.

Needle Case

A needle case is used to store needles when not in use. This can be a simple cardboard tube with a closed end and a cover, or a case with a compartment for each pair of needles. Some manufacturers sell cases that include a matched set of needles. Plain or fancy, this is one accessory that will prove its value the first time you search for the needles left in a bag of yarn and find only one needle, or none.

Needle Gauge

A needle gauge is a thin piece of metal with holes of various diameter, marked in the different sizes of your needles. The knitter often has a varied collection of U.S., English, or metric marked needles and is unable to correctly identify the size of the needle by sight. Double-pointed needles are usually unmarked and very difficult to size without a needle gauge. Many gauges include a ruler, useful for finding stitch and row gauge.

Point Protectors

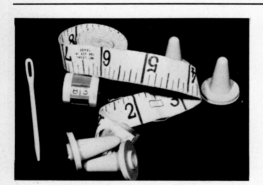

A point protector is a plastic or rubber tip that is slipped onto the point of the needle to keep the stitches from falling off the needle when the piece is not being worked. It will also prevent damage to the needle point.

Ruler and Tape Measure

Measurements have to be made when knitting any garment. All knitting projects are started by knitting a sample for gauge, which must be measured.

Tapestry or Yarn Needle

A needle with a blunt point and a large eye is used to weave together the parts of any project that were knitted separately. This needle is also used for duplicate-stitch embroidery.

Yarn Bobbins

A yarn bobbin, or bob, is a small rectangular plastic piece that is wrapped with yarn. It is used to separate colors and keep them tangle-free when knitting multicolored patterns.

YARNS

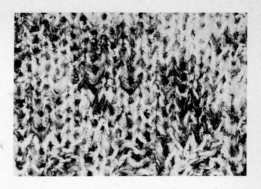

The word *yarn* as used in this book refers to any natural or synthetic fiber that is used for knitting.

In the past, the only yarns acceptable for hand knitting were derived from animals and plants.

NATURAL FIBERS

Wool

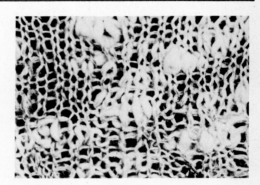

This fiber is the product of sheep shearings. It is still the most popular and well-known yarn, available in all weights and colors. Wool is an absorbent, easy-to-work insulator against heat as well as cold. A piece knitted in wool yarn must be stored carefully to protect it from the ever-present moth and should be dry cleaned or hand-washed in cold water.

Mohair is a wool yarn that comes from the Angora goat. Its light weight, warmth, and soft, fluffy appearance make it one of the more popular yarns.

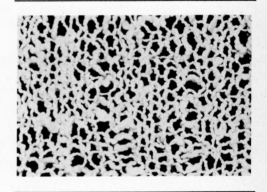

Cashmere yarns are from Himalayan goats. This prestigious yarn is soft, light, warm, and expensive.

Lamb's wool comes from the first shearings of the lamb. These short fibers are sometimes mixed with the longer fibers of other animals.

Alpaca yarn comes from the sheeplike South American relative of the llama. It is a long, silky-textured fiber.

Vicuña is another expensive yarn that comes from a South American ruminant related to the llama. It is light in weight and has a very soft nap.

Camel's hair is a natural-colored fiber known for warmth and a soft texture.

Angora yarn comes from the Angora rabbit. It is a light, fluffy yarn that has a very decorative texture. It sheds easily.

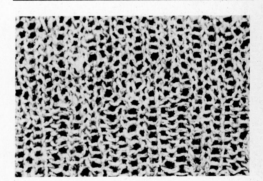

Other Natural Fibers

Linen and cotton are extracted from plant fibers. They are both strong, light, and absorbent.

Silk is a fiber obtained from the cocoon of the Chinese silkworm, *Bombyx mori*. Silk thread has a very high luster, soft texture, and high cost. It is often mixed with other fibers.

Raffia fibers come from palm trees and are used mainly for decorative accessories and beach-related articles.

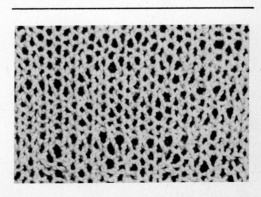

SYNTHETIC FIBERS

Today we have many new laboratory-created fibers to use for knitting. Most of them are the result of petroleum byproducts.

Nylon, polyester, and acrylic yarns resemble the natural fibers in appearance and weight. They often combine a lighter weight with high bulk, are shrink-resistant, and wash well by hand or machine.

Synthetic and natural fibers used in combination are becoming very popular with the knitters of today. These new specialty yarns have the added feature of "self-created" textures and patterns.

Lamé is a general term used to describe natural or synthetic fibers that provide a central core to support a metallic thread, which may also be natural or synthetic. They are made in the metallic gold, silver, and copper tones, as well as many lustrous colors.

Ply

The number of strands combined to make the yarn is called *ply*. Most yarn is made by combining one to four plies. The weight of each ply plus the number of plies determine the weight of the yarn.

Dye Lot

Yarn dyed at the same time will have the same dye-lot number. This number is usually printed on the label. Since it is very difficult to match yarns of different dye lots, buy a little extra yarn when you start any knitting project.

Metric Weight Equivalents

1 ounce	= 28.4 grams	25 grams =	.88 ounce
2 ounces	= 56.8 grams	40 grams =	1.04 ounces
4 ounces	= 113.6 grams	50 grams =	1.76 ounces

Yarn Categories and Corresponding Needle Sizes

Type of Yarn	Ply	Weight	Needle Size
Fingering or baby yarn	3 or 4	Light	0–4
Sport yarn	3 or 4	Medium	1–6
Knitting worsted	4	Heavy	4–10
Bulky yarns	1–4	Very heavy	7–15½
Specialty and novelty yarn	1–4	Any of the above	1–17

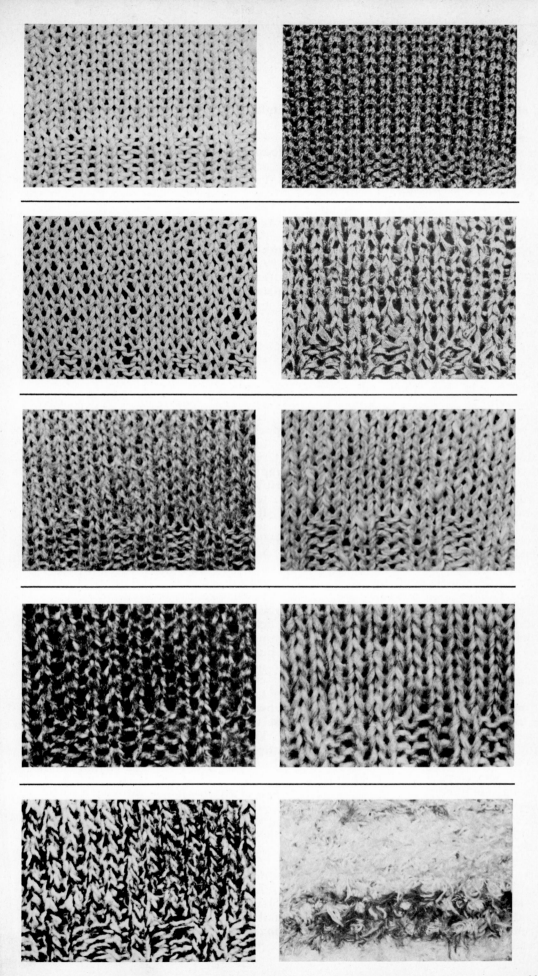

VOCABULARY

arm of stitch   The part of a stitch that joins the next stitch by a linking bar. (See diagram, p. 40.)

asterisk,*   Used in knitting as repeat signs. All instructions between two asterisks are to be repeated. (See p. 12.)

back of work   This is the side of the knitting facing away from the knitter.

bar of stitch   The part of a stitch that joins the arms of the stitch. (See diagram, p. 40.)

binding off   Method of ending the work with a finished selvage, usually at the top of the work. (See p. 15.)

cable needle   See "Tools and Accessories," p. 7.

casting on   Method of starting work. It produces a bottom selvage by putting stitches on the needle in a particular way. (See p. 18.)

circular needle   See "Tools and Accessories," p. 6.

decrease   A method of reducing the number of stitches in the work. (See p. 24.)

double-pointed needles   See "Tools and Accessories," p. 6.

dropped stitch   Intentional, see p. 26. Unintentional, see p. 27.

duplicate stitch   An imitation of a knitted stitch embroidered on the surface of the work.

elongated stitch   An enlarged stitch made by winding the yarn one or more times around the needle while the stitch is being worked. (See p. 43.)

first row   The bottom row, usually worked into cast-on stitches.

flat knitting   Knitting formed by working back and forth on two needles.

front of work   The front side of the work, facing the knitter and meant to be seen.

gauge   See p. 28.

grafting   The English term for weaving. It is the method used to join different pieces of knitted work with a row of imitation knitting. (See p. 46.)

hem   A finished edge. May also be an extra piece worked and turned to the wrong side. (See p. 29.)

increase   A method of adding stitches. (See p. 32.)

joining yarns   See p. 35.

knitting needles   See "Tools and Accessories," p. 6.

knitwise   Insert the needle from the front to the back of the loop of the stitch as if to knit.

left edge   The edge of the work at the knitter's left-hand side when the work is facing the knitter. It is also called the left-hand edge.

linking bar   The bar of yarn that joins one stitch to the next. (See diagram, p. 40.)

loop   The inverted U-shape of yarn around the needle. The front thread is usually called the front loop and the back thread the back loop. (See diagram, p. 40.)

needle (knitting)   See "Tools and Accessories," p. 6.

needle (sewing)   See "Tools and Accessories," p. 8.

over   A shortened form of "yarn over."

pattern: 1. The design or texture formed on a piece of knitting by combining different stitches in a particular sequence. 2. Instructions.

picking up stitches   Method of putting stitches lifted from any selvage on the needle so that knitting can be continued.

ply   One of the strands of yarn twisted together to form yarn.

purlwise   Insert the needle from the back to the front of loop of a stitch as if to purl.

repeat   To be done again.

ribbing   A combination of stitches used to form a stretchy edge on knitted work. It is usually used at the bottom edge, wrists, and neckline.

right edge   The edge of work at the right-hand side when the work is facing the knitter. Also called right-hand edge.

right side of work   The front side of the work, meant to be seen.

round   One row of work done on a circular needle or double-pointed needles.

round knitting   Work done on a circular needle or double-pointed needles. This is a method of producing a seamless, tubular work.

row   A line of stitches.

selvage   Any finished or closed edge of knitting.

slip knot   The knot used as a first stitch in casting on stitches. (See diagram, p. 18.)

slip or slipped stitch   Moving a stitch from one needle to the other without working it.

stitch   A worked loop used in combination to form a knitted fabric. (See diagram, p. 40.)

stitch holder   See "Tools and Accessories," p. 7.

strand   One piece of yarn.

tail of yarn   The end of a strand of yarn.

together   Knitting two or more stitches at the same time, to decrease or to form a pattern.

tubular knitting Knitting, worked on a set of double-pointed needles or on a circular needle, forming a seamless tube.

twist stitches Stitches turned or twisted while being knit.

weaving See "Grafting."

wrong side The back surface of the work, facing away from the knitter, and usually not meant to be seen.

yarn See "Yarns," p. 9.

yarn over A method of adding stitches while knitting. (See p. 47.)

zipper A closure. See p. 48.

HOW TO READ DIRECTIONS AND ABBREVIATIONS

Knitting directions use certain terms and abbreviations. The patterns on the following pages are written in an easy-to-read form. Each stitch or pattern has a name or a number of names, researched by the author. Every effort was made to identify the many alternate names of these patterns and stitches.

TOTAL NUMBER OF STITCHES

The total number of stitches necessary for the pattern to repeat are easy to calculate.

Example A: Multiple of 3
The total number of stitches must be divisible by 3 for an even repeat of the pattern. For example, in a multiple of 3, 30 stitches will form 10 even pattern repeats.
(3 x 10 = 30)

Example B: Multiple of 3 + 2
Some patterns require the addition of a number of stitches for balance. In this example, the total must be divisible by 3, with 2 left over.
(3 x 10 = 30 sts + 2 sts = 32 sts)

Example C: Multiple of 3 + 2 selvage sts
Many patterns require the addition of selvage stitches. (For ways to work them, see p. 38.) Find the correct total, as shown in example A, and add 2 stitches. One stitch is used for the right-edge selvage, the other for the left-edge selvage.
(3 x 10 = 30 + 2 = 32 sts)

REPEATS

Asterisks

Example A: *K1, p1*.
Work knit 1, purl 1 across the row.

Example B: Selv st, *k1, p1*, selv st.
Work 1 selvage stitch, work knit 1, purl 1 across the row, end with 1 selvage stitch.

Example C: Selv st, k1, *k1, p1*, selv st.
Work the first selvage stitch, knit 1 stitch, work knit 1, purl 1 across the row, end by working 1 selvage stitch.

Parentheses

This is a single direction within a general repeat instruction.

Example A: *K3, (p2 tog) 3 times, k2*.
Knit 3 stitches, purl 2 sts together, purl 2 sts together, purl 2 sts together, knit 2 stitches. Repeat everything between the asterisks across the row.

Number of Rows

A pattern or pattern stitch is formed by repeating an exact set of instructions for an exact number of rows. Each row is labeled: Row 1, Row 2, etc. These rows are repeated in a given sequence to the end of the pattern. The last direction in each pattern instructs the knitter to repeat the correct number of rows or the correct choice of rows to work the pattern.

Example A: Repeat these 4 rows for pattern.
Example B: Repeat rows 2–5 for pattern.

ABBREVIATIONS

The instructions for a stitch pattern or garment can become long and complex. To shorten them, a special vocabulary or language and a number of abbreviations have evolved. The following alphabetical list includes terms used in the United Kingdom (UK) and France (Fr) when they differ from those used in the United States.

alt alternately (Fr: alternativement)

b back (UK: back of work)
BC back cross
beg begin
BO bind off
bo bobble
but buttonhole

cab or **cabl** cable
CC contrasting color
ch chain
cm centimeter (metric)
Co cast on
col color
cont continue
Cr cross (Fr: croiser)
Cr L cross to the left
Cr R cross to the right

dbl double
dec or **decr** decrease (Fr: diminution)
diag diagonal
diam diameter
dir directions
dk dark
dpn double-pointed needle(s) (or cable needle)

ext exterior

FC front cross
fin finished
flat knit knitting worked back and forth on two needles
foll following
fr front side; side facing the knitter (Fr: endroit)

gr or **g** gram(s)

in inch
inc or **incr** increase (UK: M1; Fr: augmentation)
incl including

join attach (e.g., join yarn, join rounds)

k knit
k1-b knit 1 in the stitch below the next stitch
kwise knitwise; as if to knit

L left (Fr: gauche)
left at the left edge when the work is facing the knitter
lh left hand
lhn left-hand needle
lp loop (Fr: boucle)
lt light

MB make bobble
MC main color

med medium
mm millimeter(s)

no number

obt obtain
open opening
opp opposite
oz ounce(s)

p purl
p1-b purl 1 in the stitch below the next stitch
pat pattern
pat st pattern stitch
P.U. pick up: to lift stitches from a bound or selvage side to a needle
prec preceding
psso pass slipped stitch over
pwise purlwise; as if to purl

qual quality

r row
rem remain, remaining
rep repeat
rep *to* repeat the directions between the asterisks
rh right hand
rhn right-hand needle
right, rt at the right edge when work is facing the knitter (Fr: droite)
rnd round

selv selvage (Fr: lisière)
selv st selvage stitch
sep separate, separately
sk skip
skp slip 1 stitch, knit 1 stitch, pass slipped stitch over knit stitch
skpo slip 1 stitch, knit 1 stitch, pass slipped stitch over knit stitch
sl slip a stitch without working it (Fr: glisser)
sl st a slipped stitch (Fr: maille coulée)
st stitch(es)

tbl through back of loop (Fr: derrière)
tog together, at the same time (Fr: ensemble)

wl wool
wl bk wool back
wl fwd wool forward
wyib with yarn in back
wyif with yarn in front

yb yarn back (UK: wb, ytb)
yf yarn forward (UK: wf, ytf: Fr: jeté)
yo yarn over (UK: M1, won, wrn; Fr: jeter)
yo dbl wind yarn twice around needle

zip zipper

The Knitting Dictionary "A to Z"

Asterisks and Parentheses

These symbols are used in knitting directions to show a limited repeat of directions within a row or sequence of stitches. See "Vocabulary," p. 12.

Binding Off

After the knitting has been completed, the stitches are bound off, or finished to end the work. (British and European instructions refer to this as casting off.) There are many ways to bind off, depending on the edge desired on the finished piece. As a general rule, always keep the yarn loose when binding off.

Method I (French)

Step 1 K the first 2 st. Pass the 1st st over the 2nd, leaving 1 st on the rh needle.
Step 2 K the next st and pass the st remaining on the rh needle over this st.
Step 3 Rep these steps across the row.
This method can be used to bind off in a purl stitch or in a combination of knit and purl.

Method II (English)

Step 1 K2 tog through back loops (tbl).
Step 2 Pass this st back onto lh needle.
Step 3 Rep steps 1 and 2 across the row.

Method III (Elastic)

Step 1 K the 1st st.
Step 2 K the 2nd st, but do not let it drop off lh needle.
Step 3 Pass the 1st st over the 2nd st on the rh needle.
Step 4 K the next st on lh needle, at the same time letting the bound off st drop. Do not let the 2nd st drop off the lh needle.
Step 5 Rep steps 3 and 4 across the row.
This method works well on necklines, where an elastic edge is preferred.

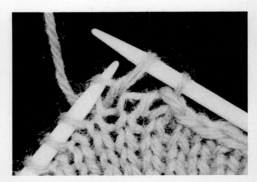

Method IV (Bias)

Step 1 Do not work the last st of the previous row. Keep it on the lh needle. Turn the work to the front side.

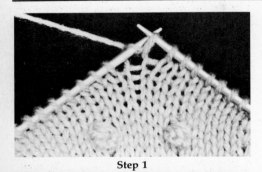

Step 2 Starting with 1 st on the rh needle, sl the first st from the lh needle pwise.

Step 3 Pass the 1st st over the 2nd st on the rh needle.

Step 4 Bind off the other sts in one of the methods already shown.

Bobble (Nope)

A bobble is made by knitting several times in sequence into the same stitch.

Step 1

Step 1 Insert the tip of the rh needle into the next st on the lh needle as if to k. Wrap the yarn over the rh needle and draw through a loop.

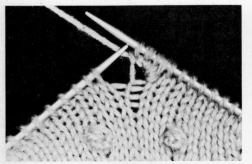

Step 2

Step 2 Sl this st back onto the lh needle and k it in the usual way.

Step 3 Rep this until you have 4 sts on the rh needle. Drop the original st from the lh needle.

Step 4 In sequence, sl the 3rd, 2nd, and 1st sts over the 4th st, leaving 1 st on the rh needle.

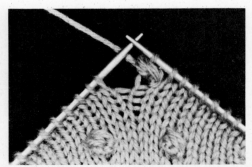

Step 3

Step 4

Borders

See "Hems and Borders," p. 29.

Buttonhole

The buttonhole is the most popular form of closure used in knitting. It can be worked with a sewing machine on the finished garment, or simply knit in while the work is in progress. Traditionally, buttonholes are placed on the left side of the garment for a female and on the right for a male.

Simple Eyelet Buttonhole
(Layette Buttonhole, Laced Buttonhole)

This buttonhole is usually used for baby or layette garments and items that will be laced with a small cord or ribbon.

Row 1 (right side): Work to the beginning of the hole. Make a yo, k2 tog, work in pattern to the end of the row.
Row 2: P all sts, including the yo.
Repeat these 2 rows for each buttonhole. Sew or embroider around the finished buttonhole for added strength.

Eyelet Buttonhole
(Alternate Method)

This method is neater and requires no additional finishing or embroidery.

Row 1 (right side): Work to the beginning of the buttonhole. Make a yo, then continue in pattern to the end of the row.
Row 2: Work to the yo, sl the yo (pwise), make another yo.
Row 3: Sl 1 st kwise (before the 2 yo), k tog the 2 yo, leaving them on the lh needle. Pass the sl st over the k st on the rh needle. K tog the 2 yos and the next st.
Row 4: P across the buttonhole sts.

Step 1

Step 2

Step 3

Horizontal Buttonhole
(Slit Buttonhole)

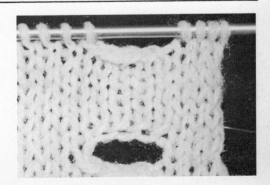

The horizontal buttonhole is used in making the closure on most knitted garments. To determine the number of stitches needed for the buttonhole, put the button on the knitted piece and count the number of stitches covered by its diameter. Do not work any more stitches than this, or the tight fit required for a neat appearance will be lost.

Row 1: Work to the beginning of the buttonhole. Bind off the required number of sts. Work in pattern to the end of the row.

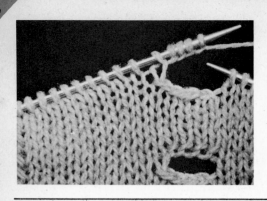

Row 2: Work in pattern until you reach the first st bound off in the previous row. Cast on the same number of sts as were bound off. Work in pattern to the end of the row.

Repeat these 2 rows for each buttonhole. Remember to work in a few stitches from the border, to allow for the tension of the button pulling against the buttonhole. The button rests at the edge of the buttonhole closest to the border.

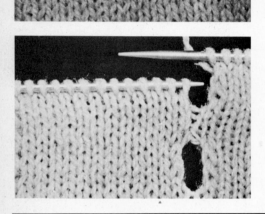

Vertical Buttonhole

Measure the number of rows to be covered by the button, to determine the height of the opening. The button will rest in the center of the slit.

At the base of the slit, join a second ball of yarn. Work each side separately for the required number of rows. Join both halves by working across both sets of stitches with one ball of yarn.

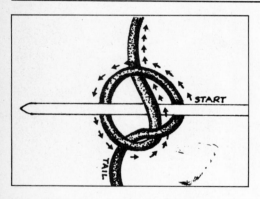

Casting On

Slip Knot

To begin the casting-on process, a loop or slip knot is the usual choice.

Follow the direction of the arrow in the diagram. Begin by placing a loop of yarn in back of the needle. Wrap the loose end of the yarn over, then under the tail end, over the needle, and through the loop. Pull the two yarn ends down. This will close the loop around the needle, forming the first stitch.

The base row of loops put on the knitting needle are called the cast-on stitches. The first row of the pattern is worked into these stitches. Any of the following methods can be used.

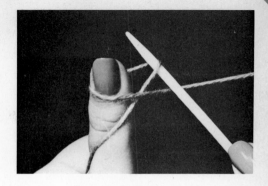

Simple Loop Casting On

Step 1 Put a slip knot on the rh needle. (See diagram, p. 18.)

Step 2 Wrap the yarn (clockwise—from front to back) around the lh thumb.

Step 3 Insert the needle in the front loop of the yarn around the thumb.

Step 4 Transfer the loop to the rh needle. Pull the yarn end to close the loop around the needle.

Repeat steps 2–4 to cast on each stitch. This method is the easiest to learn but produces a loose edge.

Reverse Simple Loop Casting On

Step 1 Put a slip knot on the rh needle.

Step 2 Wrap the yarn around the rh thumb.

Step 3 Insert the needle in the front loop of the yarn around the thumb.

Step 4 Transfer the loop to the lh needle. Pull the yarn end to close the loop around the needle.

Repeat steps 2–4 to cast on each stitch. When the required number of stitches have been cast on, turn the needle with the point to the right side. The finished edge will face the front.

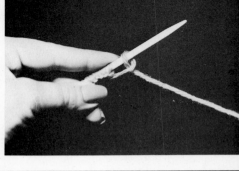

Hint: If you find that the tension in the cast-on row is too tight to knit the first row, use a pair of needles one size smaller than the size called for in the knitting instructions. Hold them together in a parallel position and cast the stitches onto both needles together. Carefully remove one needle before knitting the first row with the regular size needle. This will enlarge the stitches and produce a more elastic edge.

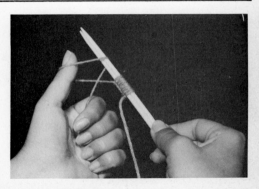

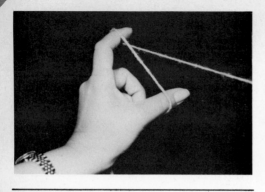

Slip Knot Cast On (Single-Needle Cast On—Italian Method)

Step 1 Measure out a piece of yarn approximately three times the length of the final finished width of the cast-on row.

Step 2 The right hand holds the needle and the yarn coming from the ball. The left hand holds the tail of the yarn passed over the thumb and index finger.

Step 3 Holding the yarn in this position, turn the left hand to cross the yarn from the thumb over the yarn from the index finger. This forms a loop.

Step 4 Insert the point of the needle in the loop, passing it in front of the yarn, over the thumb, and behind the yarn held over the rh index finger.

Step 5 Draw the loop on the index finger downward, then wrap the yarn in the right hand under and then over the needle.

(Photo 52)

Step 6 Lift the loop over the needle and the yarn wrapped around the needle. Pull the tail of the yarn gently until the stitch is closed around the needle.

Repeat steps 2–6 to cast on each stitch. This is also an alternate way to cast on the first stitch in any of the methods of casting on given.

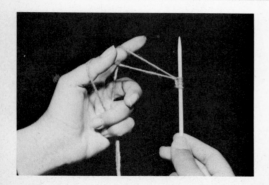

Single-Needle Thumb Casting On (English Thumb Method)

This is the most popular method used in the United States. It is easy to do and produces a neat, elastic edge.

Step 1 Measure out a piece of yarn approximately three times the length of the final finished width of the cast-on row.

Step 2 Holding the tail of the yarn in the left hand, wind the yarn once clockwise around the lh thumb, forming a loop.

Step 3 Insert the point of the needle in the loop. Wrap the yarn from the ball end around the needle, drawing the yarn through the loop as if to knit a stitch.

Step 4 Pull the yarn ends gently to tighten the stitch around the needle.

Repeat steps 2–4 for each cast-on stitch.

Step 2

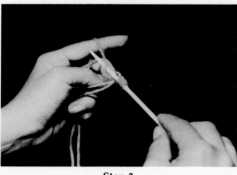

Step 3

Step 4

Two-Needle Casting On
(Knitted Casting On, French Method)

Step 1 Make a slip knot.

Step 2 Insert the rh needle in the loop of the knot and k a stitch.

Step 3 Sl the new loop onto the lh needle and tighten by pulling gently on the yarn ends. This becomes the second stitch.

Repeat steps 2 and 3 for each cast-on stitch.

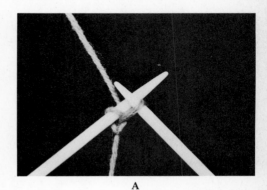

A

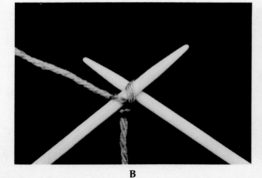

B

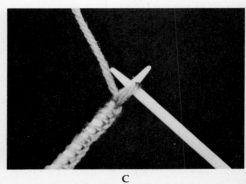

C

21

A

B   C

Two-Needle Knitted Casting On
(English Cable Method)

Step 1 Make a slip knot.
Step 2 Repeat steps 2 and 3, above.
Step 3 Insert the rh needle between the 2 sts on the lh
needle. Wind the yarn around this needle and
pull it forward as if to knit.
Step 4 Put this loop on the lh needle as the next st.
Repeat steps 3 and 4 for each cast-on stitch.

Casting On—Four- or Five-Needle Knitting

Any of the previous methods can be used to cast on
with 4 or more needles. To avoid loose stitches, keep
moving a few stitches onto the next needle when
working the rounds.

Corner

Squared Garter Stitch Corner
(Garter Stitch Corner)

Any reversible stitch can be interchanged with garter
stitch to produce this type of corner, so long as it will
give a sharp contrast to the stitch used in the body of
the work. In this sample, stockinette stitch is used for
the body of the work and garter stitch for the horizontal
and vertical bands.

The height of the horizontal band must be the same as
the width of the vertical band. When using garter stitch,
this is easily produced by working the same number of
stitches in the vertical band as there are ridges on the
right side of the horizontal band. In this sample there
are 6 stitches in the vertical band and 6 ridges in the
horizontal band.

MITERED CORNERS

A   Garter Stitch

This mitered corner is worked from the inside
outward on 11 stitches, using the center stitch as the
axis of the corner angle.

Row 1 (right side): K5, inc 1 [k the horizontal bar before
the next st], k1, inc 1, k5.
Row 2: K to the center axis, p1, k to end of row.
Row 3: K6, inc 1, k1, inc 1, k6.
Continue in this progression until the desired width is
reached. Bind off.

B Eyelet Corner (Openwork Corner)

The eyelet corner is worked on 11 stitches, using the center stitch as the axis of the angle. It is knitted from the inside outward.

Row 1 (right side): K5, yo, k1, yo, k5.
Row 2: K to axis st, p1, k to end.
Row 3: K6, yo, k1, yo, k6.
Continue in this progression until the desired width is reached. Bind off.

C Single Angle-Line Knit Mitered Corner

Row 1 (right side): K5, inc 1 [k the hor bar before the next st], k1, inc 1, k5.
Row 2: P.
Row 3: K6, inc 1, k1, inc 1, k6.
Continue in this progression until the desired width is reached. Bind off.

D Double Angle-Line Knit Mitered Corner (Knit Mitre Corner)

This knitted mitered corner is worked from the inside outward on 11 stitches, using the center stitch as the axis for the angle.

Row 1 (right side): K4, inc 1 [k into the next st of the previous row], k3, inc 1 [k into the st below the last worked st], k4.
Row 2: P.
Row 3: K5, inc 1, k3, inc 1, k5.
Continue in this progression until the desired width is reached. Bind off.

Turned Corner

Work on the number of stitches needed to produce the desired width. This example was worked on 10 stitches.

Row 1: K10.
Row 2: P9, *sl 1 pwise, yb, put sl st on lh needle, turn*.
Row 3: *Yb, pass yarn around sl st*, k9.
Row 4: P8, rep *to* in row 2.
Row 5: Rep *to* in row 3, k8.
Continue in this progression until:
Row 19: K1.
Row 20: P2, turn.
Row 21: K2.
Row 22: P3, turn.
Continue in this progression, working 1 more stitch on every purl row, until all 10 stitches are on the rh needle. Work in stockinette stitch until you reach the next corner.

Decreasing

A decrease is the reduction of a stitch or a number of stitches spaced across a row. The general rule is to follow the decrease row with a plain row, or decrease every other row.

The following examples show some of the different methods for decreasing a stitch in hand knitting.

SINGLE DECREASE (SIMPLE DECREASE, DEC)—RIGHT SIDE

Method I

Sl 1 st as if to k, k the next st, pass the sl st over the k st to the left.

Method II

Sl 2 sts to rh needle. Wind the yarn around the needle as if to k and pass both sts over the yarn and off the needle. This method makes the sl st the same size as the rest of the work.

Method III

K 2 tog tbl. This twists the sts, giving a small raised look to the decrease.

Method IV

This is the easiest and most well-known method for decreasing a stitch. K2 tog in the usual way. The sts will slant to the right.

SINGLE DECREASE—WRONG SIDE

Method I

Sl the last-worked st from the rh needle to the lh needle. Pass the 2nd st on the lh needle over the 1st st. Put this st back on the rh needle. The decrease will slant to the left on the reverse side.

Method II

P 2 tog. The decrease will slant to the right on the reverse side.

DOUBLE DECREASE—RIGHT SIDE

A double decrease reduces by 2 stitches at a time. The following methods are used in V necklines, lace, chevron, and openwork patterns. Each creates a similar decorative effect.

Method I

K3 tog tbl. The decrease will slant to the left.

Method II

K3 tog. The decrease will slant to the right.

MITERED DECREASE—RIGHT SIDE

Method I

Sl 1 st, k2 tog, pass the sl st over the st made by the k2 tog. The remaining st is the center or axis for the double decrease. You may find this decrease abbreviated as "sktpo." The decrease will slant to the left.

Method II

Sl 1 kwise, k1. Pass the sl st over the k st. Put this st back on the lh needle and pass the next st over. Put the st back on the rh needle. The decrease will slant to the right.

Method III

Sl the 1st 2 sts, k1, pass the 2 sl st over the k st. The decrease will form a straight line. This method is also known as a vertical double decrease.

MITERED DECREASE—WRONG SIDE

Method I

P2 tog. This st is now the center or axis st. Sl it back onto the lh needle. Pass the next st on the lh needle over the 1st st and put it back on the rh needle. The decrease will slant to the left on the right side.

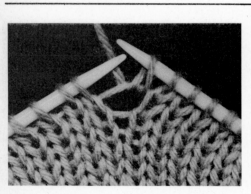

Method II

Sl 1 pwise, k1. This is the center or axis st. Twist the next st and leave it on the lh needle. Sl the axis st onto the lh needle and pass the twisted st over it. Put the axis st on the rh needle and pass the sl st over. The decrease will slant to the right on the right side.

Dropped Stitches

Intentionally Dropped Stitch

A stitch can be dropped intentionally to make a ladder that stops at a predetermined place.

Step 1 Determine the place in your work where you want the ladder to stop. At this place, k into the horizontal bar of yarn between 2 sts (inset increase).

Step 2 Work in pattern until you reach the point where the dropped st will start.

Step 3 Let the st drop from the lh needle and unravel by itself until it reaches the stop point determined in step 1. The ladder will stop here.

Step 4 Continue to work across the row.

Unintentionally Dropped Stitch

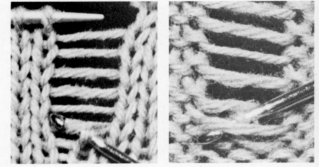

Accidents do happen in knitting. It is easy to pick up and reknit a dropped stitch, but it must be done carefully to avoid twisting the stitches. First make sure that the stitch is put in the proper position—at the front of the work if it is a knit stitch, at the back of the work if it is a purl stitch.

Lay the work on a flat surface. There will be a loose dropped stitch at the bottom and a ladder of yarn progressing up in a line to the needle. Insert a crochet hook in the dropped loop at the bottom and carefully pull the first bar through the loop to the front. Repeat for each bar of the ladder until you reach the needle. Put the last loop on the needle.

Elastic Thread

A thin piece of elastic thread can be knitted into the piece as you work. This is particularly valuable in socks and waistbands. Remember to hold the elastic at the back of the work so that it does not show on the right side. This thread can also be stitched through the finished work with a tapestry needle or crochet hook.

Gathering

Method I

The easiest way to work gathers on a knitted piece is to increase or decrease stitches evenly across a row. The rule is to increase or decrease a third to half the original number of stitches. This method is often used at a waist, wrist, or sleeve.

Method II

Alternately, simply change from the size needle you are using to the smallest size needle that can be knitted with your yarn. The pattern will continue on a smaller scale through the gathered area, since there is no change in the number of stitches. This method produces a more delicate and less gathered effect than does method I.

Gauge

Knitting instructions always give a gauge, or number of stitches and rows in 1" of work done with a particular yarn and needle size.

It is necessary to knit a sample square of at least 4" before you begin to knit the project.

To start, multiply the number of stitches per inch given in the instructions by four. Cast this number of stitches onto the size needle suggested. Use the yarn chosen for the project. Work 4" in pattern and bind off.

Pin the sample to a flat surface and measure a 3" square in the center. Mark your measure on all four sides with pins. Count the number of stitches and rows between the pins to see if the gauge is correct. It is essential to have an exact count. A difference of even ½ stitch per inch too many or too few will make a much larger or smaller overall measurement of the finished piece. If the sample has too many stitches or rows per inch, change to larger needles. If the sample has too few stitches per inch, change to smaller needles. When the sample matches the gauge given in your directions, the needle size is correct.

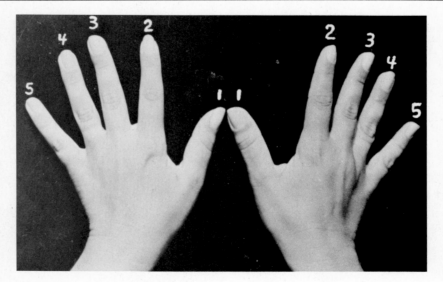

Hands

Your hands and fingers hold both the yarn and needles in knitting. In this book, the instructions use the following terminology to designate each finger: 1—Thumb. 2—Index finger. 3—Middle finger. 4—Ring finger. 5—Little finger.

Hems and Borders

A hem is used to neatly finish and give firmness to the lower edge of a garment. It is usually sewn onto the knitted garment, whereas a border is knitted on at the beginning of the work. A border will keep the edge from rolling when the piece is worked in stockinette or a similar stitch.

Stockinette Stitch Hem

Knit the desired depth of the hem in stockinette stitch, then knit 1 row on the wrong (purl) side, to mark the folding edge of the hem. Continue by working the same number of rows in stockinette stitch as you knitted before the folding edge. You can now choose to fold the hem to the back and catch the cast-on edge in the next row of knitting, or wait until the hem is finished (bound off) and sew it 1 stitch at a time to the wrong side of the work.

Picot Edge Hem

This hem is usually used on baby or layette items or as a decorative finish on the edges of lightweight sweaters and evening wear.

Work as many rows of stockinette stitch as are needed for the depth of the hem, then make the picot as follows:

Row 1: K1, *k2 tog*, rep *to* across the row.
Row 2: *P1, yo*, rep *to* across the row.

Continue in stockinette stitch, working the same number of rows as before picot rows 1 and 2. Fold the hem to the back on the picot rows. This will give a serrated or picot look to the bottom edge of the work. To finish, sew the cast-on edge to the wrong side.

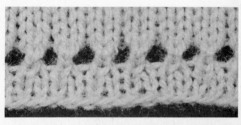

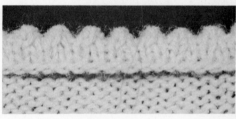

Scallop Hem

Follow the directions for the picot hem until you are ready to begin the picot rows. Then continue as follows:

Row 1: K1, *k2 tog, k2*, rep *to* across the row.
Row 2: P1, *yo, p2*, rep *to*, end row, p1.

Continue to knit in stockinette stitch and finish as for picot hem. Note: You can elongate the scallop by knitting 3 to 5 stitches between the eyelets in row 1 and purling them in row 2.

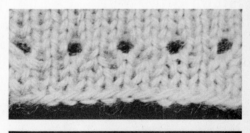

Elastic Hem (for Ribbing)

Using a knitting needle two sizes larger than the needles to be used for the ribbing, cast on half the required number of stitches plus 1. For example, if 50 sts are to be worked on size 1 needles, cast on 26 sts (25 + 1) on size 3 needles.

Step 1 Using the larger needles, work 5 rows in stockinette stitch, beginning with a p row.

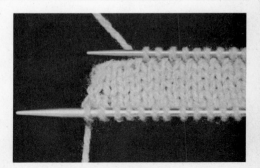

Step 2 Leave these sts on the larger needles. Using the smaller needles, pick up and k the cast-on sts.

Step 3 Fold the work in half with the needles parallel and the knit side facing out.

Step 4 Using the second smaller needle, *p1 from back needle, k1 from front needle*, rep *to*, alternating from the back to front needle across the row.

Step 5 Continue working with the smaller needles in 1 + 1 ribbing.

A channel has been formed in this tubular hem. This can be used to hold elastic and is ideal for waist and cuff hems.

Vertical-Facing Hem

The vertical-facing hem is best used as a border or facing on heavy garments and outerwear.

Pick up and knit the selvage stitches. Continue as for the horizontal hem.

Holding the Yarn

The position of the yarn and needles will control the tension or regularity of the stitches in your work. It is essential to hold your hands in a comfortable position, to avoid strain and achieve an even tension in the work.

Method I (English)

Step 1 Wrap the yarn around the little finger of the right hand, over the back of the next three fingers, and over the index finger.

Step 2 The rh needle is held between the thumb and middle finger. The index finger of the left hand pushes the loops forward on the lh needle as you work.

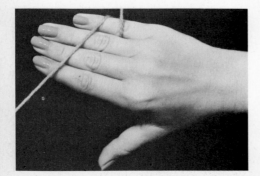

Method II (French, western European)

Step 1 Lay the yarn between the little finger and the ring finger, around the little finger, and over the back of the right hand.

Step 2 The index finger guides the yarn; the middle, ring, and little fingers hold the needle against the thumb.

Step 3 Use the tip of the rh index finger to pass the yarn around the needle for each stitch.

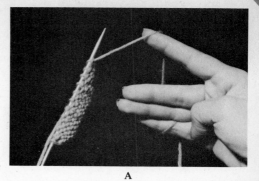

A

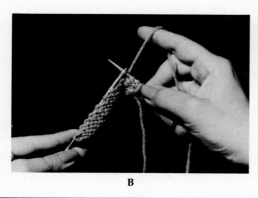

B

C

Method III (Eastern European, Swiss)

This method and several variations are used in the Central and Eastern European countries.

Step 1 Lay the yarn between the ring and little fingers of the left hand.

Step 2 Pass the yarn over the palm side of the ring and middle fingers, over the back, and around the index finger.

Step 3 The rh needle is held between the thumb and index finger and against the middle finger. The left hand is used to carry the yarn around the rh needle when knitting a stitch.

Increase

Deliberately making an extra stitch is called an increase. Methods of increasing 1 stitch are called single or simple increases. They are usually made on alternate, right-side rows. Double or multiple increases are made the same way but are separated by a central or axis stitch. The full-fashioned increase is used when a decorative effect is desired on the front side of the work.

SINGLE INCREASES (Simple Increase, Inc)

Single Barred Increase

Knit 1 stitch, but do not let it drop from the needle. Knit into the same stitch tbl, letting the stitch drop from the lh needle. A small horizontal bar is formed, creating a decorative effect when repeated in a line of even increases. This bar gives the name to the increase.

Full-Fashioned Single Barred Increase

The full-fashioned effect is produced by making the single barred increase on both the left and right sides of the knitted piece. Make the first increase in the 3rd stitch from the right side, and in the 4th stitch from the end of the row on the left side.

Single Beaded Increase

Knit 1 stitch, but do not let it drop from the needle. Put the yarn in a forward position and purl into the stitch; put the yarn back and continue in pattern. This method leaves a purled stitch and a small eyelet or hole.

Full-Fashioned Single Beaded Increase

The full-fashioned effect is produced by making a single beaded increase on both sides of the work. Begin the first increase in the 3rd stitch from the right side and in the 3rd stitch from the end of the row for the left side. On the left-side increase, reverse the order by purling into the stitch first, then knitting it.

Single Raised Increase

Using the rh needle, lift the loop from the last row behind the next stitch to be knitted. Knit this loop in the usual way. On a left-side increase, knit the stitch and then knit the lifted loop.

Full-Fashioned Single Raised Increase

This increase is often called the invisible increase, because it is the least noticeable method of increasing used. For a full-fashioned effect, start the increase under the 3rd stitch on the right side and under the 3rd stitch before the end of the row on the left side, after knitting this 3rd stitch.

Single Center-Line Increase

Knit 1 stitch into the stitch of the last row, then into the stitch to be knitted.

Full-Fashioned Center-Line Increase

On the right side, make the increase below the 3rd stitch from the beginning of the row after you first knit the stitch, and below the 3rd stitch on the left side before you knit the stitch.

Single Inset Increase

Using the lh needle, lift the horizontal bar or thread between two stitches. Twist the thread and knit 1 stitch into it. This method of increasing leaves no hole.

Full-Fashioned Single Inset Increase

For the full-fashioned effect, make the first increase on the horizontal bar after the 3rd stitch from the beginning of the row on the rh side and before the 3rd stitch from the end of the row on the left side of the work.

Single Eyelet Increase

This method is also known as an openwork increase. The decorative effect is often combined with lace patterns and used for infant or baby garments. The increase is made with a single yarn-over, which is knitted or purled on the next row in the usual way.

Full-Fashioned Single Eyelet Increase

On the rh side, make the yarn-over after the 3rd stitch from the beginning of the row, and on the lh side before the 3rd stitch from the end of the row.

DOUBLE INCREASES

Double Beaded Increase

This increase is worked on the three center stitches. Knit 1 then purl 1 into the 1st stitch, knit the 2nd stitch (also called the axis stitch), knit and purl into the 3rd stitch. Purl across the next row. All future increases are made in the stitches before and after the axis stitch.

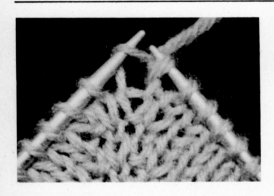

Double Barred Increase

First determine the center or axis stitch. Knit 1 into the front and back of the stitch before the axis stitch. Repeat this in the axis stitch. Purl across the next row. Make all future increases in the axis stitch and the stitch before it.

Double Center-Line Increase

Knit the first of the three stitches chosen for the increase. Next knit 1 into the row below the 2nd (axis) stitch and then knit 1 into the axis stitch. Knit 1 into the stitch below the 3rd stitch, and finally knit 1 in the 3rd stitch.

Double Inset Increase

First determine the stitch to be the center or axis stitch. Using the lh needle, lift the horizontal bar before the axis stitch. Twist this thread and knit 1 into it. Knit the axis stitch. Next lift the bar between the axis and the next stitch. Twist and then knit it.

Double Eyelet Increase

First determine the center of axis stitch. Yo before the axis stitch, knit the axis stitch, and yo after the axis stitch. Purl across the next row.

Joining Yarn

When you have finished a ball of yarn and have to start a new ball, the method of finishing off the first and adding the second is called joining.

Method I

Do not make a knot in the middle of a row. If you have miscalculated the length of yarn left for working and run out in the middle of a row, rip back to the start of the row. Take the yarn coming from the needle end and gently twist it together with the new yarn to be started. Work a few stitches with both ends, then continue to knit using only the new strand.

Method II

If you have no choice and must join a new strand of yarn in the middle of a row, do not make a knot. The best method known in this situation is splicing. Start by unraveling about 2" from both the yarn on the work and the new yarn to be attached. Then twist one end of each together to form a single strand of yarn equal to the thickness of the original yarn. If you are using three-ply yarn, use one strand from one end and two strands from the other. Knit a few stitches, leaving the extra strands of yarn at the back of the work for weaving later. Continue to knit from the new ball of yarn.
Note: It takes a length of yarn approximately three times as long as the measurement to be knitted. If you

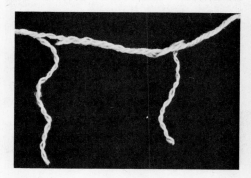

have 5" left to knit on a row, you will need about 15" of yarn to complete the row. Always add an inch or two to this measurement for safety.

Knitting (Flat)

This term describes knitting worked from right to left on two needles. The piece is turned at the end of each row, with the knitter working one row on the right side and one row on the wrong side.

Knitting (Round)

In round knitting, the stitches are cast on using three or four double-pointed needles and worked with one more needle, producing a seamless, tubular piece of work. You work only on the right side and have no seams or selvages. Larger pieces are usually worked on a single circular needle. The advantages are obvious when working socks, necklines, and turtleneck collars. A round equals a row in flat knitting.

To knit in the round:
Step 1 Cast on the required number of stitches. Divide the stitches equally onto three or four needles.

Step 2 Use the extra needle to knit the stitches from the first needle. Now take the first needle and use it to knit the stitches from the second needle. Continue in this manner.

The tail of yarn from the cast-on row marks the beginning of the round. If many rounds are to be worked or if a pattern requires a stitch count, use a marker.

Most stitches can be worked in the round if you remember that the number of stitches must be divisible by the number of stitches needed for the pattern. Jacquard patterns are especially suited to round knitting, since all the stitches are worked in stockinette and the yarn is easily carried at the back of the work. All charts are read and worked from right to left only.

Samples of round knitting and pattern instructions begin on p. 135.

Knitting Stitches Together

This term is used to describe the methods used in making a simple or single decrease by working 2 stitches together.

Simple or Single (K2 Tog)

Step 1 Insert rh needle into the 1st and 2nd loops on the lh needle at the same time.
Step 2 Draw the yarn through both loops together. The decrease st will slant to the left.

Double

Step 1 Sl the 1st st (kwise).
Step 2 K the next 2 sts together (as for a single decrease).
Step 3 Pass the sl st (1st st) over the st made in step 2. The decrease will slant to the left.

Knitting Again (K2 Tog, K 1st St Again)

Step 1 K the 1st 2 sts together; do not let them drop from the lh needle.
Step 2 Insert the rh needle in the 1st st and k it in the usual way.
Step 3 Let both sts drop from the lh needle together. Two loops will be left on the rh needle.

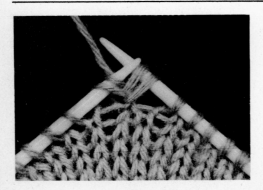

Pockets

Pockets are used both as decorative and functional additions to knitted garments. They can be knitted separately and sewn onto the finished garment or knitted at the same time as the garment.

APPLIQUÉD POCKETS (Patch Pockets)

Knitted in Stockinette Stitch

Step 1 Cast on the number of sts necessary to obtain the width of the finished pocket less 4 sts (to reduce the bulk when folding the lower edge to the back for appliqué finishing).

Step 2 Work in stockinette, increasing 1 st at each side on the 1st 4 k rows. Continue to work in stockinette until you reach the edge of the border.

Step 3 Change to needles one size larger. Work in k1, p1 ribbing for the length of the pocket. Bind off loosely.

Step 4 Fold the lower and side edges of the pocket to the back. Pin the pocket in place on the garment and appliqué, using a slipstitch around the three folded edges. Optional: Topstitch for a decorative effect.

Knitted in a Reversible Stitch (Garter, Moss, Rib, etc.)

Step 1 Cast on the number of sts necessary to obtain the width of the finished pocket.

Step 2 Work in pattern for the length of the pocket. Bind off loosely.

Step 3 Pin the pocket in place on the garment and slipstitch around the three outer edges. For a neater finish, sew the slipstitch 1 st from the outer edges of the pocket. For a decorative effect, topstitch.

KNITTED-ON POCKET

This pocket is worked on stitches picked up and knitted onto the face of the garment. It makes a very strong bottom edge and cannot rip from hard use.

Step 1 Using a needle one size smaller than the needle used for the body of the garment, pick up the number of sts required for the finished pocket size. Be exact in your measurements, as this pocket is permanently attached and cannot be moved.

Step 2 On the 1st row, add 2 sts to each side, to fold under later when finishing the pocket.

Step 3 Work in stockinette until you reach the edge for the border.

Step 4 Change to the needle size used for the body of the garment. Work k1, p1 ribbing until the finished length of the pocket is reached. Bind off loosely.

Step 5 Fold the side edges to the back and pin the pocket to the garment. Slipstitch the two sides in place.

Selvage

The knitted selvage is defined as the finished edge stitches on your work. The first and last stitches in a row are the selvage stitches.

CHAIN SELVAGE

This type of selvage forms a neat chainlike stitch that covers 2 rows to each stitch. The larger stitch formed is particularly useful when stitches are to be picked up along the selvage and worked at a later time.

Method I (French)

Row 1 (right side): Sl the 1st st kwise, work in pattern to the end of the row, k the last stitch.
Row 2: Sl the 1st st pwise, work in pattern to the end of the row, p the last stitch.

Method II (English)

Row 1 (right side): Sl the 1st st kwise, work in pattern to the end of the row, sl the last stitch.
Row 2: The yarn is now between the 1st and 2nd sts. P the 1st st, work in pattern to the end of the row, p the last st.

Method III (Inlaid Pattern)

Row 1 (right side): Sl the 1st st, p the next st, work in pattern to the last 2 sts, p the next st, sl the last st kwise.
Row 2: P.

Method IV (Garter Stitch Chain)

All rows: Yarn forward, sl the 1st st pwise, yarn back, k to the end of the row.

MOSS STITCH SELVAGE

This is the first selvage method learned by most knitters. It makes a flat seam.
All rows: K the 1st and last sts of each row.

SINGLE GARTER STITCH SELVAGE (Simple Garter Selvage)

This is another simple selvage method used by most beginning knitters. It is used when stitches will not be picked up later.

All rows: Sl the 1st st kwise, work in pattern across the row, k the last st.

DOUBLE GARTER STITCH SELVAGE

This method produces a firm, decorative selvage.
All rows: Yarn back, sl the 1st st, k the 2nd, work in pattern to the last 2 sts, k2.

PICOT SELVAGE

Row 1 (right side): Yo, k2 tog, k to end of row.
Row 2: Yo, p2 tog, p to end of row.
   On both rows, the yarn-over compensates for the knit or purl 2 together.

Stitches

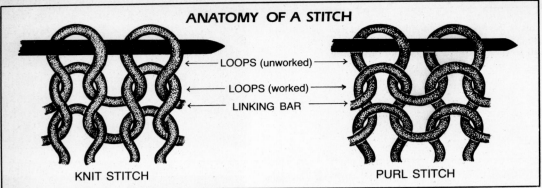

ANATOMY OF A STITCH

← LOOPS (unworked) →

← LOOPS (worked) →

LINKING BAR →

KNIT STITCH

PURL STITCH

Knit Stitch (Plain Stitch)

Step 1 The yarn is at the back of the work when knitting a plain or knit st.

Step 2 Put the point of the rh needle into the front of the st loop on the lh needle from left to right.

Step 3

Step 3 Place the yarn under and over the rh needle.

Step 4 Pull the yarn through the loop to the front.

Step 5 Sl the st off the lh needle.

Repeat steps 1–5 to knit a stitch.

Step 4

Step 5

Purl Stitch

Step 1 The yarn is at the front of the work.

Step 2 Put the point of the rh needle into the front of the st loop on the lh needle from right to left.

Step 3 Place the yarn over and around the rh needle.
Step 4 Draw the yarn back through the loop with the rh needle.
Step 5 Sl the st off the lh needle.
Repeat steps 1–5 to purl a stitch.

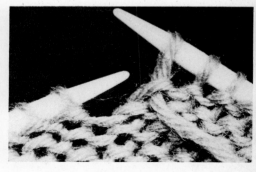

Purl a Knit Stitch

Step 1 The yarn is at the back of the work. Put it in front.
Step 2 Put the point of the rh needle into the front loop of the st on the lh needle from right to left.
Step 3 Continue from step 3 in p st directions.

Knit a Purl Stitch

Step 1 The yarn is at the front of the work. Put it in back of the work.
Step 2 Put the point of the rh needle into the front loop of the st on the lh needle from left to right.
Step 3 Continue from step 3 in k st directions.

CROSSED STITCHES

Crossed stitches are used in simple cable stitches that do not require a double-pointed or cable needle and in many decorative pattern stitches. These stitches can be crossed to the left or right, depending on the effect desired. Many directions refer to this as Cr 2 L or Cr 2 R.

Cross 2 Left
(On the Right Side of the Work)

On Knit Row

Step 1 Put the rh needle in back of the 1st st and into the front loop of the 2nd st.

Step 2 K this st without letting it drop from the lh
      needle.

Step 3 K the 1st st, letting both sts drop from the lh
      needle together.

On Purl Row

Step 1 Sl 2 sts to the rh needle pwise.

Step 2 Put the lh needle into the 1st sl st, then the 2nd,
      slipping both sts back onto the lh needle. These
      sts are now crossed.

Step 3 P each of the sts in the usual way.

Cross 2 Right
(On the Right Side of the Work)
On Knit Row

Step 1 Pass in front of the 1st st on the lh needle and k
      the 2nd st. Do not let the st drop off the lh
      needle.

Step 2 K the 1st st, letting both sts drop off the lh
      needle together.

On Purl Row

Step 1 Pass in front of the 1st st on the lh needle and p the 2nd st. Do not let the st drop off the lh needle.

Step 2 P the 1st st, letting both sts drop off the lh needle together.

A

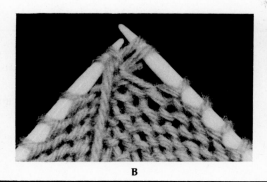

B

C

Double Stitch (Knit 1 Below or K-1 b)

Step 1 Put the rh needle into the center of the st below the next st to be worked.

Step 2 Pass the yarn around the rh needle and k a st through this st below. Both sts drop off the needle together, creating the effect of being knitted together.

Two double stitches must have a plain knit or purl stitch between them.

ELONGATED STITCHES

The elongated or lengthened stitches give a lacy or openwork effect to your knitting. They can be placed as a single inset row or repeated in various combinations. The elongated stitches are also found as part of many fancy pattern stitches.

Single Elongated Stitch

Step 1 Insert the rh needle into the st to be elongated as if to k.

Step 2 Wind yarn twice around the rh needle.

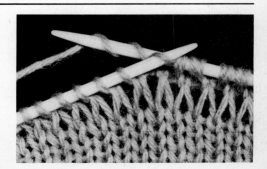

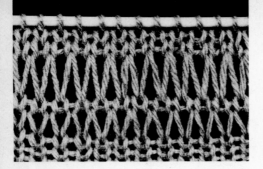

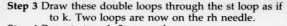

Step 3 Draw these double loops through the st loop as if
to k. Two loops are now on the rh needle.
Step 4 Repeat steps 1–3 across the row.
Step 5 On the next (return) row, drop the extra loop off
the needle.

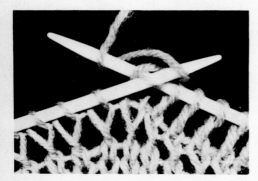

Double Elongated Stitch

Step 1 Insert the rh needle into the st to be elongated as
if to k.
Step 2 Wind yarn 3 times around the rh needle.
Step 3 Draw these 3 loops through the st loop as if to k.
Three loops are now on the rh needle.
Step 4 Repeat steps 1–3 across the row.
Step 5 On the next (return) row, drop the extra loops off
the needle.

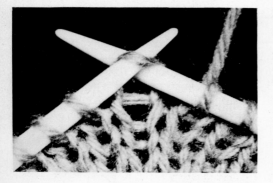

Twisted Elongated Stitch

Step 1 Insert the rh needle into the 1st st as if to k.
Step 2 Pass the yarn over the rh needle, around the lh
needle, over to the rh needle again, under and
over again.
Step 3 Draw the yarn through the k st in the usual way,
forming a twisted elongated loop.
Step 4 Repeat these 4 steps across the row.

SLIPPED STITCHES

A stitch passed from the left-hand needle to the right-hand needle without being worked is called a slipped
or slip stitch. Unless otherwise indicated, the yarn is left in front or back depending on the position of the last
worked stitch.

Slip Stitch, Knitwise

Step 1 Leave the yarn in the position of the previous st
worked.
Step 2 Put the rh needle in the loop of the st to be
slipped as if to k it, from left to right.
Step 3 Sl the lh needle out of the loop, leaving the st on
the rh needle without being worked.

Slip Stitch, Purlwise

Step 1 Leave the yarn in the position of the previous st worked.

Step 2 Put the rh needle in the loop of the st to be slipped as if to p it, from right to left.

Step 3 Sl the lh needle out of the loop, leaving the st on the rh needle without being worked.

Twisted Knit Stitch

Step 1 The yarn is in the correct position in back of the work.

Step 2 Insert the rh needle through the back loop of next st on the lh needle.

Step 3 Place the yarn under and over the rh needle.

Step 4 Pull the yarn through the loop with the rh needle.

Step 5 Let the st drop off the lh needle.

Repeat steps 1–5 to work a twisted knit stitch.

Twisted Purl Stitch

Step 1 The yarn is in the correct position at the front of the work.

Step 2 Insert the rh needle through the back loop with the rh needle in front of the lh needle.

Step 3 Place the yarn over and around the rh needle.

Step 4 Pull the yarn through the loop with the rh needle.

Step 5 Let the st drop off the lh needle.

Repeat steps 1–5 to work a twisted purl stitch.

Weaving

Weaving is the method used to join two pieces of knitting that are still on the needles or left unbound in waiting on a stitch holder. In England this is called grafting.

With the loops facing each other, the two knitted pieces are joined by forming a new row of stitches between them using a piece of yarn and a tapestry needle. This makes an invisible seam.

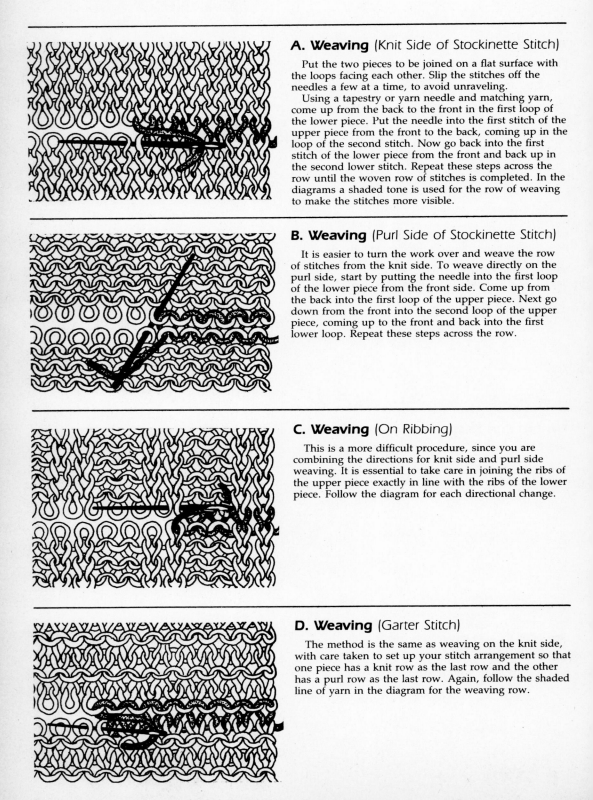

A. Weaving (Knit Side of Stockinette Stitch)

Put the two pieces to be joined on a flat surface with the loops facing each other. Slip the stitches off the needles a few at a time, to avoid unraveling.

Using a tapestry or yarn needle and matching yarn, come up from the back to the front in the first loop of the lower piece. Put the needle into the first stitch of the upper piece from the front to the back, coming up in the loop of the second stitch. Now go back into the first stitch of the lower piece from the front and back up in the second lower stitch. Repeat these steps across the row until the woven row of stitches is completed. In the diagrams a shaded tone is used for the row of weaving to make the stitches more visible.

B. Weaving (Purl Side of Stockinette Stitch)

It is easier to turn the work over and weave the row of stitches from the knit side. To weave directly on the purl side, start by putting the needle into the first loop of the lower piece from the front side. Come up from the back into the first loop of the upper piece. Next go down from the front into the second loop of the upper piece, coming up to the front and back into the first lower loop. Repeat these steps across the row.

C. Weaving (On Ribbing)

This is a more difficult procedure, since you are combining the directions for knit side and purl side weaving. It is essential to take care in joining the ribs of the upper piece exactly in line with the ribs of the lower piece. Follow the diagram for each directional change.

D. Weaving (Garter Stitch)

The method is the same as weaving on the knit side, with care taken to set up your stitch arrangement so that one piece has a knit row as the last row and the other has a purl row as the last row. Again, follow the shaded line of yarn in the diagram for the weaving row.

Yarn Forward and Yarn Back

To produce a bar or other decorative effect in many of the pattern and texture stitches, the directions will indicate a yf or yb. This instruction tells you to bring the yarn forward or to the back before the next stitch is worked. In this sample, the yarn was brought forward before the slip stitch, brought to the back in the normal position for a knit stitch, and is shown in the yarn forward position for another slip stitch. This is always a contrary direction from the normal position of the yarn. The directions would read: K1, yf, sl 1, yb, k1, yf, sl 1.

Yarn-Over

A yarn-over (yo) is a method of adding one or several stitches or holes in knitting. There are many different ways to make a stitch using this method, and just as many different names used for the general term yarn-over, depending on the country or area the instructions come from. The most common are wool round needle (wrn), wool over needle (won), make 1 stitch (M1), and yarn-over (yo).

Most lace patterns and openwork stitches are based on the use and placement of the yarn-over.

KNIT YARN-OVER (After a Knit Stitch)

Before a Knit Stitch

Bring the yarn forward under the rh needle and over toward the back of the work. This puts the yarn in the correct position to knit the next stitch.

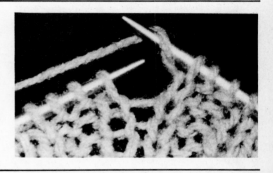

Before a Purl Stitch

Bring the yarn forward under the rh needle and over, bringing it back to the front again. This puts the yarn in the correct position to purl the next stitch.

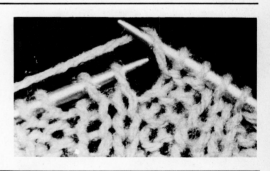

KNIT YARN-OVER (After a Purl Stitch)

Before a Knit Stitch

The yarn is in a forward position. Take the yarn from the front to the back over the rh needle. The yarn is now in the correct position to knit the next stitch.

Before a Purl Stitch

The yarn is in a forward position. Take the yarn from the front to the back over the rh needle, coming around to the front again. The yarn is once again in the correct position to purl the next stitch.

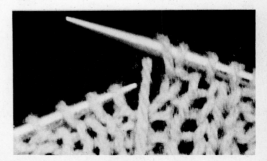

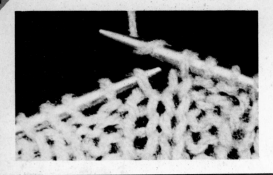

PURLED YARN-OVER
(After a Knit Stitch)

Before a Knit Stitch

The yarn is at the back of the work. Take the yarn from the back to the front over the rh needle, around the needle to the back. The yarn is again in the correct position to knit the next stitch.

Before a Purl Stitch

The yarn is at the back of the work. Insert the rh needle into the stitch to be purled. Place the yarn over the stitch and around to the front. Purl the stitch. The yarn-over will be formed when the purl stitch is slipped from the lh needle.

PURLED YARN-OVER (After a Purl Stitch)

Before a Knit Stitch

Take the yarn from the front position to the back. Place it over the rh needle, around to the front, and under to the knit position. Knit the next stitch.

Before a Purl Stitch

Take the yarn from the front position to the back. Insert the rh needle pwise in the next stitch. Place the yarn over the stitch and around the needle to the front. As you purl the stitch, the yarn-over will be formed.

MULTIPLE YARN-OVER
(Double or Triple)

A multiple yarn-over is made by winding the yarn 2 or more times around the rh needle. This is used to lengthen stitches and make lacy patterns.

Zipper

The zipper is recommended as a closure for outer wear and children's sweaters. It is added after the garment is blocked and assembled.

Measure the length of the opening. Purchase a zipper that is ½ shorter than the measurement. Pin the zipper ⅛" in from the edges on both sides of the opening on the wrong side. Using a matching thread, sew the zipper by hand or machine to the garment along the outer edge of the zipper tape. Add a second row of stitches about ⅛" from the zipper teeth.

Pattern Stitches

KNIT-PURL COMBINATIONS

All knitters should master the knit-and-purl combinations first. There are an almost infinite number of combinations that will produce a limitless variety of patterns for the beginner.

GARTER STITCH

This is the primary knitting or beginner's stitch.
Row 1: K.
Row 2: K.
Repeat these 2 rows for pattern.
Note: For a firmer texture, work into the back loop of each stitch.

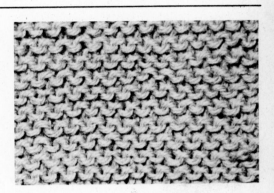

STOCKINETTE STITCH
stocking stitch, jersey stitch

This is the basic knitting stitch.
Row 1 (right side): K.
Row 2: P.
Repeat these 2 rows for pattern.

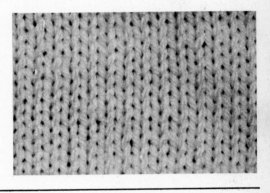

STOCKINETTE REVERSED

This is the reverse side of stockinette stitch.
Row 1 (right side): P.
Row 2: K.
Repeat these 2 rows for pattern.

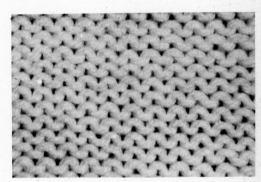

CROSSED STOCKINETTE STITCH
twisted stocking stitch, twisted continental stitch

This is the basic knitting stitch with a twist on the front side.
Row 1: K into the back loop of each st.
Row 2: P.
Repeat these 2 rows for pattern.

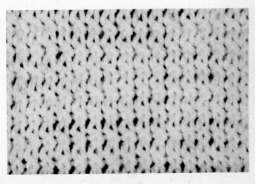

DOUBLE TWISTED STOCKINETTE STITCH
twisted stockinette

Both pattern rows are twisted.
Row 1: K into the back loop of each st.
Row 2: P into the back loop of each st.
Repeat these 2 rows for pattern.

BIAS STOCKINETTE STITCH
bias stocking stitch, oblique stocking stitch

Row 1: Inc 1 in first st, k to last 3 sts, k2 tog.
Row 2: P.
Repeat these 2 rows for pattern.

TUBULAR STOCKINETTE STITCH
tubular stocking stitch

Row 1: Cast on sts on a circular needle or set of dpn.
Join. Put a marker at beg of row.
Row 2: K.
Repeat row 2 for pattern.

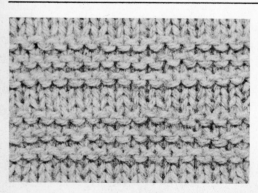

STRIPED GARTER RIDGE
striped stockinette stitch

Any number of stitches.
Rows 1, 3, and 4: K.
Row 2: P.
Repeat these 4 rows for pattern.

ALTERNATING GARTER STITCH
alternated garter stitch

Any number of stitches.
Rows 1–6: K.
Row 7: P.
Row 8: K.
Repeat these 8 rows for pattern.

BEADED GARTER RIDGE

Multiple of 2.
Rows 1–5: K.
Row 6: *K1, p1*, rep *to*.
Repeat these 6 rows for pattern.

GARTER CHECK STITCH
garter check stitch I

Multiple of 14.
Rows 1, 2, 4, 5, 6, and 8: P.
Row 3: *K7, p7*, rep *to*.
Row 7: *P7, k7*, rep *to*.
Repeat these 8 rows for pattern.

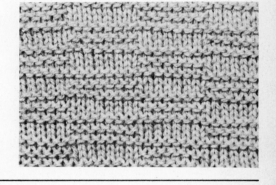

WOVEN GARTER CHECK STITCH
garter check stitch II

Multiple of 20.
Rows 1–4: *P10, k10*, rep *to*.
Row 5: K.
Rows 6–9: *K10, p10*, rep *to*.
Row 10: P.
Repeat these 10 rows for pattern.

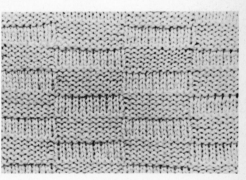

GATHERED RIDGING
gathered stitch

Any number of stitches.
Rows 1–6: Using small-size needles, k each row.
Row 7: Using larger-size needles, k twice into each st
(once in front loop, once in back loop). This will
double the number of sts on the needle.
Rows 8, 10, and 12: P.
Rows 9 and 11: K.
Row 13: (Smaller needles) *k2 tog*, rep *to*.
Repeat rows 2–13 for pattern.

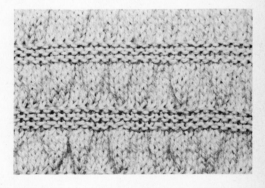

GRANITE RIDGING
granite ridges

Multiple of 2.
Rows 1, 3, and 5: K.
Rows 2, 4, and 8: P.
Row 6: *K2 tog*, rep *to*.
Row 7: (K1, p1) in every st.
Repeat these 8 rows for pattern.

GRANITE RELIEF RIDGING
granite relief stitch

Multiple of 2.
Row 1: P.
Row 2: K.
Row 3: *K2 tog*, rep *to*.
Row 4: K into the front and back of every st.
Repeat these 4 rows for pattern.

RIDGE STITCH
reversible ridge, quaker ridge, all fools' welt

Rows 1, 3, 4, and 6: K.
Rows 2 and 5: P.
Repeat these 6 rows for pattern.

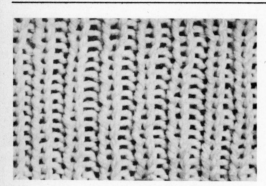

RIBBING 1 + 1

This is the basic and easiest of the ribbing group of patterns.
Odd number of stitches.
Row 1: *K1, p1*, rep *to*.
Row 2: *P1, k1* rep *to* [that is, k all k sts and p all p sts].
Repeat these 2 rows for pattern.

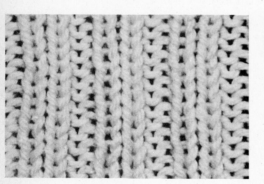

RIBBING 2 + 2

Multiple of 2.
Row 1: *K2, p2*, rep *to*.
Row 2: *K the p sts and p the k sts of preceding row*, rep *to*.
Repeat these 2 rows for pattern.

RIBBING 3 + 2
uneven rib

Multiple of 5.
Row 1: *K3, p2*, rep *to*.
Row 2: *K2, p3*, rep *to*.
Repeat these 2 rows for pattern.

FLAT RIBBING 7 + 3
flat ribs, uneven flat rib

Multiple of 10.
Row 1: *K7, p3*, rep *to*.
Row 2: *K3, p7*, rep *to*.
Repeat these 2 rows for pattern.

RIBBING—TWISTED 1 + 1
twisted ribs

Multiple of 2.
Row 1: *K1 tbl, p1*, rep *to*.
Row 2: K the k sts and p the p sts of preceding row*,
    rep *to*.
Repeat these 2 rows for pattern.

SEEDED KNIT RIBBING
seed knit rib, moss knit rib

Multiple of 4.
Row 1: *K3, p1* rep *to*.
Row 2: *K2, p1, k1*, rep *to*.
Repeat these 2 rows for pattern.

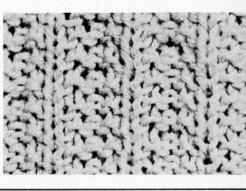

FARROWED RIBBING
farrow rib

Multiple of 3.
Row 1: *K2, p1*, rep *to*.
Row 2: Rep row 1.
Repeat these 2 rows for pattern.

MOCK RIB CABLE
ribbed cables

Multiple of 5 + 4.
Row 1: *P4, (k into the front, back, and front of next
    st)*, rep *to*, p4.
Row 2: K4, *p3, k4*, rep *to*.
Row 3: *P4, k3 tog*, rep *to*, p4.
Row 4: K4, *p1, k4*, rep *to*.
Repeat these 4 rows for pattern.

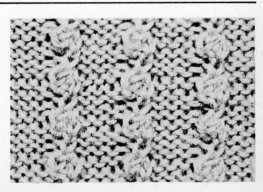

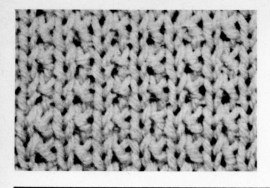

LOOSE RIBBING
supple rib

Multiple of 3.
Row 1: *K1, k next st, leave on lh needle, yf, p tog that st and the next st, yb*, rep *to*.
Row 2: P.
Repeat these 2 rows for pattern.

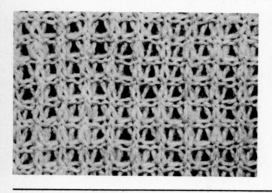

CELL RIB
cellular stitch II

Multiple of 2.
Row 1: (US size 0 needle) *k1, p1*, rep *to*.
Row 2: (Size 7 needle) *K1 tbl, pl*, rep *to*.
Repeat these 2 rows for pattern.

KNOTTED CELL RIB
cellular stitch III

Multiple of 2.
Row 1: K1, *inc 1 [k through horizontal bar before next st], k1, pass inc 1 over k1*, rep *to*.
Row 2: P.
Repeat these 2 rows for pattern.

MOSS BEADED RIB
beaded rib

Multiple of 5 + 2.
Row 1 (right side): *P2, k1, p1, k1*, rep *to* to last 2 sts, end p2.
Row 2: K2, *p3, k2*, rep *to*.
Repeat these 2 rows for pattern.

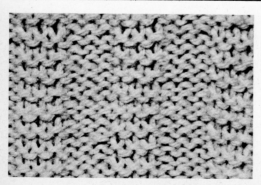

GARTER-STITCH RIBBING
garter rib, reversible garter rib

Multiple of 6.
Row 1 *K3, p3*, rep *to*.
Row 2: K.
Repeat these 2 rows for pattern.

GARTER RIBBING 2 + 2

Multiple of 4.
Row 1: *K2, p2*, rep *to*.
Row 2: K.
Repeat these 2 rows for pattern.

OBLIQUE KNIT RIB
oblique rib, right oblique rib

Multiple of 4.
Row 1: *K2, p2*, rep *to*.
Row 2: *K1, p2, k1*, rep *to*.
Row 3: *P2, k2*, rep *to*.
Row 4: *P1, k2, p1*, rep *to*.
Repeat these 4 rows for pattern.

DIAGONAL RIBBING
diagonal rib, 2 + 2 diagonal rib

Multiple of 4.
Rows 1 and 2: *K2, p2*, rep *to*.
Rows 3 and 8: *K1, p2, k1*, rep *to*.
Rows 4 and 7: *P1, k2, p1*, rep *to*.
Rows 5 and 6: *P2, k2*, rep *to*.
Repeat these 8 rows for pattern.

DIAGONAL RIBBING II
diagonal pattern rib

Multiple of 8.
Row 1: *K4, p4*, rep *to*.
Row 2: Pl, *k4, p4*, rep *to*, end p3.
Row 3: K2, *p4, k4*, rep *to*, end k2.
Row 4: P3, *k4, p4*, rep *to*, end p1.
Row 5: *P4, k4*, rep *to*.
Row 6: K1, *p4, k4*, rep *to*, end k3.
Row 7: P2, *k4, p4*, rep *to*, end p2.
Row 8: K3, *p4, k4*, rep *to*, end k1.
Repeat these 8 rows for pattern.

SPIRAL RIBBING
spiral rib

Multiple of 6.
Rows 1–3: *K3, p3*, rep *to*.
Rows 4 and 6: *P1, k3, p2*, rep *to*.
Rows 5, 8, 14, and 17: K all k sts and p all p sts.
Rows 7 and 9: *K1, p3, k2*, rep *to*.
Rows 10–12: *P3, k3*, rep *to*.
Rows 13 and 15: *P2, k3, p1*, rep *to*.
Rows 16 and 18: *K2, p3, k1*, rep *to*.
Repeat these 18 rows for pattern.

CHEVRON RIBBING PATTERN
chevron rib, chevron pattern

Multiple of 12.
Row 1: *P2, k2, p2, k1, p2, k2, p1*, rep *to*.
Rows 2, 4, 6, and 8: K all k sts and p all p sts.
Row 3: *P1, k2, p2, k3, p2, k2*, rep *to*.
Row 5: *K2, p2, k2, p1, k2, p2, k1*, rep *to*.
Row 7: *K1, p2, k2, p3, k2, p2*, rep *to*.
Repeat these 8 rows for pattern.

RIDGED RIB
piqué rib, stripe rib

Multiple of 10.
Row 1 (right side): *P3, k1, p3, k3*, rep *to*.
Row 2: *P3, k3, p1, k3*, rep *to*.
Row 3: Rep row 1.
Row 4: K.
Repeat these 4 rows for pattern.

SEED STITCH
moss stitch, rice stitch

Multiple of 2 + 1.
If a row ends with a k1, the next row must begin with k1.
Row 1: *K1, p1*, rep *to*, end k1.
Row 2: Rep row 1.
Repeat these 2 rows for pattern.

GRAIN OF SAND STITCH
sand stitch

Multiple of 2.
Row 1 (right side): *K1, p1*, rep *to*.
Row 2: K.
Repeat these 2 rows for pattern.

MOSS KNIT 1 RIB STITCH
reverse side of sand stitch, reverse side of grain of sand stitch

Multiple of 2.
Row 1 (right side): K.
Row 2: *K1, p1*, rep *to*.
Repeat these 2 rows for pattern.

ANDALUSIAN STITCH PATTERN
Andalusian stitch

Multiple of 2.
Row 1 (right side): K.
Rows 2 and 4: P.
Row 3: *K1, p1*, rep *to*.
Repeat these 4 rows for pattern.

DOUBLE ANDALUSIAN PATTERN
double Andalusian stitch

Multiple of 6 + 2.
Rows 1 and 3: K.
Row 2: *K2, p4*, rep *to*, end k2.
Row 4: P3, *k2, p4*, rep *to*, k2, p1, k2.
Repeat these 4 rows for pattern.

SINGLE SEED STITCH
simple seed stitch

Multiple of 4.
Row 1 (right side): *K3, p1*, rep *to*.
Rows 2, 4, 6, and 8: P.
Rows 3 and 7: K.
Row 5: K1, *p1, k3*, rep *to*, end p1, k2.
Repeat these 8 rows for pattern.

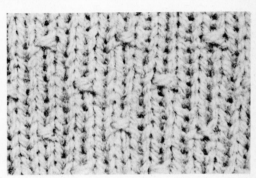

DOUBLE SEED STITCH
alternating double seed stitch

Multiple of 5.
Row 1: *P3, k2*, rep *to*.
Rows 2 and 4: P.
Row 3: *P1, k2, p2*, rep *to*.
Repeat these 4 rows for pattern.

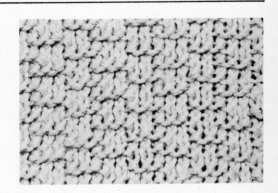

DOUBLE SEED STITCH RIB

Multiple of 9 + 4.
Row 1: P1, *k2, p1, k2, p4*, rep *to*, end K2, p1.
Rows 2, 4, and 6: P.
Row 3: *P1, k2, p4, k2*, rep *to*, end p1, k2, p1.
Row 5: *P4, k2, p1, k2*, rep *to*, end p4.
Repeat these 6 rows for pattern.

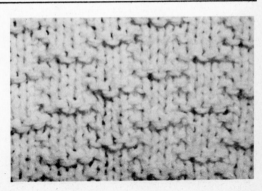

OBLIQUE SEED STITCH
seed stitch oblique, seeded oblique

Multiple of 5.
Row 1: *K4, p1*, rep *to*.
Row 2: *P1, k1, p3*, rep *to*.
Row 3: *K2, p1, k2*, rep *to*.
Row 4: *P3, k1, p1*, rep *to*.
To continue pattern, work seed stitch 1 st farther to the right on each odd-numbered row, to the left on each even-numbered row.

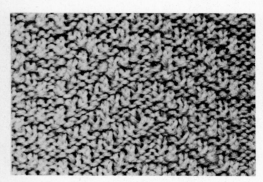

CHEVRON PATTERN SEED STITCH
chevron seed, seeded chevron

Multiple of 8.
Row 1: *P1, k3*, rep *to*.
Row 2: *K1, p5, k1, p1*, rep *to*.
Row 3: *K2, p1, k3, p1, k1*, rep *to*.
Row 4: *P2, k1, p1, k1, p3*, rep *to*.
Repeat these 4 rows for pattern.

HERRINGBONE SEEDED CHEVRON STITCH
broken chevron stitch

Multiple of 18.
Row 1: *K1, p2, k2, p2, k1, p1*, rep *to*.
Row 2: *K3, p2, k2, p2, k1, p2, k2, p2, k2*, rep *to*.
Row 3: *P1, k2, p2, k2, p3, k2, p2, k2, p2*, rep *to*.
Row 4: *K1, p2, k2, p2, k5, p2, k2, p2*, rep *to*.
Repeat these 4 rows for pattern.

HORIZONTAL CATERPILLAR PATTERN
garter dash stitch, caterpillar stitch horizontal

Multiple of 10.
Row 1 (right side): *K4, p6*, rep *to*.
Rows 2, 4, 6, and 8: P.
Rows 3 and 7: K.
Row 5: *P5, k4, p1*, rep *to*.
Repeat these 8 rows for pattern.

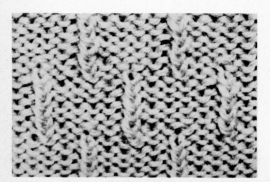

VERTICAL CATERPILLAR STITCH
caterpillar stitch vertical, alternating garter bars

Multiple of 6.
Rows 1, 3, and 5: *K3, p1 tbl, k2*, rep *to*.
Rows 2, 4, and 6: *P2, k1 tbl, p3*, rep *to*.
Rows 7, 9, and 11: *P1 tbl, k5*, rep *to*.
Rows 8, 10, and 12: *P5, k1 tbl*, rep *to*.
Repeat these 12 rows for pattern.

OBLIQUE CATERPILLAR STITCH
caterpillar stitch oblique

Multiple of 8.
Row 1 (right side): *K6, p2*, rep *to*.
Row 2: *P1, k2, p5*, rep *to*.
Row 3: *K4, p2, k2*, rep *to*.
Row 4: *P3, k2, p3*, rep *to*.
Row 5: *K2, p2, k4*, rep *to*.
Row 6: P.
Repeat these 6 rows for pattern.

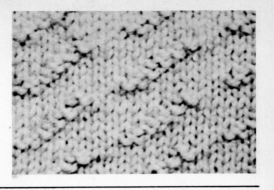

SEEDED DIAMOND PATTERN
grating stitch

Multiple of 8.
Row 1: *P1, k7*, rep *to*.
Rows 2 and 8: *K1, p5, k1, p1*, rep *to*.
Rows 3 and 7: *K2, p1, k3, p1, k1*, rep *to*.
Rows 4 and 6: *P2, k1, p1, k1, p3*, rep *to*.
Row 5: *K4, p1, k3*, rep *to*.
Repeat these 8 rows for pattern.

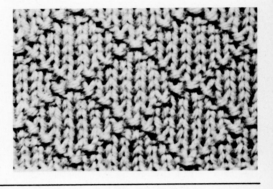

SEEDED LOZENGE STITCH
lozenge seed stitch, lozenge diamond seed stitch

Multiple of 12 + 2.
Row 1: *K6, p2, k4*, rep *to*, k2.
Rows 2 and 6: P2, *p2, k2, p2, k2, p4*, rep *to*.
Rows 3 and 5: *K2, p2, k6, p2*, rep *to*, end k2.
Row 4: K2, *p10, k2*, rep *to*.
Repeat these 6 rows for pattern.

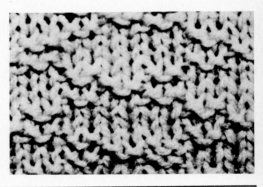

PETIT DIAMOND SEED STITCH
diamond seed stitch

Multiple of 6.
Rows 1 and 5: *K1, p1, k4*, rep *to*.
Row 2 and all even-numbered rows: K all k sts and p all
    p sts.
Row 3: *P1, k1, p1, k3*, rep *to*.
Rows 7 and 11: *K4, p1, k1*, rep *to*.
Row 9: *K3, p1, k1, p1*, rep *to*.
Repeat these 12 rows for pattern.

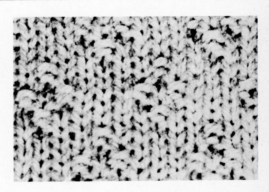

LARGE DIAMOND SEED STITCH
diamond seed stitch II, diamond knit-seed stitch

Multiple of 8.
Rows 1 and 15: *P1, k6, p1*, rep *to*.
Row 2 and all even-numbered rows: K all k sts and p all
    p sts.
Rows 3 and 13: *K1, p1, k4, p1, k1*, rep *to*.
Rows 5 and 11: *K2, pl, k2, p1, k2*, rep *to*.
Rows 7 and 9: *K3, p2, k3*, rep *to*.
Repeat these 16 rows for pattern.

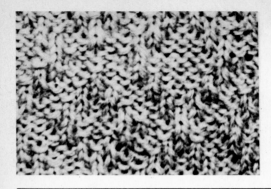

INLAID DIAMOND LOZENGE STITCH
lozenge diamond, inlaid lozenge stitch

Multiple of 12.
Row 1: *K2, p5, k2, p3*, rep *to*.
Row 2 and all even-numbered rows: K all k sts and p all
        p sts.
Rows 3 and 19: *P1, k2, p3, k2, p2, k1, p1*, rep *to*.
Rows 5 and 17: *P2, k2, p1, k2, p2, k3*, rep *to*.
Rows 7 and 15: *K1, p2, k3, p2, k2, p1, k1*, rep *to*.
Rows 9 and 13: *K2, p2, k1, p2, k2, p3*, rep *to*.
Row 11: *P1, k2, p3, k2, p4*, rep *to*.
Repeat these 20 rows for pattern.

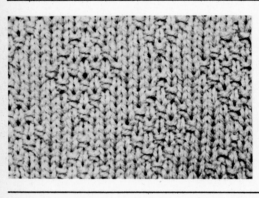

MOSS DIAMOND STITCH
Irish moss diamond stitch, inlaid moss diamonds

Multiple of 14.
Row 1: *(P1, k1) 4 times, k6*, rep *to*.
Row 2: *P6, (p1, k1) 4 times*, rep *to*.
Rows 3 and 15: *(K1, p1) 3 times, k4, p1, k3*, rep *to*.
Rows 4 and 16: *P3, k1, p4, (k1, p1) 3 times*, rep *to*.
Rows 5 and 13: *K2, p1, k1, p1, k4, p1, k1, p1, k2*, rep *to*.
Rows 6 and 14: *P2, k1, p1, k1, p4, k1, p1, k1, p2*, rep *to*.
Rows 7 and 11: *K3, p1, k4, (p1, k1) 3 times*, rep *to*.
Rows 8 and 12: *(P1, k1) 3 times, p4, k1, p3*, rep *to*.
Row 9: *K6, (k1, p1) 4 times*, rep *to*.
Row 10: *(K1, p1) 4 times, p6*, rep *to*.
Repeat these 16 rows for pattern.

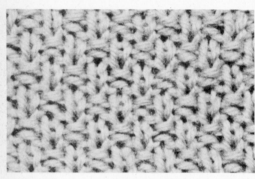

OBLIQUE MOSS STITCH
Irish moss stitch

Multiple of 2.
Row 1: *K1, p1*, rep *to*.
Rows 2 and 4: K all k sts and p all p sts.
Row 3: *P1, k1*, rep *to*.
Repeat these 4 rows for pattern.

VERTICAL STRIPE MOSS STITCH
vertical stripe seed stitch, stripe moss stitch

Multiple of 11 + 5.
Row 1 (right side): K5, *(k1, p1) 3 times, k5*, rep *to*.
Row 2: *P5, (p1, k1) 3 times*, rep *to*, p5.
Repeat these 2 rows for pattern.

ALTERNATING MOSS CHECKER STITCH
alternating moss oblong, alternating oblong stitch

Multiple of 6 + 4.
Rows 1, 3, 5, and 7: *K4, p2*, rep *to*, end k4.
Row 2 and all even-numbered rows: P.
Rows 9, 11, 13, and 15: K1, *p2, k4*, end p2, k1.
Repeat these 16 rows for pattern.

DOUBLE SEED STITCH
double moss stitch

Multiple of 4.
Rows 1 and 2: *K2, p2*, rep *to*.
Rows 3 and 4: *P2, k2*, rep *to*.
Repeat these 4 rows for pattern.

HURDLE STITCH
hurdle pattern stitch

Multiple of 2.
Rows 1 and 2: K.
Rows 3 and 4: *K1, p1*, rep *to*.
Repeat these 4 rows for pattern.

BASKETWEAVE STITCH
basket stitch

Multiple of 6.
Rows 1 and 7: K.
Rows 2 and 8: P.
Rows 3 and 5: *K1, p4, k1*, rep *to*.
Rows 4 and 6: *P1, k4, p1*, rep *to*.
Rows 9 and 11: *P2, k2, p2*, rep *to*.
Rows 10 and 12: *K2, p2, k2*, rep *to*.
Repeat these 12 rows for pattern.

WIDE BASKETWEAVE STITCH
wide basket stitch

Multiple of 9 + 6.
Rows 1, 3, and 5: *P6, k3*, rep *to*, end p6.
Row 2 and all even-numbered rows: K all k sts and p all
    p sts.
Rows 7 and 9: *K6, p3*, rep *to*, end k6.
Repeat these 10 rows for pattern.

WIDE MOSS DIAMOND RIB

Multiple of 9 + 2.
Rows 1 and 7: *P2, k7*, rep *to*, end p2.
Rows 2, 6, and 8: P.
Rows 3 and 5: *P2, k3, p1, k3*, rep *to*, end p2.
Row 4: P2, *p2, k1, p1, k1, p4*, rep *to*.
Repeat these 8 rows for pattern.

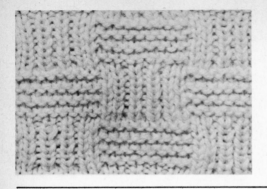

GIANT BASKETWEAVE STITCH
double basket stitch

Multiple of 18 + 1.
Rows 1, 3, 5, and 7: P1, *k1, p1, k2, p9, k2, p1, k1, p1*, rep *to*.
Rows 2, 4, 6, and 8: K1, *p1, k1, p13, k1, p1, k1*, rep *to*.
Rows 9, 11, 13, and 15: *P5, k2, p1, k1, p1, k1, p1, k2, p4*, rep *to*, end p1.
Rows 10, 12, 14, and 16: *P7, k1, p1, k1, p1, k1, p6*, rep *to*, end p1.
Repeat these 16 rows for pattern.

CHECKERBOARD
chessboard, woven squares

Multiple of 12 + 1.
Rows 1, 3, and 5: *K7, p5*, rep *to*, end k1.
Rows 2, 4, and 6: P1, *k5, p7*, rep *to*.
Rows 7, 9, and 11: K1, *p5, k7*, rep *to*.
Rows 8, 10, and 12: *P7, k5*, rep *to*, end p1.
Repeat these 12 rows for pattern.

SEEDED CHECKERBOARD
piqué squares II

Multiple of 10.
Rows 1, 3, 5, and 7: *K5, p1, k1, p1, k1, p1*, rep *to*.
Rows 2, 4, 6, and 8: *P1, k1, p1, k1, p6*, rep *to*.
Rows 9, 11, 13, and 15: *P1, k1, p1, k1, p1, k5*, rep *to*.
Rows 10, 12, 14, and 16: *P6, k1, p1, k1, p1*, rep *to*.
Repeat these 16 rows for pattern.

PARQUET-FLOOR STITCH
inlaid-floor stitch

Multiple of 20.
Rows 1, 5, and 9: *(P2, k2) twice, p2, k10*, rep *to*.
Rows 2, 6, and 10: *P10, (k2, p2) twice, k2*, rep *to*.
Rows 3 and 7: *(P2, k2) twice, p12*, rep *to*.
Rows 4 and 8: *K12, (p2, k2) twice*, rep *to*.
Rows 11, 15, and 19: *K10, (p2, k2) twice, p2*, rep *to*.
Rows 12, 16, and 20: *(K2, p2) twice, k2, p10*, rep *to*.
Rows 13 and 17: *P12, (k2, p2) twice*, rep *to*.
Rows 14 and 18: *(K2, p2) twice, k12*, rep *to*.
Repeat these 20 rows for pattern.

OBLONG SQUARES
broken 2 + 2 rib, alternating rectangles

Multiple of 4.
Rows 1–6: *K2, p2*, rep *to*.
Rows 7–12: *P2, k2*, rep *to*.
Repeat these 12 rows for pattern.

WEAVING RIBBONS
window stitch

Multiple of 12.
Rows 1 and 11: *K2, p6, k4*, rep *to*.
Rows 2, 4, 6, 8, 10, 12: K all k sts and p all p sts.
Rows 3, 5, 7, and 9: *P2, k6, p2, k2*, rep *to*.
Row 13: K.
Row 14: P.
Repeat these 14 rows for pattern.

TRIANGLE PIQUÉ
piqué triangle stitch

Multiple of 12.
Row 1: *K6, p1, k5*, rep *to*.
Row 2: *P4, k3, p5*, rep *to*.
Row 3: *K4, p5, k3*, rep *to*.
Row 4: *P2, k7, p3*, rep *to*.
Row 5: *K2, p9, k1*, rep *to*.
Rows 6 and 12: P.
Row 7: *P1, k11*, rep *to*.
Row 8: *K1, p9, k2*, rep *to*.
Row 9: *P3, k7, p2*, rep *to*.
Row 10: *K3, p5, k4*, rep *to*.
Row 11: *P5, k3, p4*, rep *to*.
Repeat these 12 rows for pattern.

TRIANGLE PIQUÉ STRIPE
piqué triangle stripe

Multiple of 15 + 2.
Rows 1, 3, 5, and 7: P2, *k13, p2*, rep *to*.
Rows 2, 4, and 6: *K2, p13*, rep *to*, end k2.
Row 8: *K2, p6, k1, p6*, rep *to*, end k2.
Row 9: P2, *k5, p3, k5, p2*, rep *to*.
Row 10: *K2, p4, k5, p4*, rep *to*, end k2.
Row 11: P2, *k3, p7, k3, p2*, rep *to*.
Row 12: *K2, p2, k9, p2*, rep *to*, end k2.
Row 13: P2, *k1, p11, k1, p2*, rep *to*.
Row 14: K.
Repeat these 14 rows for pattern.

EMBOSSED LEAF BORDER STITCH
embossed leaf stitch

Multiple of 10.
Rows 1, 3, 4, and 16: P.
Rows 2 and 10: K.
Rows 5 and 15: *P5, k5*, rep *to*.
Rows 6 and 11: *K1, p5, k4*, rep *to*.
Rows 7 and 12: *P3, k5, p2*, rep *to*.
Rows 8 and 13: *K3, p5, k2*, rep *to*.
Rows 9 and 14: *P1, k5, p4*, rep *to*.
Repeat these 16 rows for pattern.

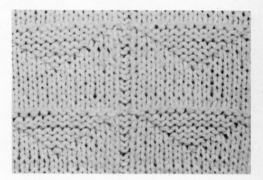

MOCK STARFISH PATTERN
starfish stitch

Multiple of 7 + 5.
Rows 1: *P5, k2 tbl*, rep *to*, end p5.
Row 2: K5, *p2 tbl, k5*, rep *to*.
Repeat these 2 rows for pattern.
Using a tapestry needle and yarn, sew alternate k2 ribs
together every 10 rows. (See photo for placement.)

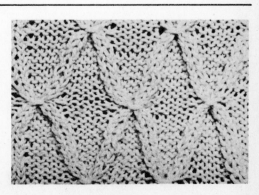

MOCK SMOCKING STITCH
smocking stitch, smocked cable

Multiple of 6 + 2.
Row 1: P2, *k4 in next st (k into the front and back twice), p2, k1, p2*, rep *to*.
Rows 2 and 4: *K2, p1, k2, (k4, winding yarn twice around needle each time)*, rep *to*, end k2.
Rows 3 and 5: P2, *k4 (let the extra loops drop), p2, k1, p2*, rep *to*.
Row 6: *K2, p1, k2, p4 tog*, rep *to*, end k2.
Row 7: P2, *k1, p2, k4 in next st, p2*, rep *to*.
Rows 8 and 10: *K2, (k4, winding yarn twice around needle each time), k2, p1*, rep *to*, end k2.
Rows 9 and 11: P2, *k1, p2, k4 (let the extra loops drop), p2*, rep *to*.   •
Row 12: *K2, p4 tog, k2, p1*, rep *to*, end k2.
Repeat these 12 rows for pattern.
The smocked effect is made by sewing 2 ribs together every 12th row. (See photo for placement of smocking.)

LOLLIPOPS
reverse side of mock smocking stitch

Work rows 1–12 as above. Omit smocking.

LINKING STITCH PATTERN
alternating link stitch

Multiple of 7 + 4.
Rows 1 and 3: *P5, k1, p1*, rep *to*, end p4.
Rows 2 and 4: K4, *k1, p1, k5*, rep *to*.
Rows 5 and 7: *P4, k1, p1, k1*, rep *to*, end p4.
Rows 6 and 8: K4, *p1, k1, p1, k4*, rep *to*.
Repeat these 8 rows for pattern.

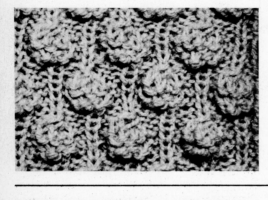

ATTACHED-CROSSES STITCH
brick stitch

Multiple of 8.
Rows 1 and 3 (right side): *P6, k2*, rep *to*.
Rows 2 and 4: *P2, k6*, rep *to*.
Rows 5 and 7: K2, *p2, k6*, rep *to*, end p2, k4.
Rows 6 and 8: P4, *k2, p6*, rep *to*, end k2, p2.
Repeat these 8 rows for pattern.

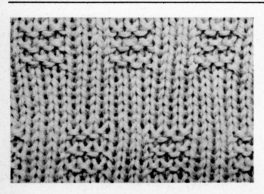

WOVEN PIQUÉ CHECK STITCH
piqué check stitch

Multiple of 6.
Rows 1, 3, 5, 13, 15, and 17: K.
Rows 2 and all even-numbered rows: P.
Rows 7, 9, and 11: *K3, p3*, rep *to*.
Rows 19, 21, and 23: *P3, k3*, rep *to*.
Repeat these 24 rows for pattern.

PIQUÉ CHECKER STITCH
piqué check stitch II

Multiple of 6.
Rows 1 and 3: *P2, k4*, rep *to*.
Rows 2, 4, 6, and 8: P.
Rows 5 and 7: K3, *p2, k4*, rep *to*, end p2, k1.
Repeat these 8 rows for pattern.

PIQUÉ TRIANGLE RIB STITCH
piqué triangles, piqué triangle shadow

Multiple of 5.
Row 1 (right side): *K1, p4*, rep *to*.
Rows 2 and 3: *K3, p2*, rep *to*.
Row 4: Rep row 1.
Repeat these 4 rows for pattern.

PIQUÉ DIAMOND PATTERN
piqué diamonds, garter diamond pattern

Multiple of 10.
Row 1: *K9, p1*, rep *to*.
Rows 2 and 8: K2, *p7, k3*, rep *to*, end p7, k1.
Rows 3 and 7: P2, *k5, p5*, rep *to*, end k5, p3.
Rows 4 and 6: K4, *p3, k7*, rep *to*, end p3, k3.
Rows 5: P4, *k1, p9*, rep *to*, end k1, p5.
Repeat these 8 rows for pattern.

EMBOSSED GIANT DIAMOND STITCH
giant diamond pattern

Multiple of 28.
Row 1 (right side): P13, k2, p13.
Rows 2 and 14: P1, k11, p4, k11, p1.
Rows 3 and 13: K2, p9, k6, p9, k2.
Rows 4 and 12: P3, k7, p8, k7, p3.
Rows 5 and 11: K4, p5, k10, p5, k4.
Rows 6 and 10: P5, k3, p5, k2, p5, k3, p5.
Rows 7 and 9: P1, k5, p1, k5, p4, k5, p1, k5, p1.
Row 8: K2, p9, k6, p9, k2.
Repeat these 14 rows for pattern.

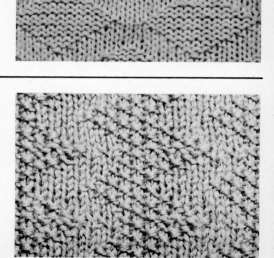

ALTERNATING PIQUÉ ZIGZAG
piqué zigzag, piqué jacquard

Multiple of 10.
Row 1: *K5, (p1, k1) twice, p1*, rep *to*.
Rows 2 and 10: *(P1, k1) 3 times, p4*, rep *to*.
Rows 3 and 9: *K3, (p1, k1) twice, p1, k2*, rep *to*.
Rows 4 and 8: *P3, (k1, p1) twice, k1, p2*, rep *to*.
Rows 5 and 7: *(K1, p1) 3 times, k4*, rep *to*.
Row 6: *(P1, k1) twice, p1, k5*, rep *to*.
Repeat these 10 rows for pattern.

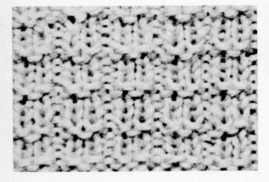

GARTER ZIGZAG STITCH
piqué zigzag

Multiple of 6 + 2 selvage stitches
Row 1 (right side): K1, *k3, p3*, rep *to*, end k1.
Row 2 and all even-numbered rows: K1, p across row,
end k1.
Row 3: K1, p1, *k3, p3*, rep *to*, end k3, p2, k1.
Row 5: K1, p2, *k3, p3*, rep *to*, end k3, p1, k1.
Row 7: K1, *p3, k3*, rep *to*, end k1.
Row 9: K1, p2, *k3, p3*, rep *to*, end k3, p1, k1.
Row 11: K1, p1, *k3, p3*, rep *to*, end k3, p2, k1.
Repeat these 12 rows for pattern.

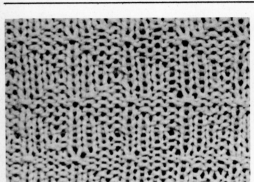

SMALL WAFFLE STITCH
waffle stitch, shadow check stitch

Multiple of 3.
Rows 1 and 3: *K2, p1*, rep *to*.
Row 2: *K1, p1*, rep *to*.
Row 4: K.
Repeat these 4 rows for pattern.

TRIANGULAR RIBBED STITCH
triangular rib I

Multiple of 4.
Row 1: P.
Rows 2 and 8: *P1, k3*, rep *to*.
Rows 3 and 7: *P2, k2*, rep *to*.
Rows 4 and 6: *P3, k1*, rep *to*.
Row 5: K.
Repeat these 8 rows for pattern.

TRIANGULAR RIBBED STITCH—LARGE
triangular rib II

Multiple of 16.
Rows 1 and 9: *K3, p1, k4, p3, k4, p1*, rep *to*.
Rows 2 and 8: *K2, p3, k3, p3, k2, p3*, rep *to*.
Rows 3 and 7: *K3, p3, k2, p3, k2, p3*, rep *to*.
Rows 4 and 6: *K4, p1, k3, p1, k4, p3*, rep *to*.
Row 5: *K3, p13*, rep *to*.
Row 10: *P5, k3, p8*, rep *to*.
Repeat these 10 rows for pattern.

TILE SQUARES
tile stitch

Multiple of 5.
Rows 1, 3, 5, and 7: K.
Rows 2, 4, and 6: *P4, k1*, rep *to*.
Row 8: K.
Repeat these 8 rows for pattern.

MOSAIC TILE STITCH
mosaic stitch

Multiple of 20.
Rows 1, 5, and 9: *K2, p2*, rep *to*.
Row 2 and all even-numbered rows: K all k sts and p all
    p sts.
Rows 3 and 7: (K2, p2) twice, *k4, p2, k2, p2*, rep *to*,
    end k2.
Rows 11, 15, and 19: *P2, k2*, rep *to*.
Rows 13 and 17: Repeat row 3.
Repeat these 20 rows for pattern.

ALTERNATING CHECKED RECTANGLES
rectangular checks

Multiple of 6.
Row 1 and all odd-numbered rows: K.
Rows 2, 4, 6, 8, 10, and 12: *K3, p3*, rep *to*.
Rows 14, 16, 18, 20, 22, and 24: *P3, k3*, rep *to*.
Repeat these 24 rows for pattern.

STEPPED STITCH
steps, piqué steps, diagonal steps

Multiple of 5.
Row 1: *P2, inc 1 (k into the front and back of next st) 3
    times*, rep *to*.
Row 2: *(K2 tog tbl) 3 times, k2*, rep *to*.
Row 3: *P1, (inc 1 in next st) 3 times, p1*, rep *to*.
Row 4: *K1, (k2 tog tbl) 3 times, k1*, rep *to*.
Row 5: *(Inc 1 in next st) 3 times, p2*, rep *to*.
Row 6: *K2, (k2 tog tbl) 3 times*, rep *to*.
Continue to move pattern 1 stitch to the right on every
alternate row.

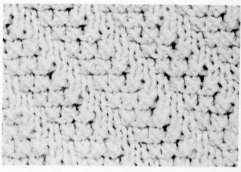

CHEVRON PATTERN
chevron rib II, zigzag pattern

Multiple of 12.
Row 1: *K3, p5, k3, p1*, rep *to*.
Row 2 and all even-numbered rows: K all k sts and p all
    p sts.
Row 3: P1, *k3, p3*, rep *to*, end k3, p2.
Row 5: P2, *k3, p1, k3, p5*, rep *to* to last 10 sts, k3,
    p1, k3, p3.
Row 7: *P3, k5, p3, k1*, rep *to*.
Row 9: K1, *p3, k3*, rep *to*, end p3, k2.
Row 11: K2, *p3, k1, p3, k5*, rep *to*, p3, k1.
Repeat these 12 rows for pattern.

STEPS
steps II, woven steps

Multiple of 18.
Rows 1 and 3: *K15, p3*, rep *to*.
Row 2 and all even-numbered rows: K all k sts and p all
    p sts.
Rows 5 and 7: *K3, p15*, rep *to*.
Rows 9 and 11: *K3, p3, k12*, rep *to*.
Rows 13 and 15: *P6, k3, p9*, rep *to*.
Rows 17 and 19: *K9, p3, k6*, rep *to*.
Rows 21 and 23: *P12, k3, p3*, rep *to*.
Repeat these 24 rows for pattern.

WOVEN REVERSED RIDGE STITCH
piqué reversed ridge stitch

Multiple of 12.
Rows 1 and 3: K.
Rows 2 and 4: P.
Rows 5 and 7: K3, *p6, k6*, rep *to*, end p6, k3.
Rows 6 and 8: K all k sts and p all p sts.
Repeat these 8 rows for pattern.

BASKETWEAVE RIDGED CHAIN STITCH
ridged chain stitch, garter chain stitch

Multiple of 14 + 3.
Rows 1, 3, 5, 15, 17, and 19: K.
Rows 2, 4, 6, 16, 18, and 20: P.
Rows 7 and 13: *K3, p11*, rep *to*, end k3.
Rows 8 and 14: P3, *k11, p3*, rep *to*.
Row 9: *K3, p2, k7, p2*, rep *to*, end k3.
Row 10: *K5, p7, k2*, rep *to*, end k3.
Row 11: P3, *p2, k7, p5*, rep *to*.
Row 12: *P3, k2, p7, k2*, rep *to*, end p3.
Rows 21 and 27: P7, *k3, p11*, rep *to*, end k3, p7.
Rows 22 and 28: K7, p3, *k11, p3*, rep *to*, end k7.
Row 23: K5, p2, *k3, p2, k7, p2*, rep *to*, end k3, p2, k5.
Row 24: P5, *k7, p7*, rep *to*, end k7, p5.
Row 25: K5, p7, *k7, p7*, rep *to*, end k5.
Row 26: P5, k2, p3, *k2, p7, k2, p3*, rep *to*, end k2, p5.
Repeat these 28 rows for pattern.

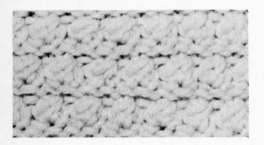

PEBBLE RIDGE STITCH
horizontal ridge stitch, berry ridge

Multiple of 2.
Rows 1 and 5: P.
Row 2: *K1, (k1, p1, k1) in next st*, rep *to*.
Row 3: *K3, p1*, rep *to*.
Row 4: *K1, p3 tog*, rep *to*.
Row 6: *(K1, p1, k1) in next st, k1*, rep *to*.
Row 7: *P1, k3*, rep *to*.
Row 8: *P3 tog, k1*, rep *to*.
Repeat these 8 rows for pattern.

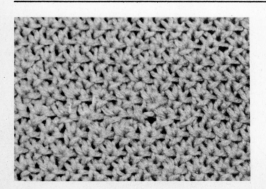

PEBBLE PATTERN
pebble stitch

Multiple of 2.
Row 1 (wrong side): P.
Row 2: *K2 tog*, rep *to*.
Row 3: *K1, inc 1 [lift horizontal thread before next st and k it]*, rep *to*, k into front and back of last st.
Row 4: K.
Repeat these 4 rows for pattern.

DIAGONAL STAR PATTERN
rizotto stitch

Multiple of 2 + 2 selvage stitches
Rows 1, 3, and 5: K.
Row 2: Selv st, *p2 tog, do not let sts drop from lh needle, k2 tog in same sts*, rep *to*, selv st.
Row 4: Selv st, p1, *p2 tog, do not let sts drop from lh needle, k2 tog in same sts*, rep *to*, p1, selv st.
Repeat rows 2–5 for pattern.

TRINITY STITCH
astrakhan stitch

Multiple of 4.
Row 1: *(K1, p1, k1) in 1st st, p3 tog*, rep *to*.
Rows 2 and 4: P.
Row 3: *P3 tog, (k1, p1, k1) in next st*, rep *to*.
Repeat these 4 rows for pattern.

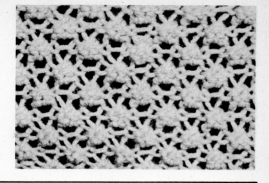

BLACKBERRY OR BLUEBERRY RIB

Multiple of 9.
Row 1: *P5, k4*, rep *to*.
Rows 2 and 4: *P4, inc 1 [k into back of horizontal
    thread before next st], k2 tog, k1, k2 tog tbl, inc
    1*, rep *to*.
Row 3: *P5, p3 tog, (k1, p1, k1) in next st*, rep *to*.
Row 5: *P5, (k1, p1, k1) in next st, p3 tog*, rep *to*.
Repeat rows 2–5 for pattern.

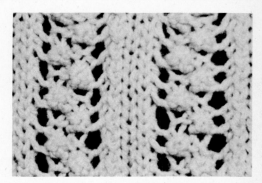

OPEN TRIANGLE PATTERN
valve stitch

Multiple of 3.
Rows 1 and 4: K.
Row 2: *K3 tog (leave sts on lh needle), k the 1st st, k
    the next 2 tog tbl*, rep *to*.
Row 3: P.
Repeat these 4 rows for pattern.

PENNANT RIB
triangle on pleats, ribbed triangles, pennant pleats

Multiple of 10.
Row 1: *P2, k8*, rep *to*.
Rows 2 and 12: *P7, k3*, rep *to*.
Rows 3 and 11: *P4, k6*, rep *to*.
Rows 4 and 10: *P5, k5*, rep *to*.
Rows 5 and 9: *P6, k4*, rep *to*.
Rows 6 and 8: *P3, k7*, rep *to*.
Row 7: *P8, k2*, rep *to*.
Repeat these 12 rows for pattern.

HATCHETS

Multiple of 6 + 3.
Rows 1 and 5: *K3, p1, k1, p1*, rep *to*, end k3.
Rows 2 and 6: P3, *k1, p1, k1, p3*, rep *to*.
Row 3: K1, *p1, k2*, rep *to*, end p1, k1.
Row 4: P1, k1, *p2, k1*, rep *to*, end p1.
Row 7: *P1, k1, p1, k3*, rep *to*, end p1, k1, p1.
Row 8: K1, p1, k1, *p3, k1, p1, k1*, rep *to*.
Repeat these 8 rows for pattern.

SPOOL STITCH
the spindle, spool of thread

Multiple of 6 + 2.
Rows 1 and 3: *P2, k4*, rep *to*, end p2.
Rows 2 and 4: K2, *p4, k2*, rep *to*.
Rows 5 and 7: P3, *k2, p4*, rep *to*, end k2, p3.
Rows 6 and 8: K3, p2, *k4, p2*, rep *to*, end k3.
Row 9: P.
Row 10: K.
Repeat these 10 rows for pattern.

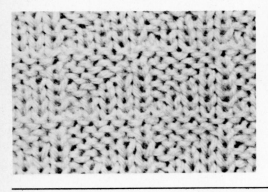

HALF-PENNANT STITCH
pennant pattern

Multiple of 5.
Rows 1 and 6: K.
Rows 2 and 5: *K1, p4*, rep *to*.
Rows 3 and 4: *K3, p2*, rep *to*.
Repeat these 6 rows for pattern.

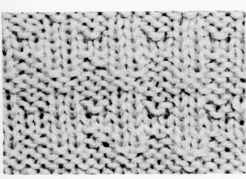

KNIT TWEED STITCH
Harris Tweed stitch

Multiple of 4.
Rows 1, 2, 5, and 6: *K2, p2*, rep *to*.
Rows 3 and 8: K.
Rows 4 and 7: P.
Repeat these 8 rows for pattern.

WOVEN BANDS

Multiple of 16 + 3.
Row 1 (right side): K.
Rows 2, 4, and 6: P3, *(k1, p1) twice, k1, p3*, rep *to*.
Rows 3, 5, and 7: K3, *(k1, p1) twice, k4*, rep *to*.
Row 8: P3, *k13, p3*, rep *to*.
Row 9: K3, *p13, k3*, rep *to*.
Row 10: P.
Rows 11, 13, and 15: K3, *(k1, p1) twice, p1, k3*, rep
    to.
Rows 12, 14, and 16: P3, *(p1, k1) twice, p4*, rep *to*.
Row 17: P8, *k3, p13*, rep *to*, end p8.
Row 18: K8, *p3, k13*, rep *to*, end k8.
Repeat these 18 rows for pattern.

RIPPLE STITCH

Multiple of 8.
Row 1: K7, *p2, k6*, rep *to*, k1.
Rows 2 and 9: K2, *p4, k4*, rep *to*, p4, k2.
Row 3: K1, *p2, k2*, rep *to*, p2, k1.
Rows 4 and 7: K1, p1, *k4, p4*, rep *to*, k4, p1, k1.
Row 5: K3, *p2, k6*, rep *to*, p2, k3.
Row 6: K1, *p6, k2*, rep *to*, p6, k1.
Row 8: K3, *p2, k2*, rep *to*, k1.
Row 10: K1, p2, *k2, p6*, rep *to*, k2, p2, k1.
Repeat these 10 rows for pattern.

CLOSED SHELL STITCH
shell stitch

Multiple of 11.
Row 1 (wrong side): P.
Row 2: *(P2 tog) twice, (inc 1 [inset inc, p. 33], k1) 3
times, inc 1, (p2 tog) twice*, rep *to*.
Repeat these 2 rows for pattern.

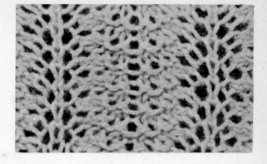

OPEN SHELL STITCH
shell stitch

Multiple of 11.
Row 1: K.
Rows 2 and 4: P.
Row 3: *(P2 tog) twice, (inc 1 [inset inc, p. 33], k1) 3
times, inc 1, (p2 tog) twice*, rep *to*.
Repeat these 4 rows for pattern.

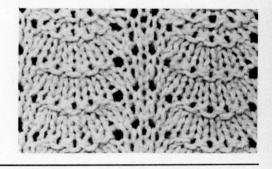

ALMOND RIDGES
the almonds, willow ridge

Multiple of 6 + 2.
Row 1: P2, *(k1, p1, k1) in next st, p3*, rep *to*, end p2.
Row 2 and all even-numbered rows: P.
Rows 3 and 5: P2, *k3, p3*, rep *to*, end p2.
Row 7: P2, *k3 tog tbl, p3*, rep *to*, end p2.
Rows 9 and 11: K.
Repeat these 12 rows for pattern.

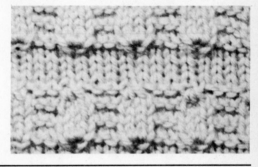

PASTURES PATTERN
the fences

Multiple of 14.
Rows 1, 3, and 5: *P4, k6, p4*, rep *to*.
Rows 2 and 4: K.
Rows 6 and 12: *K3, p1, k6, p1, k3*, rep *to*.
Rows 7 and 11: *P2, k1, p8, k1, p2*, rep *to*.
Rows 8 and 10: *K1, p1, k10, p1, k1*, rep *to*.
Row 9: *K1, p12, k1*, rep *to*.
Repeat these 12 rows for pattern.

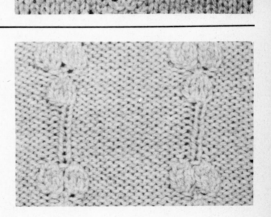

KNOTTED VINES *knotted ropes*

Multiple of 14 + 1.
Rows 1, 3, 5, and 19: P7, *k1, p13*, rep *to*, k1, p7.
Rows 2, 4, 6, and 20: K7, p1, *k13, p1*, rep *to*, k7.
Row 7: P7, *(k into front, back, and front of next st),
p13*, rep *to*, k 3 times in next st, p7.
Row 8: K7, *p3, k13*, rep *to*, p3, k7.
Row 9: P7, k3, *p13, k3*, rep *to*, p7.
Row 10: K7, p3, *k13, p3*, rep *to*, k7.
Row 11: P7, *k3 tog, p13*, rep *to*, k3 tog.
Row 12: K7, p1, *k13, p1*, rep *to*, k7.
Row 13: P6, k 3 times in next st, *p1, k 3 times in next
st, p11, k 3 times in next st*, rep *to*, p1, k 3
times in next st, p6.
Row 14: K6, p3, k1, *p3, k11, p3, k1*, rep *to*, p3, k6.
Row 15: P6, k3, *p1, k3, p11, k3*, rep *to*, p1, k3, p6.
Row 16: K6, p3, k1, *p3, k11, k1*, rep *to*, p3, k6.
Row 17: P6, k3 tog, *p1, k3 tog, p11, k3 tog*, rep *to*, p1, k3 tog, p6.
Row 18: K7, p1, *k13, p1*, rep *to*, k7.
Repeat these 20 rows for pattern.

BOBBLE STITCHES

BOBBLE STITCH

Multiple of 6 + 5.
Rows 1, 3, and 5: P.
Rows 2 and 4: K.
Row 6: K5, *(yo, k1) 3 times in next st [6 bobble sts are formed]; turn to wrong side, sl 1, p5 across the 6 bobble sts; turn to right side, sl 1, k5; turn to wrong side, (p2 tog) 3 times; turn to right side, sl 1, k2 tog, psso [bobble completed], k5*, rep *to*.
Repeat these 6 rows for pattern.

ALTERNATING BOBBLE STITCH
bobble stitch

Multiple of 6 + 5.
Rows 1, 3, and 5: P.
Rows 2 and 4: K.
Row 6: K5, *make bobble in next st [see previous pattern, row 6], k5*, rep *to*.
Rows 7, 9, and 11: P.
Rows 8 and 10: K.
Row 12: K8, *make bobble, k5*, rep *to*, end k8.
Repeat these 12 rows for pattern.

SIMPLE ALTERNATING BOBBLE STITCH

Multiple of 6 + 5.
Rows 1–5: K.
Row 6 (right side): K5, *(k1, yo, k1, yo, k1) in next st, [5 bobble sts formed]; turn to wrong side, p5 across bobble sts; turn to right side, k5, next pass the 4th, 3rd, 2nd, and 1st sts separately in order over last k st [bobble completed], k5*, rep *to*.
Rows 7–11: K.
Row 12: K8, *make bobble, k5*, rep *to*, end k8.
Repeat these 12 rows for pattern.

SIMPLE BOBBLE STITCH

Multiple of 6 + 5.
Rows 1–5: K.
Row 6: K5, *(k1, yo, k1, yo, k1) in next st [5 bobble sts formed]; turn to wrong side, p5 across bobble sts; turn to right side, k5, next pass the 4th, 3rd, 2nd, and 1st sts separately in order over last st [bobble completed], k5*, rep *to*.
Repeat these 6 rows for pattern.

BOBBLE RIB

Multiple of 8 + 5.
Rows 1, 3, and 5: P5, *k3, p5*, rep *to*.
Rows 2 and 4: *K5, p3*, rep *to*, end k5.
Row 6: *K2, MB [see bobble stitch, row 6], k2, p3*, rep *to*, end k2.
Repeat these 6 rows for pattern.

VERTICAL BOBBLE RIB STITCH
vertical bobble stitch

Multiple of 8 + 3.
Row 1: *K3, p2, MB [(p1, k1) twice in next st, pass 2nd,
    3rd, and 4th sts over first st], p2*, rep *to*, end
    k3.
Rows 2 and 4: P3, *k2, p1, k2, p3*, rep *to*.
Row 3: *K3, p2, k1, p2*, rep *to*, end k3.
Repeat these 4 rows for pattern.

DIAGONAL BOBBLE STITCH
oblique bobble stitch

Multiple of 6.
Row 1: *K2, MB [k into front and back of next st 3
    times, pass 2nd, 3rd, 4th, 5th, and 6th sts over
    1st st], p3*, rep *to*.
Rows 2 and 4: *K3, p3*, rep *to*.
Row 3: *P1, k2, MB, p2*, rep *to*.
Repeat these 4 rows for pattern, moving 1 st to the left
on row 1 each time.

PETIT ALTERNATING BOBBLE STITCH
alternating bobble stitch

Multiple of 6.
Rows 1 and 3: K.
Row 2: P.
Row 4: *P4, MB [p2, turn, sl 1, k1, turn, sl 1, p1] 3
    times*, rep *to*.
Repeat these 4 rows for pattern. Work each bobble row
3 sts farther to the left than in row 4.

SLIP-STITCH PATTERNS

This technique is used to draw yarn horizontally, vertically, or diagonally over the knitted
fabric, forming beautiful textures and patterns. It is simple to master and works up
quickly.

SLIP STITCH RIB 3 + 1

Multiple of 4.
Row 1: *K3, sl 1 pwise*, rep *to*.
Row 2: P.
Repeat these 2 rows for pattern.

CENTER SLIP STITCH RIB 3 + 2
fancy slip stitch rib

Multiple of 5.
Row 1: *P2, k1, sl 1, k1*, rep *to*.
Row 2: *P3, k2*, rep *to*.
Repeat these 2 rows for pattern.

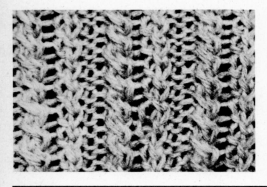

DOUBLE-TWIST RIB
double twisted ribbing, doubled rib twist

Multiple of 6.
Row 1: *P2, sl 1, k1 (do not slip st off lh needle), pass sl st over k st, then k into back of k st again, k into back of 2nd st on lh needle, then k the 1st st in the normal manner*, rep *to*.
Row 2: *P4, k2*, rep *to*.
Repeat these 2 rows for pattern.

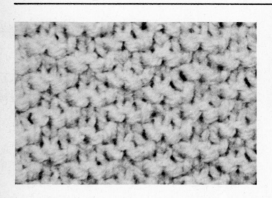

MOCKED RIBS
mock rib, mocked ribbing

Multiple of 2.
Row 1: *P1, yb, sl 1 pwise, yf*, rep *to*.
Row 2: P.
Repeat these 2 rows for pattern.

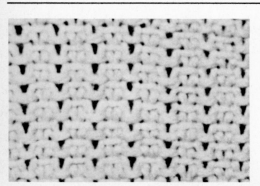

ANT TRAILS
ant egg, ant track stitch

Multiple of 4.
Row 1: *K2, sl 2 pwise*, rep *to*.
Row 2: *P2, k2*, rep *to*.
Row 3: *Sl 2 pwise, k2*, rep *to*.
Row 4: *K2, p2*, rep *to*.
Repeat these 4 rows for pattern.

LINEN STITCH
fabric stitch

Multiple of 2.
Row 1: *K1, yf, sl 1 pwise, yb*, rep *to*.
Row 2: *P1, yb, sl 1 pwise, yf*, rep *to*.
Repeat these 2 rows for pattern.

WOVEN BARRED STITCH
tweed stitch, single darning pattern

Multiple of 2.
Row 1: *K1, yf, sl 1 pwise, yb*, rep *to*.
Rows 2 and 4: P.
Row 3: *Yf, sl 1 pwise, yb, k1*, rep *to*.
Repeat these 4 rows for pattern.

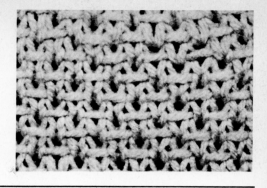

WOVEN BARRED RIBBING
barred rib, tweed rib

Odd number of stitches.
Row 1 (right side): P1, *yf, sl 1 pwise, p1*, rep *to*.
Row 2: K1, *p1, k1*, rep *to*.
Repeat these 2 rows for pattern.

REVERSE SIDE BARRED RIBBING
1 + 1 bead rib

Odd number of stitches.
Row 1: K1, *p1, k1*, rep *to*.
Row 2: P1, *yf, sl 1 pwise, p1*, rep *to*.
Repeat these 2 rows for pattern.

DOUBLE BARRED RIBBING
double tweed stitch rib

Multiple of 4 + 2.
Row 1: P2, *yf, sl 2 pwise, p2*, rep *to*.
Row 2: K2, *p2, k2*, rep *to*.
Repeat these 2 rows for pattern.

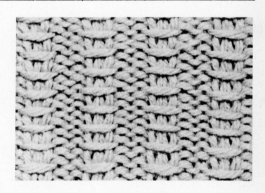

BARRED VARIATION
darning pattern

Multiple of 4 + 2 selvage stitches.
Row 1: Selv st, *k2, yf, sl 2 pwise, yb*, rep *to*, selv st.
Rows 2 and 4: P.
Row 3: Selv st, *yf, sl 2 pwise, yb, k2*, rep *to*, selv st.
Repeat these 4 rows for pattern.

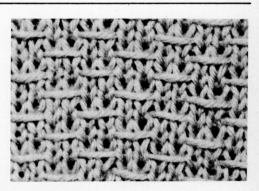

BARRED VARIATION II
double darning pattern

Multiple of 4 + 2 selvage stitches.
Rows 1 and 3: Selv st, *k2, yf, sl 2 pwise, yb*, rep *to*,
    selv st.
Row 2 and all even-numbered rows: P.
Rows 5 and 11: K.
Rows 7 and 9: *Yf, sl 2 pwise, yb, k2*, rep *to*.
Repeat these 12 rows for pattern.

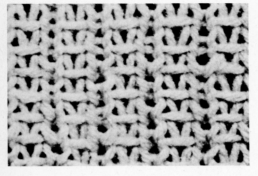

WOVEN BARRED RIB
woven rib, darning pattern rib

Multiple of 2 + 1.
Row 1: *K1, yf, sl 1 pwise, yb*, rep *to*, end k1.
Row 2: P.
Repeat these 2 rows for pattern.

WIDE WOVEN BARRED RIB
tweed stitch rib, double darning pattern rib

Multiple of 6.
Row 1: *P3, sl 1 pwise, yb, k1, yf, sl 1 pwise*, rep *to*.
Rows 2 and 4: *P3, k3*, rep *to*.
Row 3: *P3, k1, yf, sl 1 pwise, yb, k1*, rep *to*.
Repeat these 4 rows for pattern.

ECCENTRIC BARRED PATTERN
grain of powder stitch

Multiple of 2.
Row 1: *P1, yb, sl 1 pwise, yf*, rep *to*.
Rows 2 and 4: P.
Row 3: *Yf, sl 1 pwise, yf, p1*, rep *to*.
Repeat these 4 rows for pattern.

BARRED DIAGONAL RIB
embossed diagonal rib

Multiple of 4.
Row 1: *K3, yf, sl 1 pwise, yb*, rep *to*.
Rows 2, 4, 6, and 8: P.
Row 3: *K2, yf, sl 1 pwise, yf, k1*, rep *to*.
Row 5: *K1, yf, sl 1 pwise, yf, k2*, rep *to*.
Row 7: *Yf, sl 1 pwise, yb, k3*, rep *to*.
Repeat these 8 rows for pattern.

BARRED DIAGONAL HERRINGBONE
diagonal tweed stitch

Multiple of 4 + 2.
Row 1: *K2, yf, sl 2 pwise, yb, rep *to*, k2.
Row 2 and all even-numbered rows: P.
Row 3: Yf, sl 1 pwise, yb, *k2, yf, sl 2 pwise, yb*, rep *to*, k1.
Row 5: Yf, sl 2 pwise, yb, *k2, yf, sl 2 pwise, yb*, rep *to*.
To continue in pattern, move 1 stitch to the left every right-side row.

STAMEN PATTERN STITCH
stamen stitch

Multiple of 2.
Sample I: Use large needles.
Sample II: Use normal size needles.
Rows 1 and 3: K.
Row 2: *K1, sl 1 pwise*, rep *to*, end k2.
Row 4: K2, *sl 1 pwise, k1*, rep *to*.
Repeat these 4 rows for pattern.

Sample I

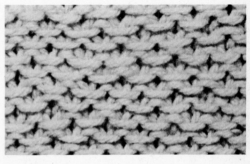

Sample II

STAMEN RIDGE PATTERN
stamen and ridge

Multiple of 2.
Row 1: K.
Row 2 and all even-numbered rows: P.
Rows 3 and 7: *P1, yf, sl 1 pwise*.
Rows 5 and 9: Yf, sl 1 pwise, p1*.
Repeat these 10 rows for pattern.

STAMEN OBLIQUE PATTERN

Multiple of 12.
Row 1: *K6, (p1, yf, sl 1 pwise) 3 times*.
Row 2 and all even-numbered rows: P.
Row 3: K5, *(p1, yf, sl 1 pwise) 3 times, k6*, end k1.
Row 5: K4, *(p1, yf, sl 1 pwise) 3 times, k6*, end k2.
Row 7: K3, *(p1, yf, sl 1 pwise) 3 times, k6*, end k3.
Row 9: K2, *(p1, yf, sl 1 pwise) 3 times, k6*, end k4.
Row 11: K1, *(p1, yf, sl 1 pwise) 3 times, k6*, end k5.
Row 13: *(P1, yf, sl 1 pwise) 3 times, k6*.
Row 15: (Yf, sl 1 pwise, p1) 2 times, sl 1 pwise, *k6, (p1, yf, sl 1 pwise) 3 times*, end k6, p1.
Row 17: (P1, yf) 2 times, *k6, (p1, yf, sl 1 pwise) 3 times*, end p1, yf, sl 1 pwise.
Row 19: P1, yf, sl 1 pwise, p1, *k6, (p1, yf, sl 1 pwise) 3 times*, end p1, yf, sl 1 pwise, p1.
Row 21: P1, yf, sl 1 pwise, *k6, (p1 yf, sl 1 pwise) 3 times*, end (p1, yf, sl 1 pwise) 2 times.
Row 23: P1, *k6, (p1, yf, sl 1 pwise) 3 times, end (p1, yf, sl 1 pwise) 2 times, p1.
Repeat these 24 rows for pattern.

CLASSIC SOCK HEEL STITCH

Any number of stitches.
Row 1: *K1, sl 1*, rep *to*.
Row 2: P.
Repeat these 2 rows for pattern.

SWARM STITCH

Multiple of 4.
Rows 1, 2, 5, 6, 8, 11, 12, and 14: *P2, k2*, rep *to*.
Rows 3 and 9: *P2, yf, sl 2 pwise*, rep *to*.
Rows 4 and 10: *Yb, sl 2, k2*, rep *to*.
Row 7: *P2, k tog (the 2 sl loops of the 2 previous sl st
    rows and the next st), k1*, rep *to*.
Row 13: *P2, k1, k tog (as row 7)*, rep *to*.
Repeat rows 3–14 for pattern.

KNOT STITCH
knotted stitch, knotting stitch

Multiple of 3 + 1.
Row 1: *K1, sl 1 pwise, k1, pass sl st over k1 and put it
    back on lh needle and k the st*, rep *to*, end
    k1.
Row 2: P.
Repeat these 2 rows for pattern.

HORSESHOE STITCH
medallion stitch

Multiple of 4.
Row 1: *Yb, sl 2 pwise, k into the back of the 4th st,
    then 3rd st*, rep *to*.
Row 2: *Yf, sl 2 pwise, p the 4th st, then p the 3rd st,
    rep *to*.
Row 3: K.
Row 4: P.
Repeat these 4 rows for pattern.

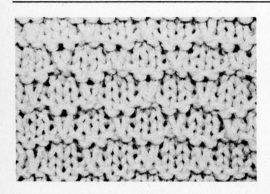

SLIP STITCH RIDGED
ridge slip stitch, ridged V

Multiple of 4.
Rows 1 and 5: K.
Rows 2 and 4: *K3, yb, sl 1 pwise*.
Row 3: *Yf, sl 1 pwise, p3*.
Rows 6 and 8: *K1, yb, sl 1 pwise, k2*.
Row 7: *P2, yf, sl 1 pwise, p1*.
Repeat these 8 rows for pattern.

LITTLE FISHTAIL PATTERN
fishtail stitch 1, guppy tail

Multiple of 10 + 1 + 2 selvage stitches.
Row 1: K1 selv st, *k1, yf, k3, sl 1, k2 tog, psso, k3, yf*, k1, k1 selv st.
Rows 2, 4, and 6: P.
Row 3: K1 selv st, *k2, yf, k2, sl 1, k2 tog, psso, k2, yf, k1*, k1, k1 selv st.
Row 5: K1 selv st, k2 tog, *yf, k1, yf, k1, sl 1, k2 tog, psso, k1, yf, k1, yf, sl 1, k2 tog, psso*, k2 tog, k1 selv st.
Repeat these 6 rows for pattern.

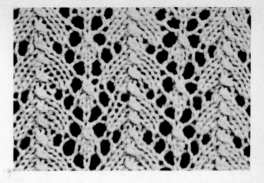

ALTERNATING SLIP STITCH RIB
changing rib

Multiple of 8.
Rows 1 and 3 (wrong side): *K3, yf, sl 1 pwise, k3, p1*, rep *to*.
Row 2: *K1, p3, sl 1 pwise, p3*, rep *to*.
Row 4: *K1, p3, k1, p3*, rep *to*.
Repeat these 4 rows for pattern.

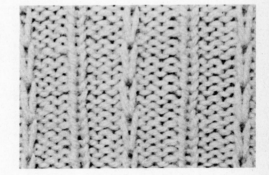

SLIP STITCH COLUMN RIB
slip stitch rib

Multiple of 3.
Row 1 (wrong side): P2, inc 1 [take up yarn after last st and before next st], k1*, rep *to*.
Row 2: *P1, sl 1 pwise, k2, psso the k2 sts*, rep *to*.
Repeat these 2 rows for pattern.

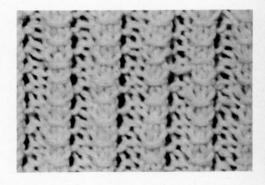

HORIZONTAL CHEVRON SLIP STITCH
horizontal chevron

Multiple of 10 + 2 selvage stitches.
Rows 1 and 11: Selv st, *k1, yf, sl 3 pwise, yb, k2, yf, sl 3 pwise, yb, k1*, selv st.
Rows 2 and 10: Selv st, *(yb, sl 3 pwise, yf, p2) twice*, selv st.
Rows 3 and 9: Selv st, *yf, sl 1 pwise, yb, k2, yf, sl 3 pwise, yb, k2, yf, sl 2 pwise*, selv st.
Rows 4 and 8: Selv st, *yb, sl 1 pwise, p2, yb, sl 3 pwise, yf, p2, yb, sl 2 pwise*, selv st.
Rows 5 and 7: Selv st, *(yf, sl 3 pwise, yb, k2) twice*, selv st.
Row 6: Selv st, *(p1, yb, sl 3 pwise, yf, p1) twice*, selv st. **Rows 12 and 14:** P. **Row 13:** K.
Repeat these 14 rows for pattern.

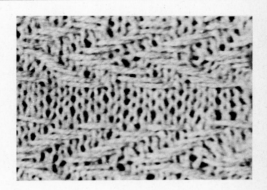

BARRED WOVEN CHECK STITCH
woven check stitch, barred check

Multiple of 12.
Rows 1, 3, 5, 7, and 9: *K9, yf, sl 3 pwise, yb*, rep *to*.
Row 2 and all even-numbered rows: P.
Rows 11, 13, and 15: *(K1, yf, sl 3 pwise, yb) 3 times*, rep *to*.
Repeat these 16 rows for pattern.

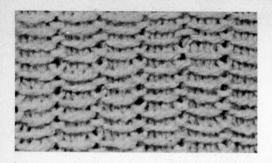

HORIZONTAL BAR STITCH
bat stitch, horizontal bat stitch

Multiple of 3 + 1.
Row 1: K.
Row 2: *K1, sl 2 pwise*, rep *to*, end k1.
Repeat these 2 rows for pattern.

ELONGATED STITCHES

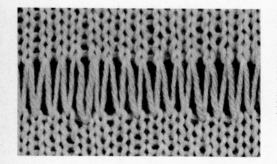

SIMPLE DROP INSERTION
simple drop, single drop stitch

Any number of stitches.
Rows 1, 3, 5, 7, and 9: K.
Rows 2, 4, 6, 8, and 10: P.
Row 11: *K (wind yarn 3 times around needle for each st)*, rep *to*.
Row 12: *P (let the extra loops drop)*, rep *to*.
Repeat these 12 rows for pattern.

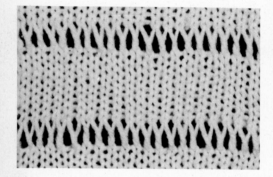

TWISTED DROP INSERTION
twisted drop stitch

Any number of stitches.
Rows 1, 3, 5, and 7: K.
Rows 2, 4, 6, and 8: P.
Row 9: *K (wind yarn around both needles once, then around the rh needle as if to knit in the normal manner)*, rep *to*.
Row 10: *P (let the extra loops drop)*, rep *to*.
Repeat these 10 rows for pattern.

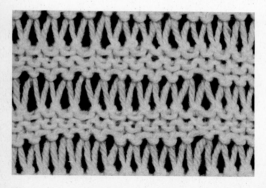

DOUBLE TWIST DROP INSERTION
double twisted drop stitch, double crested insertion

Any number of stitches.
Rows 1, 3, 5, and 7 (right side): K.
Rows 2, 4, and 6: P.
Row 8: *K (wind yarn around both needles once, then around the rh needle once as if to knit in the normal manner)*, rep *to*.
Row 9: Repeat row 8, letting the extra loops of row 8 drop.
Row 10: *k (let the extra loop of the preceding row drop)*, rep *to*.
Repeat these 10 rows for pattern.

GARTER STITCH DROP INSERTION
garter drop stitch

Any number of stitches.
Rows 1–4: K.
Row 5: *K (wind yarn twice around needle)*, rep *to*.
Row 6: *K (let the extra loops drop)*, rep *to*.
Repeat these 6 rows for pattern.

MOSS STITCH DROP INSERTION
moss drop stitch

Multiple of 2 + 1.
Rows 1–6: *K1, p1*, rep *to*, end p1. [See "Seed
    Stitch," p. 56.]
Row 7: *Work in moss st k1, p1 (wind yarn twice round
    needle on each stitch)*, rep *to*.
Row 8: *Work in moss st (let the extra loop drop)*, rep
    to.
Repeat these 8 rows for pattern.

HARROWED STITCH
harrow stitch

Multiple of 10.
Rows 1 and 3: K.
Row 2: *P1, k1, k5 elongated [see "Elongated Stitches,"
    p. 43], k1, p2*, rep *to*.
Row 4: *K3 elongated, k1, p3, k1, k2 elongated*, rep
    to.
Repeat these 4 rows for pattern.

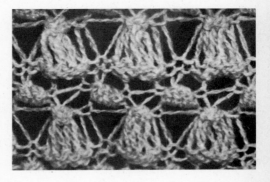

DROOPING FLORAL STITCH
hyacinth stitch

Multiple of 6 + 2.
Row 1: K1, *p5 tog, (k1, p1, k1, p1, k1) in next st*, rep
    to, end k1.
Rows 2 and 4: P.
Row 3: K1, *(k1, p1, k1, p1, k1) in next st, p5 tog*, rep
    to, end k1.
Row 5: K (wind yarn around needle 3 times for each st).
Row 6: P (let the extra loops drop off needle).
Repeat these 6 rows for pattern.

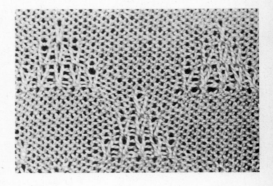

ALTERNATING LOOP STITCH TRIANGLES
loop triangle

Multiple of 18.
Row 1: *P5, (k1, winding yarn around needle twice, p1)
    5 times, p3*, rep *to*.
Row 2: Knit the k sts, yf, sl the p sts, dropping the extra
    loop.
Rows 3, 7, 11, 15, 19, and 23: Purl the p sts, yb, sl the k
    sts pwise.
Rows 4, 8, 12, 16, 20, and 24: Knit the k sts, yf, sl the p
    sts.
Row 5: *P5, k1, (p1, k1, winding yarn around needle
    twice) 3 times, p1, k1, p4*, rep *to*.
Rows 6, 10, 18, and 22: Rep row 2 but k the 1st and last
    sl sts of previous triangle.
Row 9: *P7, k1, p1, k1, winding yarn around needle
    twice, p1, k1, p6*, rep *to*.
Row 13: P2, (k1, winding yarn around needle twice, p1)
    2 times, *p3, k1, p4, (k1, winding yarn around
    needle twice, p1) 5 times*, rep *to*.
Row 14: Rep row 2.
Row 17: P2, k1, winding yarn around needle twice, p1,
    k1, *p9, k1, p1, (k1, winding yarn around
    needle twice, p1) 3 times, k1*, rep *to*.
Row 21: P2, k1, *p13, k1, p1, k1, winding yarn around
    needle twice, p1, k1*, rep *to*.
Row 25: P5, *(k1, winding yarn around needle twice, p1)
    5 times, p3, k1, p4*, rep *to*, end p3.
Repeat rows 2–25 for pattern.

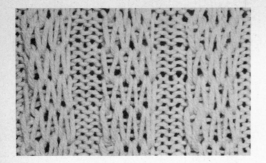

ELONGATED LOOP RIBBING
loop stitch rib

Multiple of 8 + 4.
Row 1: *P4, k4 elongated (k the st winding yarn around rh needle 3 times)*, rep *to*, p4.
Rows 2 and 4: K4, *yf, sl 4 pwise (let extra loops drop), k4*, rep *to*.
Row 3: *P4, yb, sl 4, yf*, rep *to*, p4.
Row 5: Rep row 1 (knit the elongated sts and wind yarn 3 times around rh needle).
Repeat rows 2–5 for pattern.

GIANT BASKET CROSS
cross stitch, giant woven stitch

Multiple of 8 + 2 selvage stitches.
Row 1: K.
Row 2: Selv st, *p6 (wind yarn twice around the needle for each stitch), p2*, rep *to*, selv st.
Row 3: Selv st, *k2, cross the next 6 sts (sl the 6 sts to rh needle, drop the extra loops, return the sts to the lh needle, then k the 4th, 5th, and 6th sts, then the 1st, 2nd, and 3rd, letting all sts drop off lh needle tog)*, rep *to*, selv st.
Row 4: Selv st, p2, k2, *p6 (wind yarn twice around the needle for each st), k2*, rep *to*, p4, selv st.
Row 5: Selv st, k4, *k2, cross the next 6 sts [as in row 3]*, rep *to*, k4, selv st.
Repeat rows 2–5 for pattern.

CROSSED DROP INSERTION
crossed insertion

Multiple of 6.
Rows 1, 3, 5, and 6: K.
Rows 2 and 4: P.
Row 7: *K1 (winding yarn twice around rh needle)*, rep *to*.
Row 8: *Sl 3 to dpn (let extra loops drop), k3 (let extra loop drop), k3 from dpn*, rep *to*.
Repeat these 8 rows for pattern.

DIAMOND PATTERN QUILT STITCH
diamond quilting stitch

Multiple of 4 + 2.
Row 1: *K1, yf, sl 3 pwise, place yarn in front of the 3 sl sts, wind around rh needle once*, rep *to*, end k2.
Rows 2 and 6: *P (let extra loop drop to the back of the work)*, rep *to*.
Rows 3 and 7: K.
Rows 4 and 8: P.
Row 5: K1, *(with rh needle, lift up long yarn from row 2 and k it with the next st), yf, sl 3, take yarn across the 3 sl sts and wind once around rh needle*, rep *to*, end k1.
Repeat these 8 rows for pattern.

RENAISSANCE TILES
Renaissance pattern

Multiple of 8 + 2 + 2 selvage stitches.
Rows 1, 2, 3, 4, 6, and 10: K.
Row 5: Selv st, *K2, p6*, rep *to*, k2, selv st.
Row 7: Selv st, *K2, p1, p4 (wind yarn twice around needle for each st), p1*, rep *to*, k1, selv st.
Row 8: Selv st, k2, *k1, sl next 4 sts to rh needle, drop the extra loops. Return the 4 sts to the lh needle and (k4 tog, p4 tog, k4 tog, p4 tog) into these 4 sts, k3*, rep *to*, selv st.
Row 9: Selv st, *k2, p6*, rep *to*, k2, selv st.
Repeat these 10 rows for pattern.

CLAMSHELL STITCH
clam stitch, shell stitch

Multiple of 6 + 1 + 2 selvage stitches.
Rows 1 and 5: K.
Row 2: Selv st, *p1, p5 (wind yarn twice around needle)*, rep *to*, p1, selv st.
Row 3: Selv st, k1, *sl next 5 sts to rh needle (drop extra loop of each st). Put the 5 sts back on lh needle and work them together as follows (once kwise, once pwise, once kwise, once pwise, once kwise, winding yarn twice around needle each time; you now have 5 sts again), k1*, rep *to*, k1, selv st.
Row 4: Selv st, *p1, k5 (drop the extra loops)*, rep *to*, p1, selv st.
Row 6: Selv st, p4, *p5 (wind yarn twice around needle), p1* rep *to*, p3, selv st.
Row 7: Selv st, k3, *k1, work next 5 sts as in row 3*, rep *to*, k4, selv st.
Row 8: Selv st, p4, *k5 (drop the extra loops), p1*, rep *to*, p3, selv st.
Repeat these 8 rows for pattern.

DOUBLE STITCHES

This is a group of increase stitches often included with the yarn-over grouping. They all contain the instruction "k1-b," an increase made in a stitch of the preceding row.

K1-b: Insert rh needle through the center of the stitch in the preceding row, below the stitch to be knitted, so that both are knitted at the same time.

REVERSIBLE BRIOCHE STITICH
brioche rib

Row 1: K.
Row 2: *K1, k1-b*, rep *to*, end k2.
Repeat row 2 for pattern.

HALF BRIOCHE

Multiple of 2.
Rows 1 and 3: K.
Row 2: *K1, k1-b*, rep *to*.
Row 4: *K1-b, k1*, rep *to*.
Repeat these 4 rows for pattern.

ALTERNATING BRIOCHE STITCH
contrary brioche stitch

Multiple of 2.
Row 1 (base row): K.
Rows 2–5: *K1, k1-b*, rep *to*.
Rows 6–9: *K1-b, k1*, rep *to*.
Repeat rows 2–9 for pattern.

HUNTERS RIB
hunters stitch

Multiple of 11 + 4.
Row 1: *P4, (k1-b, p1) 3 times, k1-b*, rep *to*, end p4.
Row 2: *K4, p1, (k1-b, p1) 3 times*, rep *to*, end k4.
Repeat these 2 rows for pattern.

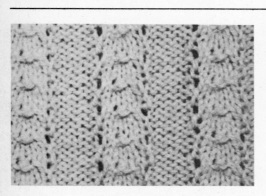

WHEAT GERM PATTERN
wheat germ stitch

Multiple of 2 + 2 selvage stitches.
Rows 1, 3, 7, and 9: K.
Row 2 and all even-numbered rows: P.
Row 5: Selv st, *k1, k1-b*, rep *to*, selv st.
Row 11: Selv st, *k1-b, k1*, rep *to*, selv st.
Repeat these 12 rows for pattern.

BRAIDED RIBS
braid stitch

Multiple of 10.
Row 1: *P3, k5, p2*, rep *to*.
Rows 2 and 4: *K2, p5, k3*, rep *to*.
Row 3: *P3, inc 1 by knitting into the loop below the last st, k1, p3 tog, k1, k1-b, p2*, rep *to*.
Repeat these 4 rows for pattern.

YARN-OVER STITCHES

This technique basically constitutes a series of increases and decreases that produce lacy and openwork patterns. It is important to remember that all increases must be compensated for by a decrease either in the same row or in a later row.

Both eyelet and lace patterns use the yarn-over techniques, although they are often put in separate categories.

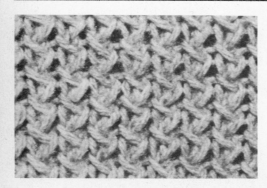

TWEEDED MOCK RIBBING
tweed mock rib, tweed ribs

Multiple of 2.
Row 1: *Yb, sl 1 pwise, k1, yo, psso the k1 and the yo*, rep *to*.
Row 2: P.
Repeat these 2 rows for pattern.

DIAGONAL TWEEDED CROSSED STITCH
diagonal crossed stitch

Multiple of 2.
Row 1: *Sl 1 pwise, k1, yo, psso the k1 and the yo*, rep
    to.
Rows 2 and 4: P.
Row 3: K1, *sl 1 pwise, k1, yo, psso the k1 and the yo*,
    rep *to*, k1.
Repeat these 4 rows for pattern.

TWEEDED OBLIQUE CROSSED STITCH
oblique crossed stitch

Multiple of 8.
Row 1: *(Sl 1 pwise, k1, yo, psso the k1 and the yo)
    twice, k4*, rep *to*.
Row 2 and all even-numbered rows: P.
Row 3: *K2, (sl 1 pwise, k1, yo, psso the k1 and the yo)
    twice, k2*, rep *to*.
To continue in pattern, move 2 stitches to the left on
every odd-numbered row.

BRAIDED CORDED RIB
plaited cord, braided cord stitch

Multiple of 5 + 3.
Row 1: *K3, sl 1 pwise, k1, yo, psso the k1 and the yo*,
    rep *to*, k3.
Row 2: P.
Repeat these 2 rows for pattern.

DOUBLE BRAIDED CORDED RIB
double corded rib

Multiple of 7 + 3.
Row 1: *K3, (sl 1 pwise, k1, yo, pass the sl st over the
    k1 and the yo) twice*, rep *to*, k3.
Row 2: K3, *p4, k3*, rep *to*.
Repeat these 2 rows for pattern.

BAMBOO PATTERN STITCH
bamboo stitch

Multiple of 2.
Row 1: *Yo, k2, pass yo over k2*, rep *to*.
Row 2: P.
Repeat these 2 rows for pattern.

BAMBOO DIAGONAL CROSS
crossed openwork, diagonal bamboo

Multiple of 3 + 1.
Row 1: *P1, yo, p2 tog*, rep *to*, p1.
Row 2: K1, *sl 1 pwise, k2, psso*, rep *to*.
Row 3: *P2, yo*, rep *to*, p1.
Row 4: *Sl 1, k2, psso*, rep *to*, k1.
Row 5: P1, *yo, p2*, rep *to*.
Repeat rows 2–5 for pattern.

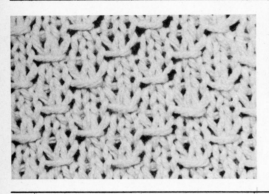

ELM STITCH
elm grain

Multiple of 4.
Rows 1 and 3: K.
Row 2: *Yo, p2, pass yo over p2, p2*, rep *to*.
Row 4: *P2, yo, p2, pass yo over p2*, rep *to*.
Repeat these 4 rows for pattern.

ST. JOHN'S WORT

Multiple of 6.
Row 1: *Sl 1 pwise, k2, psso the k2, k3*, rep *to*.
Row 2: *P4, yo, p1*, rep *to*.
Row 3: *K3, sl 1 pwise, k2, psso the k2*, rep *to*.
Row 4: *P1, yo, p4*, rep *to*.
Repeat these 4 rows for pattern.

TILE PATTERN
tile stitch, petit tile

Multiple of 2 + 1.
Row 1: K1, *yo, k2*, rep *to*.
Row 2: P1, *p3, pass 3rd st on rh needle over 1st 2 sts*, rep *to*.
Row 3: *K2, yo*, rep *to*, k1.
Row 4: *P3, pass 3rd st on rh needle over 1st 2 sts*, rep *to*, p1.
Repeat these 4 rows for pattern.

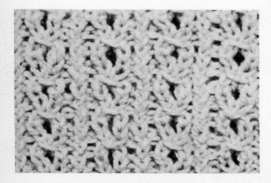

OPEN MOCK CABLE RIB
open twisted rib, mock eyelet rib

Multiple of 5 + 3.
Row 1: *P1, k1 tbl, p1, k2*, rep *to*, end p1, k1 tbl, p1.
Row 2: K1, p1 tbl, k1, *p2, k1, p1 tbl, k1*, rep *to*.
Row 3: *P1, k1, tbl, p1, k1, yo, k1*, rep *to*, end p1, k1 tbl, p1.
Row 4: K1, p1 tbl, k1, *p3, k1, p1 tbl, k1*, rep *to*.
Row 5: *P1, k1 tbl, p1, k3, pass 3rd st on rh needle over 1st 2 sts*, rep *to*, end p1, k1 tbl, p1.
Repeat rows 2–5 for pattern.

LADDER CORD STITCH
corded ladder stitch, open cord ladder

Multiple of 4.
Row 1: *Yo, k4*, rep *to*.
Row 2: P.
Row 3: *Yo, k into 3rd st on lh needle, k 1st and 2nd sts tog, from the back side, k into the front side of the 2nd st on the lh needle, k the 1st st in the normal manner*, rep *to*.
Repeat rows 2 and 3 for pattern.

MOCK CABLE RIBBING
mock cable rib

Multiple of 8.
Row 1: *P5, k3*, rep *to*.
Rows 2 and 4: *P3, k5*, rep *to*.
Row 3: *P5, sl 1, k2, yo, psso the k2 and the yo*, rep *to*.
Repeat these 4 rows for pattern.

SHELL LACE RIB PATTERN
shell lace

Multiple of 14 + 2.
Row 1: K2, *k2 tog, k2, yo, k1, yo, k5, sl 1, k1, psso, k2*, rep *to*.
Row 2 and all even-numbered rows: P.
Row 3: K2, *k2 tog, k1, yo, k3, yo, k4, sl 1, k1, psso, k2*, rep *to*.
Row 5: K2, *k2 tog, yo, k5, yo, k3, sl 1, k1, psso, k2*, rep *to*.
Row 7: K2, *k2 tog, k5, yo, k1, yo, k2, sl 1, k1, psso, k2*, rep *to*.
Row 9: K2, *k2 tog, k4, yo, k3, yo, k1, sl 1, k1, psso, k2*, rep *to*.
Row 11: K2, *k2 tog, k3, yo, k5, yo, sl 1, k1, psso, k2*, rep *to*.
Repeat these 12 rows for pattern.

OPEN ALTERNATING FEATHER STITCH
alternating feather stitch

Multiple of 6 + 1.
Rows 1, 3, 5, 7, 9, and 11: *K1, k2 tog, yo, k1, yo, sl 1, k1, psso*, rep *to*, end k1.
Row 2 and all even-numbered rows: P.
Rows 13, 15, 17, 19, 21, and 23: *K1, yo, sl 1, k1, psso, k1, k2 tog, yo*, rep *to*, end k1.
Repeat these 24 rows for pattern.

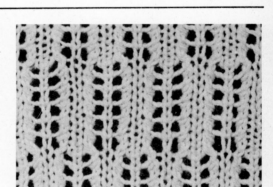

OPEN FEATHER STITCH
feather stitch, eyelet feather stitch

Multiple of 7.
Row 1: *P1, p2 tog, yo, k1, yo, p2 tog, p1*, rep *to*.
Rows 2 and 4: P.
Row 3: K.
Repeat these 4 rows for pattern.

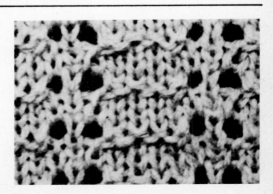

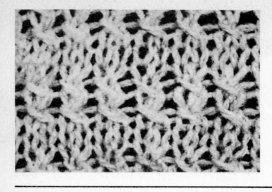

MOCK MOIRÉ PATTERN STITCH
moiré stitch, mock moiré

Multiple of 2.
Rows 1 and 3: *Sl 1 pwise, k1, yo, psso the k1 and the
           yo*, rep *to*.
Rows 2, 4, and 6: P.
Row 5: K.
Repeat these 6 rows for pattern.

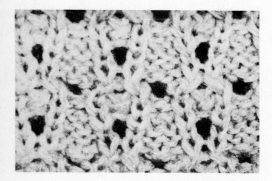

OPEN FANCY CHAINS
openwork fancy stitch, reverse open fancy chains
(wrong side)

Multiple of 5 + 3.
Row 1: K3, *p2, k3*, rep *to*.
Row 2: *P3, k1, yo, k1*, rep *to*, end p3.
Row 3: K3, *p1, k1, p1, k3*, rep *to*.
Row 4: *P3 tog, (k1, yo) twice, k1*, rep *to*, end p3 tog.
Row 5: (K1, yo, k1) in 1st st, *p1, p3 tog, p1, (k1, yo,
           k1) in next st*, rep *to*.
Row 6: *P3, yb, sl 1 kwise, k the next st (leave on lh
           needle), psso the st just worked, then k yarn on
           lh needle and the next st tog*, rep *to*, end p3.
Repeat these 6 rows for pattern.

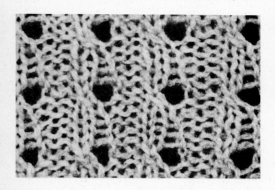

OPEN LONG RIB
openwork 2 × 2 rib

Multiple of 4 + 2.
Rows 1, 3, and 5: *K2, p2*, rep *to*, end k2.
Rows 2 and 4: P2, *k2, p2*, rep *to*.
Row 6: P2, *yo, sl 1, k1, psso, p2*, rep *to*.
Repeat these 6 rows for pattern.

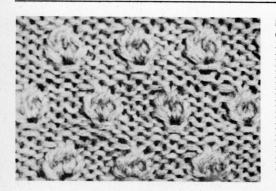

NUT STITCH
cob nut stitch, nut pattern

Multiple of 4.
Row 1: *P3, (k1, yo, k1) in next stitch*, rep *to*.
Rows 2 and 3: *P3, k3*, rep *to*.
Row 4: *P3 tog, k3*, rep *to*.
Rows 5 and 11: P.
Rows 6 and 12: K.
Row 7: *P1, (k1, yo, k1) in next stitch, p2*, rep *to*.
Row 8: K2, *p3, k3*, rep *to*, end p3, k1.
Row 9: P1, *k3, p3*, rep *to*, end k3, p2.
Row 10: K2, *p3 tog, k3*, rep *to*, end p3 tog, k1.
Repeat these 12 rows for pattern.

RIBBED GARTER COLUMNS
ribbed garter stitch

Multiple of 4.
Row 1 (wrong side): *K3, yo, sl 1*, rep *to*.
Row 2: *K2 tog tbl (the sl 1 and yo of row 1), k3*, rep
to.
Repeat these 2 rows for pattern.

SHELL RIB
tile stitch

Multiple of 12 + 2.
Row 1: K1, *sl 1, k1, psso, k3, yo, p2, yo, k3, k2 tog*,
rep *to*, k1.
Row 2: K1, *p2 tog, p2, yo, k4, yo, p2, p2 tog tbl*, rep
to, k1.
Row 3: K1, *sl 1, k1, psso, k1, yo, p6, yo, k1, k2 tog*,
rep *to*, k1.
Row 4: K1, *p2 tog, yo, k8, yo, p2 tog tbl*, rep *to*, k1.
Row 5: K1, *p1, yo, k3, k2 tog, sl 1, k1, psso, k3, yo,
p1*, rep *to*, k1.
Row 6: K1, *k2, yo, p2, p2 tog tbl, p2 tog, p2, yo, k2*,
rep *to*, k1.
Row 7: K1, *p3, yo, k1, k2 tog, sl 1, k1, psso, k1, yo,
k3*, rep *to*, k1.
Row 8: K1, *k4, yo, p2 tog tbl, p2 tog, yo, k4*, rep *to*, k1. Repeat these 8 rows for pattern.

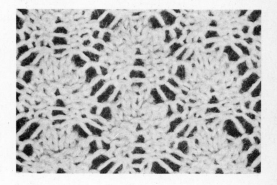

2 + 2 RIB WITH EYELET
perforated 2 × 2 rib

Multiple of 6 + 1.
Row 1: P1, *k1, yo, p3 tog, yo, k1, p1*, rep *to*.
Rows 2 and 4: *K1, p1, k3, p1*, rep *to*, end k1.
Row 3: P1, *k1, p3, k1, p1*, rep *to*.
Repeat these 4 rows for pattern.

PERFORATED RIB STITCH
perforated stitch

Multiple of 3 + 2 selvage stitches.
Row 1: Selv st, *k1, p2*, rep *to*, selv st.
Row 2: Selv st, *k1, yo, k2 tog*, rep *to*, selv st.
Row 3: Selv st, *p1, k yo of preceding row, p1*, rep *to*,
selv st.
Row 4: Selv st, *k1, k2 tog, yo*, rep *to*, selv st.
Row 5: Selv st, *k yo of preceding row, p2*, rep *to*,
selv st.
Repeat rows 2–5 for pattern.

CAMPANULA STITCH
eyelet bells

Multiple of 5.
Row 1: *K3, p2*, rep *to*.
Rows 2, 4, and 6: *K2, p3*, rep *to*.
Row 3: *K3, p2*, rep *to*.
Row 5: *Yo, sl 1, k2 tog, psso, yo, p2*, rep *to*.
Repeat these 6 rows for pattern.

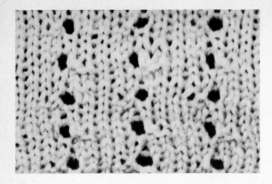

ALTERNATING EYELET COLUMNS
zigzag layette stitch, eyelet vine

Multiple of 5.
Row 1: *K2, p2 tog, yf, k1*, rep *to*.
Rows 2, 4, 6, and 8: P.
Rows 3 and 7: K.
Row 5: *K3, yf, p2 tog*, rep *to*.
Repeat these 8 rows for pattern.

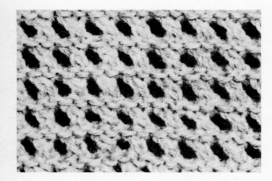

BUTTERFLY EYELET
butterfly stitch, 4 dice

Multiple of 10.
Rows 1 and 3: *K2 tog, yo, k1, yo, sl 1, k1, psso, k5*,
    rep *to*.
Rows 2 and 4: *P7, sl 1 pwise, p2*, rep *to*.
Rows 5 and 11: K.
Rows 6 and 12: P.
Rows 7 and 9: *K5, k2 tog, yo, k1, yo, sl 1, k1, psso*,
    rep *to*.
Rows 8 and 10: *P2, sl 1 pwise, p7*, rep *to*.
Repeat these 12 rows for pattern.

EYELET LACE BORDER
horizontal lace stitch I, garter eyelet lace

Multiple of 2.
Rows 1, 2, and 3: P.
Row 4 (right side): *Yo, sl 1, k1, psso*, rep *to*.
Repeat these 4 rows for pattern.

RIBBON EYELET BORDER STITCH
horizontal lace stitch II, goffer stitch

Multiple of 2.
Rows 1, 3, 5, 7, 9, 10 and 12: K.
Rows 2, 4, 6, and 8: P.
Row 11: *Yo, p2 tog*, rep *to*.
Repeat these 12 rows for pattern.

RIDGED ARROW POINT
arrow point ridge

Multiple of 6 + 5.
Rows 1 and 3: K.
Rows 2 and 4: P.
Row 5: *P5, yo, k1, yo*, rep *to*, end p5.
Row 6: K5, *p3, k5*, rep *to*.
Row 7: *P5, k3*, rep *to*, end p5.
Row 8: K5, *p3 tog, k5*, rep *to*.
Repeat these 8 rows for pattern.

OPEN RIDGING
ridged openwork

Multiple of 6 + 1.
Row 1: K1, *k3, k2 tog, yo, k1*, rep *to*.
Rows 2 and 5: P.
Rows 3 and 6: K.
Row 4: *K4, k2 tog, yo*, rep *to*, end k1.
Repeat these 6 rows for pattern.

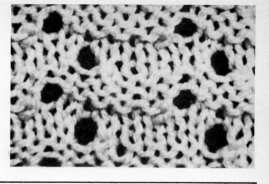

EYELET TRELLIS PATTERN
fancy trellis stitch

Multiple of 7.
Row 1: *K2, k2 tog, yo, k3*, rep *to*.
Row 2: *P1, p2 tog tbl, yo, p1, yo, p2 tog, p1*, rep *to*.
Row 3: *K2 tog, yo, k3, yo, sl 1, k1, psso*, rep *to*.
Rows 4 and 8: P.
Row 5: *Yo, sl 1, k1, psso, k5*, rep *to*.
Row 6: *Yo, p2 tog, p2, p2 tog tbl, yo, p1*, rep *to*.
Row 7: *K2, yo, sl 1, k1, psso, k2 tog, yo, k1*, rep *to*.
Repeat these 8 rows for pattern.

OPENWORK OBLIQUE STITCH
oblique openwork I

Multiple of 2.
Row 1: K1, *yo, k2 tog*, rep *to*, end k1.
Rows 2 and 4: P.
Row 3: K2, *yo, k2 tog*, rep *to*.
Repeat these 4 rows for pattern.

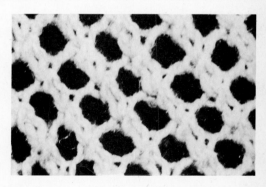

OPENWORK OBLIQUE STITCH II
oblique openwork II

Multiple of 9.
Row 1: *K4, inc 1 [simple inset inc, p. 33], k2 tog, pass
    the inc st over the k2 tog, inc 1, k3*, rep *to*.
Row 2: P.
Row 3: *K3, inc 1, k2 tog, pass the inc st over the k2
    tog, inc 1, k4*, rep *to*.
To continue in pattern, work the 1st stitch farther to the
right on every odd-numbered row.

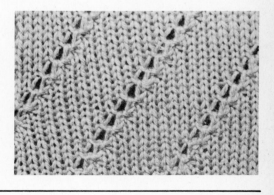

OPENWORK OBLIQUE STITCH III
oblique openwork III

Multiple of 2.
Row 1: K1, p1, *yo, k1, p1*, rep *to*.
Row 2: *K1, k2 tog [the yo and next st of preceding
    row], p1*, rep *to*.
Row 3: K1, p1, *yo, k2 tog [the yo and next st of
    preceding row], p1*, rep *to*.
Repeat rows 2 and 3 for pattern.

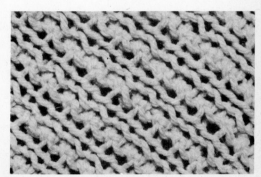

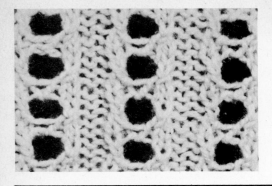

EYELET RIBBING I
openwork rib I

Multiple of 6 + 2.
Row 1: *P2, k2 tog, double yo, sl 1, k1, psso*, rep *to*, end p2.
Rows 2 and 4: K2, *p1, (k1, p1) in double yo, p1, k2*, rep *to*.
Row 3: *P2, k4*, rep *to*, p2.
Repeat these 4 rows for pattern.

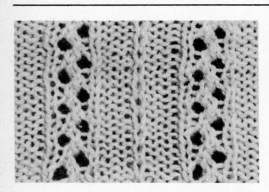

EYELET RIBBING II
openwork rib II, double eyelet rib

Multiple of 7 + 2.
Row 1: *P2, k2 tog, yo, k1, yo, sl 1, k1, psso*, rep *to*, end p2.
Rows 2 and 4: K2, *p5, k2*, rep *to*.
Row 3: *P2, k5*, rep *to*, end p2.
Repeat these 4 rows for pattern.

EYELET RIBBING III
openwork rib III, alternating eyelet rib

Multiple of 11.
Row 1: *P3, sl 1 pwise, p3, k1, yo, k2 tog, k1*, rep *to*.
Rows 2 and 4: *P4, k3, p1, k3*, rep *to*.
Row 3: *P3, sl 1, p3, k1, sl 1, k1, psso, yo, k1*, rep *to*.
Repeat these 4 rows for pattern.

LACE GARTER INSET STITCH
garter lace stitch

Multiple of 2.
Rows 1–6: K.
Row 7: *Yo, k2 tog*, rep *to*.
Row 8: *Yo, p2, tog*, rep *to*.
Row 9: Rep row 7.
Row 10: Rep row 8.
Repeat these 10 rows for pattern.

EYELET SLIP STITCH RIB
openwork slip stitch

Multiple of 4.
Row 1: K.
Row 2: *P4, yo*, rep *to*.
Row 3: *Let the yo sts of row 2 drop, yo, sl 1 kwise, k3, psso*, rep *to*.
Row 4: P.
Repeat these 4 rows for pattern.

OPEN RIBBED GRANITE STITCH
granite-stitch rib, open granite

Multiple of 7.
Row 1: *K1, p1, k1, (yo, k2 tog tbl) twice*, rep *to*.
Row 2: *(Yo, p2 tog) twice, k1, p1, k1*, rep *to*.
Repeat these 2 rows for pattern.

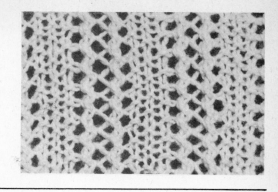

EYELET LACE RIB
lace rib

Multiple of 7 + 2.
Row 1: P2, *yo, sl 1, k1, psso, k1, sl 1, k1, psso, yo, p2*, rep *to*.
Rows 2 and 4: *K2, p5*, rep *to*, end k2.
Row 3: P2, *k1, yo, sl 1, k2 tog, psso, yo, k1, p2*, rep *to*.
Repeat these 4 rows for pattern.

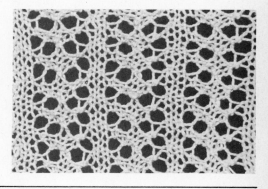

EYELET ZIGZAG GARTER RIB
zigzag garter rib

Multiple of 14 + 7.
Row 1 and all odd-numbered rows: K7, *p7, k7*, rep *to*.
Row 2: *K11, k2 tog, yo, k1*, rep *to*, k7.
Row 4: *K10, k2, tog, yo, k2*, rep *to*, k7.
Row 6: *K9, k2, tog, yo, k3*, rep *to*, k7.
Row 8: *K8, k2 tog, yo, k4*, rep *to*, k7.
Row 10: *K7, k2 tog, yo, k5*, rep *to*, k7.
Row 12: *K8, yo, k2 tog, k4*, rep *to*, k7.
Row 14: *K9, yo, k2 tog, k3*, rep *to*, k7.
Row 16: *K10, yo, k2 tog, k2*, rep *to*, k7.
Row 18: *K11, yo, k2 tog, k1*, rep *to*, k7,
Row 20: *K12, yo, k2 tog*, k7.
Repeat these 20 rows for pattern.

LABURNUM STITCH

Multiple of 5 + 2.
Row 1 (wrong side): P.
Row 2: P2, *yf, sl 1 pwise, yb, k2 tog, psso, yo dbl [wind yarn twice around needle], p2*, rep *to*.
Row 3: *K2, p into front and back of dbl st, p1*, rep *to*, end k2.
Row 4: P2, *k3, p2*, rep *to*.
Row 5: *K2, p3*, rep *to*, end k2.
Repeat rows 2–5 for pattern.

LACY PATTERN I
imitation embroidery I

Multiple of 3 + 2.
Row 1: *P2, yo, k1, yo*, rep *to*, end p2.
Row 2: K2, *p3, k2*, rep *to*.
Row 3: *P2, k3*, rep *to*, end p2.
Row 4: K2, *p3 tog, k2*, rep *to*.
Repeat these 4 rows for pattern.

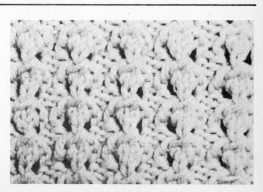

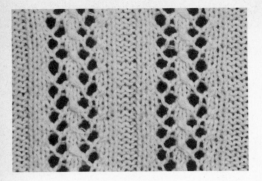

LACY PATTERN II
imitation embroidery II

Multiple of 12 + 3.
Rows 1 and 3: *K3, p9*, rep *to*, end k3.
Row 2: *P3, k3, yo, sl 1, k2 tog, psso, yo, k3*, rep *to*, end p3.
Row 4: *P3, k1, k2 tog, yo, k3, yo, k2 tog, k1*, rep *to*, end p3.
Repeat these 4 rows for pattern.

LACY PATTERN III
imitation embroidery V

Multiple of 13.
Row 1: *(K2 tog, yo) twice, k1, yo, (k2 tog) twice, k2, yo, k2 tog, yo*, rep *to*.
Rows 2 and 4: P.
Row 3: *(Yo, k2 tog) twice, yo, k2, (k2 tog) twice, yo, k1, yo, k2 tog*, rep *to*.
Repeat these 4 rows for pattern.

LACY PATTERN IV
imitation embroidery III

Multiple of 6.
Row 1: *P2, yo, sl 1, k1, psso, k2 tog, yo*, rep *to*.
Rows 2 and 4: *P4, k2*, rep *to*.
Row 3: *P2, k4*, rep *to*.
Repeat these 4 rows for pattern.

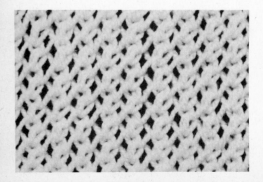

STAR PATTERN
star stitch

Multiple of 3 + 1.
Row 1: K1, *yo, k3, pass the 1st st over the next 2 sts*, rep *to*.
Rows 2, 4, and 6: P.
Row 3: *Yo, k3, pass 1st st over the next 2 sts*, rep *to*, end k1.
Row 5: K2, *yo, k3, pass 1st st over the next 2 sts*, rep *to*, end yo, k2 tog.
Repeat these 6 rows for pattern.

MOCK TURK STITCH I
mock Turkish stitch

Multiple of 2.
Row 1: K1, *yo, k2 tog*, rep *to*, end k1.
Row 2: Rep row 1.
Repeat these 2 rows for pattern.

MOCK TURK STITCH WITH LEFT BIAS
Turkish stitch with bias to left

Multiple of 2.
Row 1 (base row): K.
Row 2: P1, *yo, p2 tog tbl*, rep *to*, end p1.
Row 3: K1, *sl 1, k1, psso, yo*, rep *to*, end k1.
Repeat rows 2 and 3 for pattern.

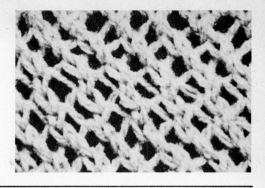

MOCK TURK STITCH WITH RIGHT BIAS
Turkish stitch with bias to the right

Multiple of 2.
Row 1: K.
Row 2: P1, *yo, p2 tog*, rep *to*, end p1.
Row 3: K2, *yo, k2 tog*, rep *to*.
Row 4: P2, *yo, p2 tog*, rep *to*.
Row 5: K1, *yo, k2 tog*, rep *to*, end k1.
Repeat rows 2–5 for pattern.

NETTING STITCH I
Turkish stitch

Multiple of 2.
All rows: *Yo, sl 1, k1, psso*, rep *to*.

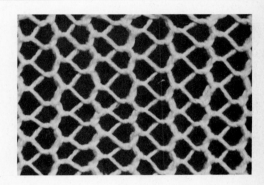

NETTING STITCH II
purse stitch

Multiple of 2.
All rows: *Yo, p2 tog*, rep *to*.

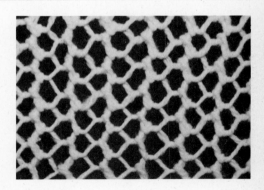

CAT EYE NETTING
cat's eye stitch

Multiple of 4.
Row 1: P2, *yo, p4 tog*, rep *to*, end p2.
Row 2: K2, *k1, (k1, p1, k1) in yo of preceding row*, rep *to*, end k2.
Row 3: K.
Repeat these 3 rows for pattern.

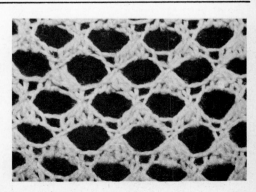

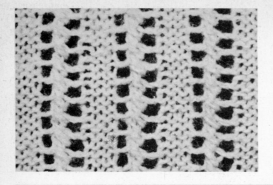

OPENWORK COLUMNS
vertical openwork I

Multiple of 6 + 3.
Row 1: *P3, yo, sl 1, k2 tog, psso, yo*, rep *to*, end p3.
Row 2: K3, *p3, k3*, rep *to*.
Repeat these 2 rows for pattern.

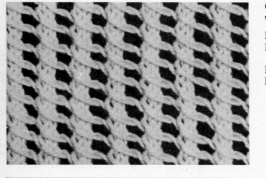

OPENWORK COLUMNS II
vertical openwork II

Multiple of 3.
Row 1: *Yo, sl 1 pwise, k2, pass sl st over the k2*, rep
to.
Row 2: P.
Repeat these 2 rows for pattern.

OPENWORK COLUMNS III
vertical openwork III

Multiple of 3.
Row 1: *K1, yo, k2 tog*, rep *to*.
Row 2: *K1, yo, k2 tog [the yo and k1 of the preceding
row]*, rep *to*.
Repeat row 2 for pattern.

OPENWORK COLUMNS IV
vertical openwork IV

Multiple of 4.
Row 1: *K1, yo, sl 1 pwise, k1, p1*, rep *to*.
Row 2: *K1, p1, k2 tog [into the back of yo and sl st of
the preceding row], p1*, rep *to*.
Repeat these 2 rows for pattern.

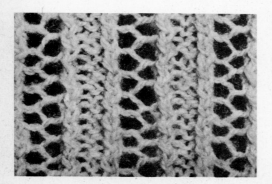

OPENWORK COLUMNS V
vertical openwork V

Multiple of 6 + 2.
Row 1: *P2, k2 tog, yo, k2*, rep *to*, end p2.
Row 2: K2, *p2 tog, yo, p2, k2*, rep *to*.
Repeat these 2 rows for pattern.

OPENWORK COLUMNS VI
vertical openwork VI

Multiple of 4.
Row 1: *K2, yo, sl 1, k1, psso*, rep *to*.
Row 2: *P2, yo, p2 tog*, rep *to*.
Repeat these 2 rows for pattern.

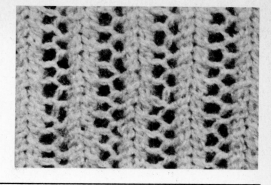

EYELET LACE STITCH
perforated stitch

Multiple of 4 + 2.
Row 1: K2, *sl 1, k1, psso, yo dbl, k2 tog*, rep *to*.
Rows 2 and 4: P, but k into front and back of yo sts.
Row 3: *Sl 1, k1, psso, yo dbl, k2 tog*, rep *to*, end k2.
Repeat these 4 rows for pattern.

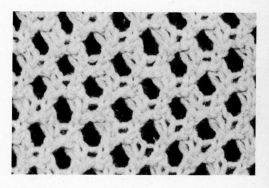

EYELET LACE STITCH I
eyelet stitch I

Multiple of 4.
Row 1: *K2, (yo) twice, k2*, rep *to*.
Row 2: *P2 tog, k1, p1 [in yo], p2 tog*, rep *to*.
Row 3: *Yo, k4, yo*, rep *to*.
Row 4: *P1, (p2 tog) twice, k1*, rep *to*.
Repeat these 4 rows for pattern.

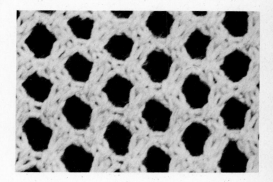

EYELET LACE STITCH II
eyelet stitch II

Multiple of 4.
Row 1: K.
Row 2: *P4, (yo) twice*, rep *to*, end p4.
Row 3: *(K2 tog) twice, k into the front and back of yo
       st*, rep *to*, end (k2 tog) twice.
Row 4: P1, *(yo) twice, p4*, rep *to*, end (yo) twice, p1.
Row 5: K1, *k into the front and back of yo st, (k2 tog)
       twice*, rep *to*, end k into the front and back
       of yo, p1.
Repeat rows 2–5 for pattern.

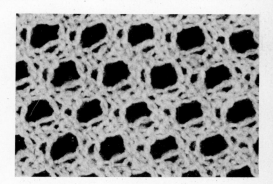

EYELET LACE STITCH III
eyelet stitch III

Multiple of 5.
Row 1: *K3, yo, k2 tog*, rep *to*.
Row 2 and all even-numbered rows: P.
Row 3: K1, *yo, k2 tog, k3*, rep *to*.
Row 5: K4, *yo, k2 tog, k3*, rep *to*.
Row 7: K2, *yo, k2 tog, k3*, rep *to*.
Row 9: *Yo, k2 tog, k3*, rep *to*.
Repeat these 10 rows for pattern.

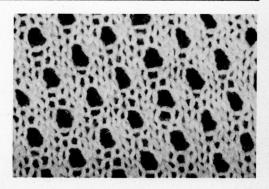

CELL STITCH
cellular stitch I

Multiple of 4.
Rows 1 and 3: P.
Row 2: Yo, sl 1, k2 tog, psso, *yo, k1, yo, sl 1, k2 tog, psso*, rep *to*, end yo, k1.
Row 4: Yo, k2 tog, *yo, sl 1, k2 tog, psso, yo, k1*, rep *to*, end yo, sl 1, k1, psso.
Repeat these 4 rows for pattern.

TURTLE LACE PATTERN
tortoise stitch

Multiple of 6 + 1.
Row 1: *K1, yo, sl 1, k1, psso, k1, k2 tog, yo*, rep *to*, end k1.
Row 2 and all even-numbered rows: P.
Rows 3 and 9: *K2, yo, k3, yo, k1*, rep *to*, end k1.
Row 5: K2 tog, *yo, sl 1, k1, psso, k1, k2 tog, yo, sl 1, k2 tog, psso*, rep *to*, end sl 1, k1, psso.
Row 7: *K1, k2 tog, yo, k1, yo, sl 1, k1, psso*, rep *to*, end k1.
Row 11: *K1, k2 tog, yo, sl 1, k2 tog, psso, yo, sl 1, k1, psso*, rep *to*, end k1.
Repeat these 12 rows for pattern.

VINE LACE
chevron lace stitch, lace vine

Multiple of 6.
Row 1: *Yo, k2, k2 tog, k2*, rep *to*.
Rows 2 and 4: P [including yo sts].
Row 3: *K2, k2 tog, k2, yo*, rep *to*.
Repeat these 4 rows for pattern.

VINE LACE II
lace vine alternate

Multiple of 9 + 4.
Row 1: K3, *yo, k2, sl 1, k1, psso, k2 tog, k2, yo, k1*, rep *to*, end k1.
Rows 2 and 4: P.
Row 3: K2, *yo, k2, sl 1, k1, psso, k2 tog, k2, yo, k1*, rep *to*, end k2.
Repeat these 4 rows for pattern.

OPEN RIBBING
openwork rib

Multiple of 4.
Row 1: *K3, p1*, rep *to*.
Row 2: *K1, p3*, rep *to*.
Row 3: *Yo, sl 1, k2 tog, psso, yo, p1*, rep *to*.
Row 4: *K1, p3*, rep *to*.
Repeat these 4 rows for pattern.

PORTHOLE RIB
fancy rib, eyelet rib

Multiple of 4.
Rows 1 and 3 (right side): *K1, p3*, rep *to*.
Rows 2, 4, and 6: *K3, p1*, rep *to*.
Row 5: *K1, p2 tog, yo, p1*, rep *to*.
Repeat these 6 rows for pattern.

PORTHOLE KNIT RIB
fancy rib reverse, reverse porthole

Multiple of 4.
Rows 1, 3, and 5: *K3, p1*, rep *to*.
Rows 2 and 4: *K1, p3*, rep *to*.
Row 6: *K1, p2 tog, yo, p1*, rep *to*.
Repeat these 6 rows for pattern.

BLUEBERRY STITCH
blackberry stitch, berry stitch

Multiple of 4.
Row 1: *(K1, yo, k1) in 1st st, p3*, rep *to*.
Row 2: *P3 tog, k3*, rep *to*.
Row 3: *P3, (k1, yo, k1) in next st*, rep *to*.
Row 4: *K3, p3 tog*, rep *to*.
Repeat these 4 rows for pattern.

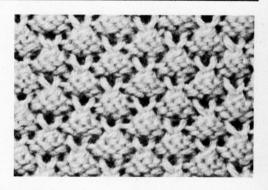

RIPPLED LADDERS
ladders

Multiple of 8 + 1.
Rows 1 and 3: *K5, yf, sl 3 pwise, yo*, rep *to*, end k1.
Row 2: P1, *yb, sl 3 pwise, yf, p5*, rep *to*.
Rows 4 and 8: P.
Rows 5 and 7: K1, *yf, sl 3 pwise, k5, yo*, rep *to*.
Row 6: *P5, yb, sl 3 pwise, yf*, rep *to*, end p1.
Repeat these 8 rows for pattern.

ALTERNATING KNOTTED RIB
flagon stitch

Multiple of 6.
Row 1 and all odd-numbered rows: *P2, k1, p2, k1*, rep *to*.
Rows 2, 4, 6, and 8: *P1, k2, p1, yf, sl 1 pwise, p1, yo, psso the p1 and the yo, p1, k2*, rep *to*.
Rows 10, 12, 14, and 16: *P1, yf, sl 1 pwise, p1, yo, psso the p1 and the yo, p1, k2*, rep *to*.
Repeat these 16 rows for pattern.

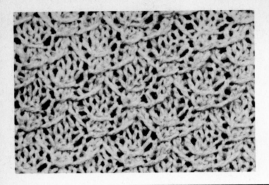

TERRAPIN STITCH

Multiple of 6.
Row 1: *Yo, k3, pass yo over the k3, sl 3 pwise*, rep *to*.
Rows 2 and 6: K.
Row 3: *Yo, k3, pass yo over the k3, p3*, rep *to*.
Row 4: *K1, lift yarn in front of sl sts of row 1, put on lh needle, and k it with the next st, k4*, rep *to*.
Row 5: *Sl 3 pwise, yo, k3, pass yo over the k3*, rep *to*.
Row 7: *P3, yo, k3, pass yo over the k3*, rep *to*.
Row 8: *K4, lift yarn in front of sl sts of row 5, put on lh needle, and k it with the next st. k1*, rep *to*.
Repeat these 8 rows for pattern.

CABLED MOSS STITCH
moss stitch cable

Multiple of 9 + 5.
Rows 1 and 3: (K1, p1) twice, k1, *k1 tbl, p2, k1 tbl, (k1, p1) twice, k1*, rep *to*.
Rows 2, 4, and 6: *(K1, p1) 3 times, k2, p1*, rep *to*, end (k1, p1) twice, k1.
Row 5: (K1, p1) twice, k1, *yo, k1, p2, k1, pass yo over 4 sts, (k1, p1) twice, k1*, rep *to*.
Repeat these 6 rows for pattern.

LOZENGE STITCH I

Multiple of 16.
Row 1: *K6, k2 tog, yo, k1, yo, k2 tog, k5*, rep *to*.
Row 2 and all even-numbered rows: K.
Row 3: *K5, k2 tog, yo, k3, yo, k2 tog, k4*, rep *to*.
Row 5: *K4, k2 tog, yo, k5, yo, k2 tog, k3*, rep *to*.
Row 7: *K3, k2 tog, yo, k7, yo, k2 tog, k2*, rep *to*.
Row 9: *K2, k2 tog, yo, k9, yo, k2 tog, k1*, rep *to*.
Row 11: *K1, k2 tog, yo, k11, yo, k2 tog*, rep *to*.
Row 13: *K1, yo, k2 tog, k11, k2 tog, yo*, rep *to*.
Row 15: *K2, yo, k2 tog, k9, k2 tog, yo, k1*, rep *to*.
Row 17: *K3, yo, k2 tog, k7, k2 tog, yo, k2*, rep *to*.
Row 19: *K4, yo, k2 tog, k5, k2 tog, yo, k3*, rep *to*.
Row 21: *K5, yo, k2 tog, k3, k2 tog, yo, k4*, rep *to*.
Row 23: *K6, yo, k2 tog, k1, k2 tog, yo, k5*, rep *to*.
Repeat these 24 rows for pattern.

OIL WELLS PATTERN
Eiffel Tower stitch

Multiple of 8.
Rows 1 and 9: P.
Row 2: *P4, yo, p2 tog, p2*, rep *to*.
Rows 3, 5, and 7: *K3, p1, k4*, rep *to*.
Rows 4, 6, and 8: *P4, k1, p3*, rep *to*.
Row 10: *Yo, p2 tog, p6*, rep *to*.
Rows 11, 13, and 15: *K7, p1*, rep *to*.
Rows 12, 14, and 16: *K1, p7*, rep *to*.
Repeat these 16 rows for pattern.

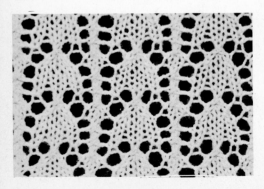

SNOWDROP STITCH
snowdrop lace stitch

Multiple of 8 + 3 + 2 selvage stitches.
Rows 1, 3, 5, and 7: P.
Rows 2 and 4: Selv st, k1, *yo, dbl dec [k2 tog tbl, put this st back on lh needle, pass next st over the k2 tog, put back on rh needle), yo, k5*, rep *to*, yo, dbl dec, yo, k1, selv st.
Row 6: Selv st, k1, *k3, yo, sl 1, k1, psso, k1, k2 tog, yo*, rep *to*, k4, selv st.
Row 8: Selv st, k1, *yo, dbl dec, yo, k1*, rep *to*, yo, dbl dec, yo, k1, selv st.
Repeat these 8 rows for pattern.

FISHTAIL STITCH
fishtail stitch II, chevron lace stitch

Multiple of 8 + 1.
Row 1: K1, *yo, k2, sl 1, k2 tog, psso, k1, yo, k1*, rep
to, end k1.
Rows 2, 4, and 6: P.
Row 3: K2, *yo, k1, sl 1, k2 tog, psso, k1, yo, k3*, rep
to, end yo, k2.
Row 5: K3, *yo, sl 1, k2 tog, psso, yo, k5*, rep *to*, end
k3.
Repeat these 6 rows for pattern.

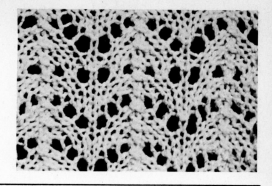

PIQUÉ DIAMOND PATTERN WITH EYELET

Multiple of 8 + 1.
Row 1: K.
Rows 2 and 8: K1, p3, *k1, p7*, rep *to*, end k1, p3, k1.
Rows 3 and 7: K3, *p3, k5*, rep *to*, end p3, k3.
Rows 4 and 6: K1, p1, *k5, p3*, rep *to*, end k5, p1, k1.
Row 5: K1, *p1, p2 tog, yo, p3, k1*, rep *to*.
Repeat these 8 rows for pattern.

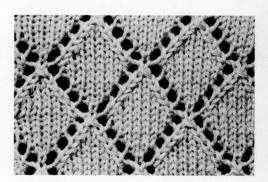

EYELET DIAMONDS
lozenge stitch III

Multiple of 10.
Row 1 and all odd-numbered rows: P.
Row 2: *Yo, sl 1, k1, psso, k5, k2 tog, yo, k1*, rep *to*.
Row 4: *K1, yo, sl 1, k1, psso, k3, k2 tog, yo, k2*, rep
to.
Row 6: *K2, yo, sl 1, k1, psso, k1, k2 tog, yo, k3*, rep
to.
Row 8: *K3, yo, sl 1, k2 tog, psso, yo, k4*, rep *to*.
Row 10: *K2, k2 tog, yo, k1, yo, sl 1, k1, psso, k3*, rep
to.
Row 12: *K1, k2 tog, yo, k3, yo, sl 1, k1, psso, k2*, rep
to.
Row 14: *K2 tog, yo, k5, yo, sl 1, k1, psso, k1*, rep *to*.
Row 16: K1, *yo, k7, yo, sl 1, k2 tog, psso*, rep *to*,
end sl 1, k1, psso.
Repeat these 16 rows for pattern.

LOZENGE STITCH BORDER VARIATION
lozenge stitch II

Multiple of 8.
Rows 1, 4, and 18: K.
Rows 2, 3, 5, 6, 16, 17, 19, and 20: P.
Rows 7 and 15: *K3, yo, sl 1, k1, psso, k3*, rep *to*.
Rows 8, 10, 12, and 14: P.
Rows 9 and 13: *K2, (yo, sl 1, k1, psso) twice, k2*, rep
to.
Row 11: *K1, (yo, sl 1, k1, psso) 3 times, k1*, rep *to*.
Repeat these 20 rows for pattern.

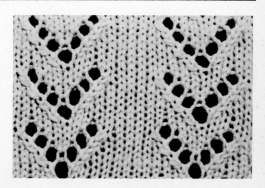

VANDYKE STITCH VARIATION
vandyke stitch III

Multiple of 13.
Row 1: *K6, yo, sl 1, k1, psso, k5*, rep *to*.
Rows 2, 4, 6, and 8: P.
Row 3: *K4, k2 tog, yo, k1, yo, sl 1, k1, psso, k4*, rep
to.
Row 5: *K3, k2 tog, yo, k3, yo, sl 1, k1, psso, k3*, rep
to.
Row 7: *K2, k2 tog, yo, k5, yo, sl 1, k1, psso, k2*, rep
to.
Repeat these 8 rows for pattern.

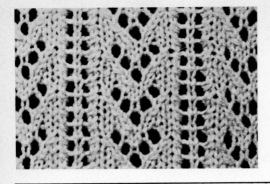

VANDYKE LACY PATTERN
vandyke stitch IV

Multiple of 12.
Row 1: *K3, yo, sl 1, k1, psso, k2, k2 tog, yo, k1, yo, sl 1, k1, psso*, rep *to*.
Rows 2, 4, and 6: P.
Row 3: *K1, k2 tog, yo, k1, yo, sl 1, k1, psso, k1, k2 tog, yo, k1, yo, sl 1, k1, psso*, rep *to*.
Row 5: *K2 tog, yo, k3, yo, sl 1, k1, psso, k2 tog, yo, k1, yo, sl 1, k1, psso*, rep *to*.
Repeat these 6 rows for pattern.

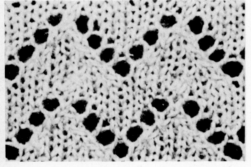

VANDYKE MOSS STRIPE
vandyke stitch V

Multiple of 8 + 1.
Rows 1–8 (moss stitch): *K1, p1*, rep *to*.
Row 9: *K1, yo, sl 1, k1, psso, k3, k2 tog, yo*, rep *to*, k1.
Rows 10, 12, and 14: P.
Row 11: *K2, yo, sl 1, k1, psso, k1, k2 tog, yo, k1*, rep *to*, k1.
Row 13: *K3, yo, sl 1, k2 tog, psso, yo, k2*, rep *to*, k1.
Repeat these 14 rows for pattern.

VANDYKE STITCH VARIATION II
vandyke stitch VI

Multiple of 8 + 1.
Row 1: *K5, yo, k2 tog, k1*, rep *to*, k1.
Row 2 and all even-numbered rows: P.
Row 3: *K3, k2 tog tbl, yo, k1, yo, k2 tog tbl*, rep *to*, k1.
Row 5: K1, *k1, k2 tog tbl, yo, k3, yo, k2 tog*, rep *to*.
Row 7: *Yo, k2 tog tbl, put st back on lh needle, pass next st on lh needle over it, put back on rh needle, yo, k5*, rep *to*, k1.
Row 9: *K1, k into front and back of next st, k6*, rep *to*, k1.
Row 11: *K2 tog tbl, k4, yo, k2 tog tbl, k1*, rep *to*, k1.
Repeat rows 3–12 for pattern.

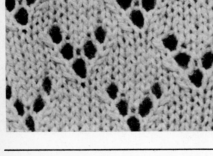

VANDYKE VARIATION III
vandyke stitch VII

Multiple of 10.
Row 1: *Yo, sl 1, k1, psso, k8*, rep *to*.
Row 2 and all even-numbered rows: P.
Row 3: *K1, yo, sl 1, k1, psso, k5, k2 tog, yo, rep *to*.
Row 5: *K2, yo, sl 1, k1, psso, k3, k2 tog, k1*, rep *to*.
Row 7: *K5, yo, sl 1, k1, psso, k3*, rep *to*.
Row 9: *K3, k2 tog, yo, k1, yo, sl 1, k1, psso, k2*, rep *to*.
Row 11: *K2, k2 tog, yo, k3, yo, sl 1, k1, psso, k1*, rep *to*.
Repeat these 12 rows for pattern.

ALTERNATE BRIOCHE STITCH
brioche rib, reversible brioche

Even number of stitches.
Row 1: *Yo, sl 1 pwise, k1*, rep *to*.
Row 2: *Yo, sl 1 pwise, k2 tog*, rep *to*.
Repeat these 2 rows for pattern.

SLIP GRANITE STITCH

Multiple of 4 + 2.
Rows 1 and 3: *K1, p1*, rep *to*.
Row 2: *P1, yb, sl 1 kwise, k2, yo, psso the k2 and yo*, rep *to*, end p1, k1.
Row 4: P1, k1, *p1, yb, sl 1 kwise, k2, yo, psso the k2 and yo*, rep *to*.
Repeat these 4 rows for pattern.

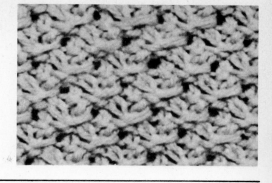

ALTERNATING VERTICAL GRANITE
vertical granite

Multiple of 4.
Rows 1, 3, and 5: *Yf, sl 2 pwise, yo, k2*, rep *to*.
Rows 2, 4, and 6: *P2, k2 tog tbl [next st and yo of preceding row], k1*, rep *to*.
Rows 7, 9, and 11: *K2, yf, sl 1 pwise, yo, yf, sl 1 pwise, yb*, rep *to*.
Rows 8, 10, and 12: *K1, k2 tog tbl, p2*, rep *to*.
Repeat these 12 rows for pattern.

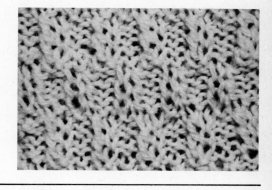

LACE CHECKER PATTERN
lace squares I

Multiple of 16.
Row 1 and all odd-numbered rows: P.
Rows 2, 4, 6, and 8: *K8, (yo, sl 1, k1, psso) 4 times*, rep *to*.
Rows 10, 12, 14, and 16: *(Yo, sl 1, k1, psso) 4 times, k8*, rep *to*.
Repeat these 16 rows for pattern.

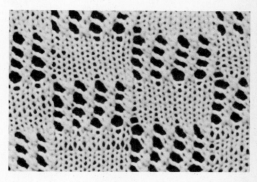

LACE SQUARE REVERSE PATTERN
lace squares II

Multiple of 8 + 5.
Rows 1 and 5: *K5, p3*, rep *to*, end k5.
Rows 2 and 4: P5, *k3, p5*, rep *to*.
Row 3: *K5, p1, yo, p2 tog*, rep *to*, end k5.
Rows 6 and 12: P.
Rows 7 and 11: *K1, p3, k4*, rep *to*, end k1, p3, k1.
Rows 8 and 10: P1, k3, p1, *p4, k3, p1*, rep *to*.
Row 9: *K1, p1, yo, p2 tog, k4*, rep *to*, end k1, p1, yo, p2 tog, k1.
Repeat these 12 rows for pattern.

LACE CHECKER II
lace squares III

Multiple of 12 + 6.
Rows 1, 3, 5, and 7: *K6, (k2 tog, yo) 3 times*, rep *to*, end k6.
Rows 2, 4, and 6: *P6, (p2 tog, yo) 3 times*, rep *to*, end p6.
Row 8: P [incl yo sts].
Repeat from row 1, working the 6 pattern sts over the st below.

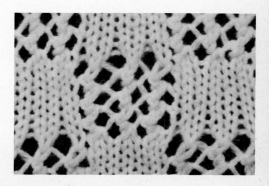

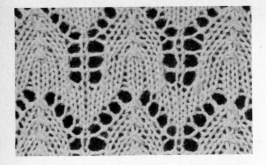

ARCH STITCH
arches

Multiple of 10.
Rows 1, 3, and 5: *K1, yo, k2 tog, k5, sl 1, k1, psso, yo*, rep *to*.
Row 2 and all even-numbered rows: P.
Row 7: *K1, yo, k3, sl 1, k2 tog, psso, k3, yo*, rep *to*.
Row 9: *K2, yo, k2, sl 1, k2 tog, psso, k2, yo, k1*, rep *to*.
Row 11: K3, yo, k1, sl 1, k2 tog, psso, k1, yo, k2*, rep *to*.
Row 13: *K4, yo, sl 1, k1 tog, psso, yo, k3*, rep *to*.
Repeat these 14 rows for pattern.

LACE KNIT RIB PATTERN

Multiple of 11 + 2 selvage stitches.
Row 1: Selv st, *(k2 tog, yo) 3 times, k5*, rep *to*, selv st.
Rows 2 and 4: P.
Row 3: Selv st, *k1, (k2 tog, yo) twice, k6*, rep *to*, selv st.
Repeat these 4 rows for pattern.

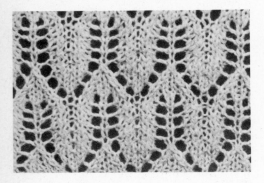

LACE TULIPS
cones

Multiple of 6 + 2 selvage stitches.
Row 1 and all odd-numbered rows: P.
Row 2 (right side): Selv st, *k1, yo, k5, yo*, rep *to*, selv st.
Row 4: Selv st, *k2, yo, sl 1, k1, psso, k1, k2 tog, yo, k1*, rep *to*, selv st.
Row 6: Selv st, *p1, k2, yo, sl 1, k2 tog, psso, yo, k2*, rep *to*, selv st.
Rows 8, 10, 12, and 14: Selv st, *p1, sl 1, k1, psso, k1, yo, k1, yo, k1, k2 tog*, rep *to*, selv st.
Row 16: Selv st, *k1, yo, sl 1, k1, psso, k3, k2 tog, yo*, rep *to*, selv st.
Repeat rows 4–17 for pattern.

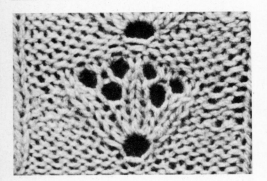

TULIP RIBS
the tulips

Multiple of 13 + 4.
Row 1 (right side): K2, *p13*, rep *to*, k2.
Row 2: P2, *k13*, rep *to*, p2.
Row 3: K2, *p6, (p1, k1, p1, k1, p1, k1) in next st, p6*, rep *to*, k2.
Rows 4 and 6: P2, *k6, p6, k6*, rep *to*, p2.
Row 5: K1, *p6, k6, p6*, rep *to*, k2.
Row 7: K2, *(p2 tog) twice, p2, k2, yo, k2, yo, k2, p2, (p2 tog) twice*, rep *to*, k2.
Row 8: P2, *k4, p8, k4*, rep *to*, p2.
Row 9: K2, *(p2 tog) twice, (k2 tog, yo, k1, yo) twice, k2 tog, (p2 tog) twice*, rep *to*, k2.
Row 10: P2, *k2, p9, k2*, rep *to*, p2.
Repeat these 10 rows for pattern.

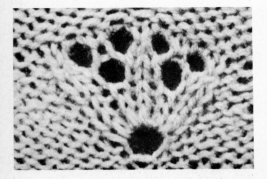

TULIP PATTERN
the tulips

Multiple of 13 + 2 selvage stitches.
Row 1 (right side): P.
Row 2: K.
Row 3: Selv st, *p6, (p1, k1, p1, k1, p1, k1) in next st, p6*, rep *to*, selv st.
Rows 4 and 6: Selv st, *k6, p6, k6*, rep *to*, selv st.
Row 5: Selv st, p6, *k6, p6*, selv st.
Row 7: Selv st, *(p2 tog) twice, p2, k2, yo, k2, yo, k2, p2, (p2 tog) twice*, rep *to*, selv st.
Row 8: Selv st, *k4, p8, k4*, rep *to*, selv st.
Row 9: Selv st, *(p2 tog) twice, (k2 tog, yo, k1, yo) twice, k2 tog, (p2 tog) twice*, rep *to*, selv st.
Row 10: Selv st, *k2, p9, k2*, rep *to*, selv st.
Repeat these 10 rows for pattern.

TILE STITCH I
tile stitch

Multiple of 10.
Row 1: *K1, yo, sl 1, k1, psso, k5, k2 tog, yo*, rep *to*.
Row 2 and all even-numbered rows: P.
Row 3: *K2, yo, sl 1, k1, psso, k3, k2 tog, yo, k1*, rep *to*.
Row 5: *K1, (yo, sl 1, k1, psso) twice, k1, (k2 tog, yo) twice*, rep *to*.
Row 7: *K2, yo, sl 1, k1, psso, yo, sl 1, k2 tog, psso, yo, k2 tog, yo, k1*, rep *to*.
Row 9: *K3, k2 tog, yo, k1, yo, sl 1, k1, psso, k2*, rep *to*.
Row 11: *K2, k2 tog, yo, k3, yo, sl 1, k1, psso, k1*, rep *to*.
Row 13: *k1, (k2 tog, yo) twice, k1, (yo, sl 1, k1, psso) twice*, rep *to*.
Row 15: *K1, yo, k2 tog, yo, k3, yo, sl 1, k1, psso, yo, sl 1, k2 tog, psso*, rep *to*, end sl 1, k1, psso.
Repeat these 16 rows for pattern.

TILE STITCH II
tile stitch

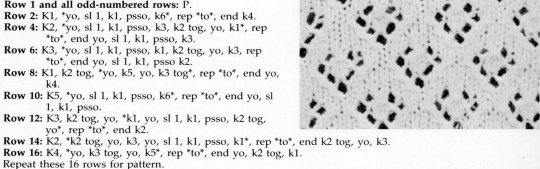

Row 1 and all odd-numbered rows: P.
Row 2: K1, *yo, sl 1, k1, psso, k6*, rep *to*, end k4.
Row 4: K2, *yo, sl 1, k1, psso, k3, k2 tog, yo, k1*, rep *to*, end yo, sl 1, k1, psso, k3.
Row 6: K3, *yo, sl 1, k1, psso, k1, k2 tog, yo, k3, rep *to*, end yo, sl 1, k1, psso k2.
Row 8: K1, k2 tog, *yo, k5, yo, k3 tog*, rep *to*, end yo, k4.
Row 10: K5, *yo, sl 1, k1, psso, k6*, rep *to*, end yo, sl 1, k1, psso.
Row 12: K3, k2 tog, yo, *k1, yo, sl 1, k1, psso, k2 tog, yo*, rep *to*, end k2.
Row 14: K2, *k2 tog, yo, k3, yo, sl 1, k1, psso, k1*, rep *to*, end k2 tog, yo, k3.
Row 16: K4, *yo, k3 tog, yo, k5*, rep *to*, end yo, k2 tog, k1.
Repeat these 16 rows for pattern.

TRAVELING LEAVES
the fountains, leaf vines

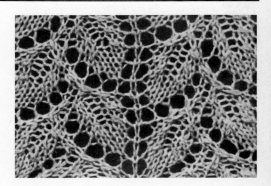

Multiple of 15 + 1.
Row 1: K1, *yo, k1, sl 1, k1, psso, p1, k2 tog, k1, yo, p1, sl 1, k1, psso, p1, k2 tog, yo, k1, yo, k1*, rep *to*.
Row 2: P1, *p4, k1, p1, k1, p3, k1, p4*, rep *to*.
Row 3: K1, *yo, k1, sl 1, k1, psso, p1, k2 tog, k1, p1, sl 1, k2 tog, psso, yo, k3, yo, k1*, rep *to*.
Row 4: P1, *p6, k2, p2, k1, p4*, rep *to*.
Row 5: K1, *yo, k1, yo, sl 1, k1, psso, p1, (k2 tog) twice, yo, k5, yo, k1*, rep *to*.
Row 6: P1, *p7, k1, p1, k1, p5*, rep *to*.
Row 7: K1, *yo, k3, yo, sl 1, k2 tog, psso, p1, yo, k1, sl 1, k1, psso, p1, k2 tog, k1, yo, k1*, rep *to*.
Row 8: P1, *p3, k1, p3, k1, p7*, rep *to*.
Row 9: K1, *yo, k5, yo, sl 1, k1, psso, k1, sl 1, k1, psso, p1, k2 tog, k1, yo, k1*, rep *to*.
Row 10: P1, *p3, k1, p2, k1, p8*, rep *to*.
Repeat these 10 rows for pattern.

LACE LEAVES AND BUDS
plumes, feather flower

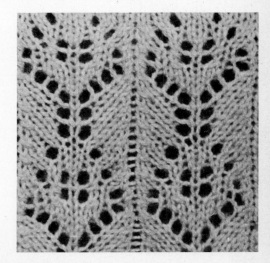

Multiple of 11 + 2 selvage stitches.
Row 1 and all odd-numbered rows: P.
Rows 2, 4, and 6: Selv st, *k2 tog, k3, yo, k1, yo, k3, sl 1, k1, psso*, rep *to*, selv st.
Row 8: Selv st, *k2 tog, k2, yo, k3, yo, k2, sl 1, k1, psso*, rep *to*, selv st.
Row 10: Selv st, *k2 tog, k1, yo, k5, yo, k1, sl 1, k1, psso*, rep *to*, selv st.
Rows 12 and 14: Selv st, *k2 tog, yo, k1, k2 tog, yo, k1, yo, sl 1, k1, psso, k1, yo, sl 1, k1, psso*, rep *to*, selv st.
Row 16: Selv st, *k2 tog, k1, yo, k5, yo, k1, sl 1, k1, psso*, rep *to*, selv st.
Row 18: Selv st, *k2 tog, k2, yo, k3, yo, k2. sl 1, k1, psso*, rep *to*, selv st.
Repeat these 18 rows for pattern.

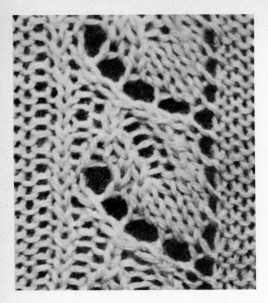

LAUREL LEAF
the laurels

Multiple of 12 + 4.
Row 1: *P4, yo, k5, yo, sl 1, k1, psso, k1 tbl*, rep *to*, p4.
Row 2: *K4, p9*, rep *to*, k4.
Row 3: *P4, yo, k1, sl 1, k1, psso, p1, k2 tog, k1, yo, p1, k1 tbl*, rep *to*, p4.
Row 4: *K4, p1, (k1, p3) twice*, rep *to*, k4.
Row 5: *P4, yo, k1, sl 1, k1, psso, p1, k2 tog, k1, p1, k1 tbl*, rep *to*, p4.
Row 6: *K4, p1, k1, p2, k1, p3*, rep *to*, k4.
Row 7: *P4, yo, k1, yo, sl 1, k1, psso, p1, k2 tog, p1, k1 tbl*, rep *to*, p4.
Row 8: *K4, (p1, k1) twice, p4*, rep *to*, k4.
Row 9: *P4, yo, k3, yo, sl 1, k2 tog, psso, p1, k1 tbl*, rep *to*, p4.
Row 10: *K4, p1, k1, p6*, rep *to*, k4.
Repeat these 10 rows for pattern.

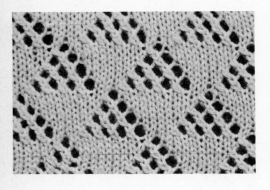

ALTERNATING LACE TRIANGLES
lace triangles

Multiple of 11 + 5.
Row 1: *K3, (yo, sl 1, k1, psso) 4 times*, rep *to*, end k5.
Row 2 and all even-numbered rows: P.
Row 3: *K4, (yo, sl 1, k1, psso) 3 times, k1*, rep *to*, end k5.
Row 5: *K5, (yo, sl 1, k1, psso) 2 times, k2*, rep *to*, end k5.
Row 7: *K6, yo, sl 1, k1, psso, k3*, rep *to*, end k5.
Row 9: K5, *k3, (yo, sl 1, k1, psso) 4 times*, rep *to*.
Row 11: K5, *k4, (yo, sl 1, k1, psso) 3 times, k1*, rep *to*.
Row 13: K5, *k5, (yo, sl 1, k1, psso) 2 times, k2*, rep *to*.
Row 15: K5, *k6, yo, sl 1, k1, psso, k3*, rep *to*.
Repeat these 16 rows for pattern.

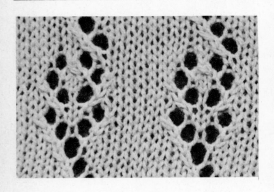

CROCUS PATTERN
crocus stitch

Multiple of 11.
Row 1: *K1, yo, sl 1, k1, psso, k8*, rep *to*.
Row 2 and all even-numbered rows: P.
Row 3: *K2, yo, sl 1, k1, psso, k7*, rep *to*.
Row 5: *K3, yo, sl 1, k1, psso, k6*, rep *to*.
Row 7: *K1, k2 tog, yo, k1, yo, sl 1, k1, psso, k5*, rep *to*.
Row 9: *K2 tog, yo, k3, yo, sl 1, k1, psso, k4*, rep *to*.
Row 11: *K1, k2 tog, yo, k1, yo, sl 1 k1, psso, k5*, rep *to*.
Row 13: *K2 tog, yo, k3, yo, sl 1, k1, psso, k4*, rep *to*.
Row 15: *K2, yo, sl 1, k2 tog, psso, yo, k6*, rep *to*.
Repeat these 16 rows for pattern.

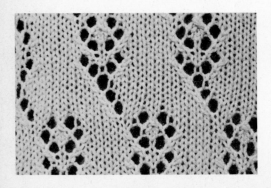

CROCUS PATTERN II

Multiple of 11.
Rows 1–16: Same as crocus pattern.
Rows 17–32: Start k6, then repeat rows 1–16.
Repeat these 32 rows for pattern.

FISH SCALE PATTERN
shell pattern, shell lace

Multiple of 7 + 4.
Row 1: K2, *yo, sl 1, k1, psso, k5*, rep *to*, end yo, k2
   tog.
Row 2, and all even-numbered rows: P.
Row 3: K2, *yo, k1, sl 1, k1, psso, k4*, rep *to*, end yo,
   k2 tog.
Row 5: K2, *yo, k2, sl 1, k1, psso, k3*, rep *to*, end yo,
   k2 tog.
Row 7: K2, *yo, k3, sl 1, k1, psso, k2*, rep *to*, end yo,
   k2 tog.
Row 9: K2, *yo, k4, sl 1, k1, psso, k1*, rep *to*, end yo,
   k2 tog.
Row 11: K2, *yo, k5, sl 1, k1, psso*, rep *to*, end yo, k2
   tog.
Repeat these 12 rows for pattern.

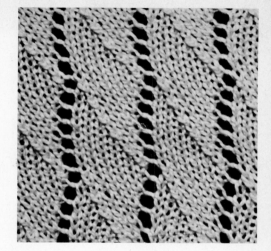

FERN LACE PATTERN
fern pattern, fern leaf stitch

Multiple of 29.
Row 1: *K1, sl 1, k2 tog, psso, k9, yo, k1, yo, p2, yo, k1,
   yo, k9, sl 1, k2 tog, psso*, rep *to*.
Row 2 and all even-numbered rows: *P13, k2, p14*, rep
   to.
Row 3: *K1, sl 1, k2 tog, psso, k8, (yo, k1) twice, p2,
   (k1, yo) 2 times, k8, sl 1, k2 tog, psso*, rep *to*.
Row 5: *K1, sl 1, k2 tog, psso, k7, yo, k1, yo, k2, p2, k2,
   yo, k1, yo, k7, sl 1, k2 tog, psso*, rep *to*.
Row 7: *K1, sl 1, k2 tog, psso, k6, yo, k1, yo, k3, p2, k3,
   yo, k1, yo, k6, sl 1, k2 tog, psso*, rep *to*.
Row 9: *K1, sl 1, k2 tog, psso, k5, yo, k1, yo, k4, p2, k4,
   yo, k1, yo, k5, sl 1, k2 tog, psso*, rep *to*.
Repeat these 10 rows for pattern.

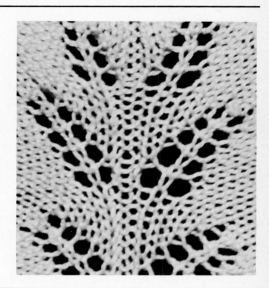

OPEN DROOPING LEAVES
falling leaves, openwork leaves

Multiple of 8 + 1.
Row 1 and all odd-numbered rows: P.
Row 2: K1, yo, *k2, sl 1, k2 tog, psso [pass sl st over k2
   tog], k2, yo, k1*, rep *to*.
Row 4: K2, yo, k1, sl 1, k2 tog, psso, k1, yo, *k3, yo, k1,
   sl 1, k2 tog, psso, k1, yo*, rep *to*, end k2.
Row 6: K3, yo, sl 1, k2 tog, psso, *yo, k5, yo, sl 1, k2
   tog, psso*, rep *to*, end yo, k3.
Row 8: K1, k2 tog, k1, yo, k1, yo, *k2, sl 1, k2 tog, psso,
   k2, yo, k1, yo*, rep *to*, k1, k2 tog, k1.
Row 10: K1, k2 tog, *yo, k3, sl 1, k2 tog, psso, k1*,
   rep *to*, end yo, k3, yo, k2 tog, k1.
Row 12: K2 tog, yo, k5, yo, *sl 1, k2 tog, psso, k5, yo*,
   rep *to*, end k2 tog.
Repeat these 12 rows for pattern.

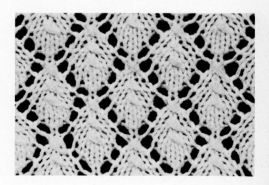

WILLOW BUDS moon stitch

Multiple of 10 + 4.
Rows 1 and 9: P4, *k6, p4*, rep *to*.
Row 2: *Yo, k2 tog, tbl, k2 tog, yo, p2, (k1, p1, k1 in
   next st) twice, p2*, rep *to*, end yo, k2 tog tbl,
   k2 tog, yo.
Rows 3, 5, and 7: P4, *k2, p6, k2, p4*, rep *to*.
Rows 4 and 6: *Yo, k2 tog tbl, k2 tog, yo, p2, k6, p2*,
   rep *to*, end yo, k2 tog tbl, k2 tog, yo.
Row 8: *Yo, k2 tog tbl, k2 tog, yo, p2, (k3 tog) twice,
   p2*, rep *to*, end yo, k2 tog tbl, k2 tog, yo.
Row 10: *Yo, k2 tog tbl, k2 tog, yo, p6*, rep *to*, end
   yo, k2 tog tbl, yo.
Repeat these 10 rows for pattern.

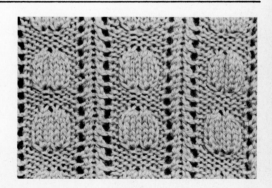

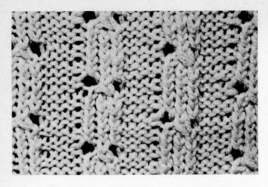

EYELET BELL RIB
little bells

Multiple of 14.
Rows 1 and 5: *P2, k3 tbl, p4, k3 tbl, p2*, rep *to*.
Rows 2 and 6: *K2, p3 tbl, k4, p3 tbl, k2*, rep *to*.
Row 3: *P2, k3 tbl, p4, yo, sl 1, k2 tog, psso, yo, p2*, rep *to*.
Row 4: *K2, p1, p1 tbl, p1, k4, p3 tbl, k2*, rep *to*.
Row 7: *P2, yo, sl 1, k2 tog, psso, yo, p4, k3 tbl, p2*, rep *to*.
Row 8: *K2, p3 tbl, k4, p1, p1 tbl, p1, k2*, rep *to*.
Repeat these 8 rows for pattern.

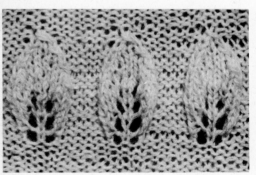

RELIEF LEAF PATTERN
embossed leaf stitch

Multiple of 7 + 6.
Row 1: P6, *yo, k1, yo, p6*, rep *to*.
Row 2: *K6, p3, k6*, rep *to*.
Row 3: P6, *k1, yo, k1, yo, k1, p6*, rep *to*.
Row 4: *K6, p5*, rep *to*, end k6.
Row 5: P6, *k2, yo, k1, yo, k2, p6*, rep *to*.
Row 6: *K6, p7*, rep *to*, end k6.
Row 7: P6, *k3, yo, k1, yo, k3, p6*, rep *to*.
Row 8: *K6, p9*, rep *to*, end k6.
Row 9: P6, *sl 1, k1, psso, k5, k2 tog, p6*, rep *to*.
Row 10: *K6, p7*, rep *to*, end k6.
Row 11: P6, *sl 1, k1, psso, k3, k2 tog, p6*, rep *to*, end p6.
Row 12: *K6, p5*, rep *to*, end k6.
Row 13: P6, *sl 1, k1, psso, k1, k2 tog, p6*, rep *to*.
Row 14: *K6, p3*, rep *to*, end k6.
Row 15: P6, *sl 1, k2 tog, psso, p6*, rep *to*.
Rows 16, 18, and 20: K.
Rows 17 and 19: P.
Repeat these 20 rows for pattern.

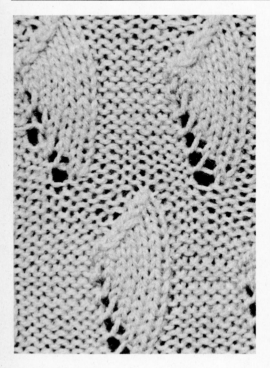

FUCHSIA STITCH

Multiple of 8.
Row 1: *P7, k1, yo*, rep *to*.
Row 2: *P2, k7*, rep *to*.
Row 3: *P7, k2, yo*, rep *to*.
Row 4: *P3, k7*, rep *to*.
Row 5: *P7, k3, yo*, rep *to*.
Row 6: *P4, k7*, rep *to*.
Row 7: *P7, k4, yo*, rep *to*.
Row 8: *P5, k7*, rep *to*.
Row 9: *P7, k5, yo*, rep *to*.
Row 10: *P6, k7*, rep *to*.
Row 11: *P7, k6, yo*, rep *to*.
Row 12: *P7, k7*, rep *to*.
Row 13: *P7, k5, k2 tog*, rep *to*.
Row 14: *P2 tog, p4, k7*, rep *to*.
Row 15: *P7, k3, k2 tog*, rep *to*.
Row 16: *P2 tog, p2, k7*, rep *to*.
Row 17: *P7, k1, k2 tog*, rep *to*.
Row 18: *P2 tog, k7*, rep *to*.
Row 19: *P3, k1, yo, p4*, rep *to*.
Row 20: *K4, p2, k3*, rep *to*.
Row 21: P3, k2, yo, p4*, rep *to*.
Row 22: *K4, p3, k3*, rep *to*.
Row 23: *P3, k3, yo, p4*, rep *to*.
Row 24: *K4, p4, k3*, rep *to*.
Row 25: *P3, k4, yo, p4*, rep *to*.
Row 26: *K4, p5, k3*, rep *to*.
Row 27: *P3, k5, yo, p4*, rep *to*
Row 28: *K4, p6, k3*, rep *to*.
Row 29: *P3, k6, yo, p4*, rep *to*.
Row 30: *K4, p7, k3*, rep *to*.
Row 31: *P3, k5, k2 tog, p4*, rep *to*.
Row 32: *K4, p2 tog, p4, k3*, rep *to*.
Row 33: *P3, k3, k2 tog, p4*, rep *to*.
Row 34: *K4, p2 tog, p2, k3*, rep *to*.
Row 35: *P3, k1, k2, tog, p4*, rep *to*.
Row 36: *K4, p2 tog, k3*, rep *to*.
Repeat these 36 rows for pattern.

TRAVELING LEAVES
traveling vine

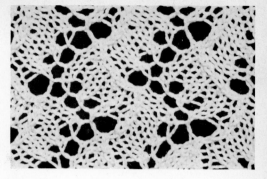

Multiple of 8 + 2 selvage stitches.
Row 1: Selv st, *yo, k1 tbl, yo, sl 1, k1, psso, k5*, rep *to*, selv st.
Row 2: Selv st, *p4, p2 tog tbl, p3*, rep *to*, selv st.
Row 3: Selv st, *yo, k1 tbl, yo, k2, sl 1, k1, psso, k3*, rep *to*, selv st.
Row 4: Selv st, *p2, p2 tog tbl, p5*, rep *to*, selv st.
Row 5: Selv st, *k1, tbl, yo, k4, sl 1, k1, psso, k1, yo*, rep *to*, selv st.
Row 6: Selv st, *p1, p2 tog tbl, p6*, rep *to*, selv st.
Row 7: Selv st, *k5, k2 tog, yo, k1 tbl, yo*, rep *to*, selv st.
Row 8: Selv st, *p3, p2, tog, p4*, rep *to*, selv st.
Row 9: Selv st, *k3, k2 tog, k2, yo, k1 tbl, yo*, rep *to*, selv st.
Row 10: Selv st, *p5, p2 tog, p2*, rep *to*, selv st.
Row 11: Selv st, *yo, k1, k2 tog, k4, yo, k1 tbl*, rep *to*, selv st.
Row 12: Selv st, *p6, p2 tog, p1*, rep *to*, selv st.
Repeat these 12 rows for pattern.

CANDLELIGHT PATTERN *candle pattern*

Multiple of 10 + 2.
Row 1 and all odd-numbered rows: K1, *p10*, rep *to*, k1.
Row 2: K3, *k2 tog, yo, k1, yo, sl 1, k1, psso, k5*, rep *to*, end k4.
Row 4: K2, *k2 tog, k1, yo, k1, yo, k1, sl 1, k1, psso, k3*, rep *to*, end k3.
Row 6: K1, *k2 tog, k2, yo, k1, yo, k2, sl 1, k1, psso, k1*, rep *to*, end k1.
Row 8: K2 tog, *k3, yo, k1, yo, k3, sl 1, k2 tog, psso*, rep *to*, end k3, yo, k1, yo, k3, sl 1, k1, psso, k1.
Row 10: K1, *yo, sl 1, k1, psso, k5, k2 tog, yo, k1*, rep *to*, end k1.
Row 12: K1, *yo, k1, sl 1, k1, psso, k3, k2 tog, k1, yo, k1*, rep *to*, end k1.
Row 14: K1, *yo, k2, sl 1, k1, psso, k1, k2 tog, k2, yo, k1*, rep *to*, end k1.
Row 16: K1, *yo, k3, sl 1, k2 tog, psso, k3, yo, k1*, rep *to*, end k1.
Repeat these 16 rows for pattern.

MOTH'S FLIGHT *pinecones*

Multiple of 19 + 9 + 2 selvage stitches.
Row 1: Selv st, *yo, k7, sl 1, k1, psso, k2 tog, k7, yo, k1*, rep *to*, end yo, k7, sl 1, k1, psso, selv st.
Row 2: Selv st, p2 tog, p6, yo, p1, *p2, yo, p6, (p2 tog) twice, p6, yo, p1*, rep *to*, end selv st.
Row 3: Selv st, *k2, yo, k5, sl 1, k1, psso, k2 tog, k5, yo, k3*, rep *to*, end k2, yo, k5, sl 1, k1, psso, selv st.
Row 4: Selv st, p2 tog, p4, yo, p3, *p4, yo, p4, (p2 tog) twice, p4, yo, p3*, rep *to*, end selv st.
Row 5: Selv st, *k4, yo, k3, sl 1, k1, psso, k2 tog, k3, yo, k5*, rep *to*, end k4, yo, k3, sl 1, k1, psso, selv st.
Row 6: Selv st, p2 tog, p2, yo, p5, *p6, yo, p2, (p2 tog) twice, p2, yo, p5*, rep *to*, end selv st.
Row 7: Selv st, *k6, yo, k1, sl 1, k1, psso, k2 tog, k1, yo, k7*, rep *to*, end k6, yo, k1, sl 1, k1, psso, selv st.
Row 8: Selv st, p2 tog, yo, p7, *p8, yo, (p2 tog) twice, yo, p7*, rep *to*, end selv st.
Row 9: Selv st, *k8, yo, sl 1, k1, psso, k7, sl 1, k1, psso*, rep *to*, end k8, yo, k1, selv st.
Row 10: Selv st, p1, yo, p7, p2 tog, *p2 tog, p7, yo, p1, yo, p7, p2 tog*, end selv st.
Row 11: Selv st, *k2 tog, k7, yo, k1, yo, k7, sl 1, k1, psso*, rep *to*, end k2 tog, k7, yo, k1, selv st.
Row 12: Selv st, p2, yo, p6, p2 tog, *p2 tog, p6, yo, p3, yo, p6, p2 tog*, rep *to*, end selv st.
Row 13: Selv st, *k2 tog, k5, (yo, k5) twice, sl 1, k1, psso*, rep *to*, end k2 tog, k5, yo, k3, selv st.
Row 14: Selv st, p4, yo, p4, p2 tog, *p2 tog, p4, yo, p7, yo, p4, p2 tog*, rep *to*, end selv st.
Row 15: Selv st, *k2 tog, k3, yo, k9, yo, k3, sl 1, k1, psso*, rep *to*, end k2 tog, k3, yo, k5, selv st.
Row 16: Selv st, p6, yo, p2, p2 tog, *p2 tog, p2, yo, p11, yo, p2, p2 tog*, rep *to*, end selv st.
Row 17: Selv st, *k2 tog, k1, yo, k13, yo, k1, sl 1, k1, psso*, rep *to*, end k2 tog, k1, yo, k7, selv st.
Row 18: Selv st, p8, yo, p2 tog, *p2 tog, yo, p15, yo, p2 tog*, rep *to*, end selv st.
Row 19: Selv st, *k1 [this st with the sl st before asterisk at end of repeat will make the sl 1, k1, psso at end of each pattern repeat, the sl st must be passed over the k1 as the beginning of the next pattern repeat], yo, k7, sl 1, k1, psso, k8, yo, sl 1*, rep *to*, k1 (pass sl st over this st), yo, k7, sl 1, k1, psso, selv st.
Row 20: Selv st, p2 tog, p7, *yo, p1, yo, p7, (p2 tog) twice, p7, yo*, rep *to*, end p1, selv st.
Repeat these 20 rows for pattern.

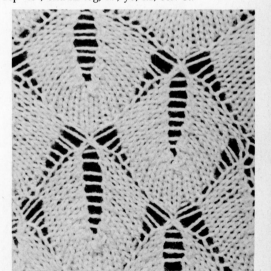

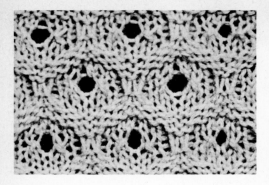

EYE OF LYNX

Multiple of 8 + 6.
Rows 1, 3, and 11: P.
Rows 2, 10, and 12: K.
Row 4: P5, *p1, sl 2 pwise, p5*, p1.
Row 5: K1, *k5, sl 2 pwise, k1*, k5.
Row 6: P5, *p1, sl 2, p5*, p1.
Row 7: K1, *sl 1, k1, psso, yo, k2 tog, k1, sl 2 pwise, k1*, sl 1, k1, psso, yo, k2 tog, k1.
Row 8: P2, p into front and back of yo of preceding row, p1, *p1, sl 2 pwise, p2, p into front and back of yo of preceding row, p1*, p1.
Row 9: K1, *k5, sl 2 pwise, k1*, k5.
Row 13: K1, *k1, sl 2 pwise, k5*, k1, sl 2 pwise, k2.
Row 14: P2, sl 2 pwise, p1, *p5, sl 2 pwise, p1*, p1.
Row 15: K1, *k1, sl 2 pwise, k5*, k1, sl 2 pwise, k2.
Row 16: P2, sl 2 pwise, p1, *p2, tog, yo, p1 and put on lh needle, pass next st on lh needle over st to the rt, put st on rh needle, p1, sl 2 pwise, p1*, p1.
Row 17: K1, *k1, sl 2 pwise, k2, k into front and back of yo of preceding row, k1*, k1, sl 2 pwise, k2.
Row 18: P2, sl 2 pwise, p1, *p5, sl 2 pwise, p1*, p1.
Repeat these 18 rows for pattern.

OPENWORK ENTRELACS
the lacy entrelacs, grapevine pattern

Multiple of 8 + 6.
Row 1 and all odd-numbered rows: P.
Row 2: K2, *k2 tog, k1, yo, k1, sl 1, k1, psso, k2*, rep *to*, end k4.
Row 4: K1, k2 tog, k1, yo, *k1, yo, k1, sl 1, k1, psso, k2 tog, k1, yo*, rep *to*, end k2.
Row 6: K3, yo, *k3, yo, k1, sl 1, k1, psso, k1, yo*, rep *to*, end k3.
Row 8: K5, *k2 tog, k1, yo, k1, sl 1, k1, psso, k2*, rep *to*, end k2.
Row 10: K4, *k2 tog, k1, yo, k1, yo, k1, sl 1, k1, psso*, rep *to*, end k3.
Row 12: K3, k2 tog, *k1, yo, k3, yo, k1, sl 1, k1, psso*, rep *to*, end k2.
Repeat these 12 rows for pattern.

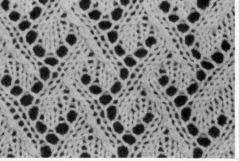

EYELET CABLE STITCH
the lacy arches

Multiple of 20 + 2.
Row 1 and all odd-numbered rows: *K2, p8, k2, p8*, rep *to*, end k2.
Row 2 (right side): *P2, k8, p2, k8*, rep *to*, end p2.
Row 4: *P2, k8, p2, k1, (sl 1, k1, psso, yo) 3 times, k1*, rep *to*, end p2.
Row 6: *P2, k8, p2, (sl 1, k1, psso, yo) 3 times, k2*, rep *to*, end p2.
Row 8: *P2, k8, p2, k1, (sl 1, k1, psso, yo) twice, k3*, rep *to*, end p2.
Rows 10 and 18: *P2, sl 2 sts to dpn, hold in back, k2, then k2 from dpn, sl 2 sts to dpn, hold in front, k2, k2 from dpn*, rep *to* once, p2.
Row 12: *P2, k1, (sl 1, k1, psso, yo) 3 times, k1, p2, k8*, rep *to*, end p2.
Row 14: *P2, (sl 1, k1, psso, yo) 3 times, k2, p2, k8*, rep *to*, end p2.
Row 16: *P2, k1, (sl 1, k1, psso, yo) twice, k3, p2, k8*, rep *to*, end p2.
Repeat rows 4–19 for pattern.

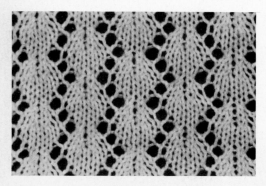

FALLING LEAF PATTERN
laced leaves, eyelet leaves

Multiple of 10.
Rows 1, 3, 5, and 7: P.
Row 2: K2, *yo, k1, (k2 tog) twice, k1, yo, k4*, rep *to*, end yo, k2.
Row 4: K3, *yo, (k2 tog) twice, yo, k6*, rep *to*, end yo, k3.
Row 6: K2 tog, *k1, yo, k4, yo, k1, (k2 tog) twice*, rep *to*, k1, yo, k4, yo, k1, k2 tog.
Row 8: K2, *yo, k6, (k2 tog) twice*, rep *to*, yo, k6, yo, k2 tog.
Repeat these 8 rows for pattern.

FLAME STITCH
candle flames

Multiple of 12 + 2.
Row 1: *P2, yo, k1, yo, p2, k2, k2 tog, k3*, rep *to*, p2.
Row 2: *K2, p6, k2, p3*, rep *to*, k2.
Row 3: *P2, (k1, yo) twice, k2, p2, k2, k2 tog, k2*, rep *to*, p2.
Row 4: *(K2, p5) twice*, rep *to*, k2.
Row 5: *P2, k2, yo, k1, yo, k2, p2, k2, k2 tog, k1*, rep *to*, p2.
Row 6: *K2, p4, k2, p7*, rep *to*, k2.
Row 7: *P2, k3, yo, k1, yo, k3, p2, k2, k2 tog*, rep *to*, p2.
Row 8: *K2, p3, k2, p9*, rep *to*, k2.
Row 9: *P2, k2, k2 tog, k5, p2, k1, k2 tog*, rep *to*, p2.
Row 10: *K2, p2, k2, p8*, rep *to*, k2.   **Row 11:** *P2, k2, k2 tog, k4, p2, k2 tog*, rep *to*, p2.   **Row 12:** *K2, p1, k2, p7*, rep *to*, k2.   **Row 13:** *P2, k2, k2 tog, k3, p2, yo, k1, yo*, rep *to*, p2.   **Row 14:** *K2, p3, k2, p6*, rep *to*, k2.   **Row 15:** *P2, k2, k2 tog, k2, p2, k1, yo, k1, yo, k1*, rep *to*, p2.   **Row 16:** *K2, p5, k2, p5*, rep *to*, k2.   **Row 17:** *P2, k2, k2 tog, k2, p2, k2, yo, k1, yo, k2*, rep *to*, p2.
Row 18: *K2, p7, k2, p4*, rep *to*, k2.   **Row 19:** *P2, k2, k2 tog, p2, k3, yo, k1, yo, k3*, rep *to*, p2.
Row 20: *K2, p9, k2, p3*, rep *to*, k2.   **Row 21:** *P2, k1, k2 tog, p2, k2, k2 tog, k5*, rep *to*, p2.
Row 22: *K2, p8, k2, p2*, rep *to*, k2.   **Row 23:** *P2, k2 tog, p2, k2, k2 tog, k4*, rep *to*, p2.
Row 24: *K2, p7, k2, p1*, rep *to*, k2.
Repeat these 24 rows for pattern.

TRELLIS FRAMED LEAVES
apple leaves, trellis leaves

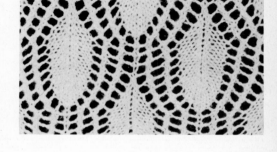

Multiple of 19 + 2.
Rows 1, 3, 5, and 7: K1, *sl 1, k1, psso, k3, (yo, sl 1, k1, psso) twice, yo, k1, yo, (k2 tog, yo) twice, k3, k2 tog*, rep *to*, k1.
Row 2 and all even-numbered rows: P.
Row 9: K1, *sl 1, k1, psso, k2, (yo, k2 tog) twice, yo, k3, yo, (sl 1, k1, psso, yo) twice, k2, k2 tog*, rep *to*, k1.
Row 11: K1, *sl 1, k1, psso, k1, (yo, k2 tog) twice, yo, k5, yo, (sl 1, k1, psso, yo) twice, k1, k2 tog*, rep *to*, k1.
Row 13: K1, *sl 1, k1, psso, (yo, k2 tog) twice, yo, k7, yo, (sl 1, k1, psso, yo) twice, k2 tog*, rep *to*, inc 1 in last st.
Row 15: Sl 1, *k1, psso, (yo, k2 tog) twice, yo, k3, k2 tog, k4, yo, (sl 1, k1, psso, yo) twice, sl 1*, rep *to*, k1, psso, k1.   **Rows 17, 19, 21, and 23:** K1, *(yo, k2 tog) twice, yo, k3, k2 tog, sl 1, k1, psso, k3, yo, (sl 1, k1, psso, yo) twice, k1*, rep *to*, k1.   **Row 25:** K1, *k1, (yo, sl 1, k1, psso) twice, yo, k2, k2 tog, sl 1 k1, psso, k2, (yo, k2 tog) twice, yo, k2*, rep *to*, k1.   **Row 27:** K1, *k2, (yo, sl 1, k1, psso) twice, yo, k1, k2 tog, sl 1, k1, psso, k1, yo, (k2 tog, yo) twice, k3*, rep *to*, k1.   **Row 29:** K1, *k3, (yo, sl 1, k1, psso) twice, yo, k2 tog, sl 1, k1, psso, yo, (k2 tog, yo) twice, k4*, rep *to*, k1.   **Row 31:** K1, *k4, (yo, sl 1, k1, psso) 3 times, yo, (k2 tog, yo) twice, k3, k2 tog*, rep *to*, k1.
Repeat these 32 rows for pattern.

DUTCH STITCH PATTERN
Dutch lace

Multiple of 16.
Row 1: *K5, k2 tog, yo, k2, yo, sl 1, k1, psso, k5*, rep *to*.
Row 2: P4, p2 tog, yo, p4, yo, p2 tog, p4*, rep *to*.
Row 3: *K3, k2 tog, yo, k6, yo, sl 1, k1, psso, k3*, rep *to*.
Row 4: *P2, p2 tog, yo, p4, yo, p2 tog, p2, yo, p2 tog, p2*, rep *to*.
Row 5: *K1, k2 tog, yo, k5, yo, sl 1, k1, psso, k3, yo, sl 1, k1, psso, k1*, rep *to*.
Row 6: *P2 tog, yo, p6, yo, p2 tog, p4, yo, p2 tog*, rep *to*.
Row 7: Sl 1 pwise, k1, yo, sl 1, k1, psso, k4, yo, sl 1, k1, psso, k2, k2 tog, yo, k1, sl 1 pwise*, rep *to*.
Row 8: *P3, yo, p2 tog, p3, yo, p2 tog, p1, p2 tog, yo, p3*, rep *to*.
Row 9: *Yo, sl 1, k1, psso, k2, yo, sl 1, k1, psso, k4, k2 tog, yo, k4*, rep *to*.
Row 10: *Yo, p2 tog, p3, yo, p2 tog, p2, p2 tog, yo, p5*, rep *to*.
Row 11: *Yo, sl 1, k1, psso, k4, yo, sl 1, k1, psso, k2 tog, yo, k6*, rep *to*.
Row 12: *Yo, p2 tog, p2, p2 tog, yo, p1, sl 2 pwise, p1, yo, p2 tog, p4*, rep *to*.
Row 13: *Yo, sl 1, k1, psso, k1, k2 tog, yo, k2, Cr 2 R [see p. 42], k2, yo, sl 1, k1, psso, k3*, rep *to*.
Row 14: *P2, p2 tog, yo, p4, yo, p2 tog, p2, yo, p2 tog, p2*, rep *to*.
Row 15: *K1, k2 tog, yo, k5, yo, sl 1, k1, psso, k3, yo, sl 1, k1, psso, k1*, rep *to*.
Row 16: *P2 tog, yo, p6, yo, p2 tog, p4, yo, p2 tog*, rep *to*.
Repeat rows 7–15 for pattern.

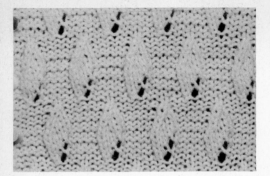

LITTLE CANDLE FLAMES
teardrop

Row 1: P3, *yo, k1, p5*, rep *to*, yo, k1, p2.
Rows 2 and 10: K2, *p2, k5*, rep *to*, p2, k3.
Row 3: P3, *yo, k2, p5*, rep *to*, yo, k2, p2.
Rows 4 and 8: K2, *p3, k5*, rep *to*, p3, k3.
Row 5: P3, *yo, k3, p5*, rep *to*, yo, k3, p2.
Row 6: K2, *p4, k5*, rep *to*, p4, k3.
Row 7: P3, *k2, k2 tog, p5*, rep *to*, k2, k2 tog, p2.
Row 9: P3, *k1, k2 tog, p5*, rep *to*, k1, k2 tog, p2.
Row 11: P3, *k2 tog, p5*, rep *to*, k2 tog, p2.
Row 12: K2, *p1, k5*, rep *to*, p1, k3.
Row 13: P6, *yo, k1, p5*, rep *to*.
Rows 14 and 22: K5, *p2, k5*, rep *to*, k1.

Row 15: P6, *yo, k2, p5*, rep *to*.   **Rows 16 and 20:** K5, *p3, k5*, rep *to*, k1.   **Row 17:** P6, *yo, k3, p5*, rep *to*.   **Row 18:** K5, *p4, k5*, rep *to*, k1.   **Row 19:** P6, *k2, k2 tog, p5*, rep *to*.   **Row 21:** P5, *k1, k2 tog, p5*, rep *to*.   **Row 23:** P6, *k2 tog, p5*, rep *to*.   **Row 24:** K5, *p1, k5*, rep *to*, k1.
Repeat these 24 rows for pattern.

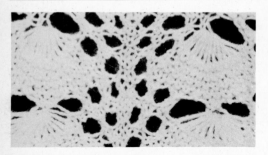

RIPPLE WITH SHELL
ripple with bell

Multiple of 31.
Row 1: K2, *yo, k2, p3, p3 tog, p3, k2, yo, k1*, rep *to*, end k1.
Row 2: *P5, k7, p7, k7, p5*, rep *to*.
Row 3: K3, *yo, k2, p2, p3 tog, p2, k2, yo, k3*, rep *to*.
Row 4: *P6, k5, p9, k5, p6*, rep *to*.
Row 5: K4, *yo k2, p1, p3 tog, p1, k2, yo, k5*, rep *to*, end k4.
Row 6: *P7, k3, p11, k3, p7*, rep *to*.
Row 7: K5, *yo, k2, p3 tog, k2, yo, k7*, rep *to*, end k5.
Row 8: *P8, k1, p13, k1, p8*, rep *to*.
Row 9: K1, *p3 tog, p3, k2, yo, k1, k2, p3*, rep *to*, end p2 tog, k1.

Row 10: *P1, k4, p7, k7, p7, k4, p1*, rep *to*.   **Row 11:** K1, *p3 tog, p2, k2, yo, k3, yo, k2, p2*, rep *to*, end p2 tog, k1.   **Row 12:** *P1, k3, p9, k5, p9, k3, p1*, rep *to*.   **Row 13:** K1, *p3 tog, p1, k2, yo, k5, yo, k2, p1*, rep *to*, end p2 tog, k1.   **Row 14:** *P1, k2, p11, k3, p11, k2, p1*, rep *to*.   **Row 15:** K1, *p3 tog, k2, yo, k7, yo, k2*, rep *to*, end p2 tog, k1.   **Row 16:** *P1, k1, p13, k1, p13, k1, p1*, rep *to*.
Repeat these 16 rows for pattern.

SEASHELLS
cockle shells

Multiple of 19.
Rows 1, 2, 5, 6, and 9: K.
Row 3: *K1, yo dbl (wind yarn around needle 2 times counterclockwise), p2 tog tbl, k13, p2 tog, yo dbl, k1*, rep *to*.
Row 4: *K1, (k1, p1) in yo sts, k15, (p1, k1) in yo sts, k1*, rep *to*.
Row 7: *K1, (yo dbl, p2 tog tbl) twice, k11, (p2 tog, yo dbl) twice, k1*, rep *to*.
Row 8: *(K1, then k1, p1 in yo sts) twice, k13, (p1, k1 in yo sts, k1) twice, rep *to*.

Row 10: *K6, (yo dbl, k1) 14 times, k5*, rep *to*.   **Row 11:** *K1, (yo dbl, p2 tog tbl) twice, yo dbl, (drop the yo loops of the preceding row), p all 15 sts tog, (yo dbl, p2 tog tbl) twice, yo dbl, k1*, rep *to*.   **Row 12:** *(K1, then p1, k1 in yo sts) 3 times, k1, (k1, p1 in yo sts, k1) 3 times*, rep *to*.
Repeat these 12 rows for pattern.

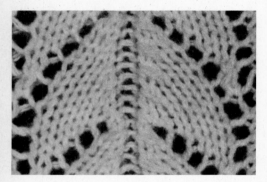

ARCHES PATTERN
horseshoe pattern, deer clove

Multiple of 16 + 1.
Rows 1 and 3: K1, *p7, k1*, rep *to*.
Row 2: *K2 tog, yo, k6, p1, k6, yo, k2 tog*, rep *to*.
Row 4: *K1, yo, k1, yo, k4, sl 1, k1, psso, p1, k2 tog, k4, (yo, k1) twice*, rep *to*.
Rows 5, 7, 9, 11, and 13: K1, *p8, k1*, rep *to*.
Row 6: *K2, yo, k2 tog, yo, k3, sl 1, k1, psso, p1, k2 tog, k3, yo, k2 tog, yo, k2*, rep *to*.
Row 8: *K1, k2 tog, (yo, k2) twice, sl 1, k1, psso, p1, k2 tog, (k2, yo) twice, k2 tog, k1*, rep *to*.
Row 10: *K1, k2 tog, yo, k3, yo, k1, sl 1, k1, psso, p1, k2 tog, k1, yo, k3, yo, k2 tog, k1*, rep *to*.
Row 12: *K1, k2 tog, yo, k4, yo, sl 1, k1, psso, p1, k2 tog, yo, k4, yo, k2 tog, k1*, rep *to*.
Row 14: *K2 tog, yo, k1, yo, k4, sl 1, k1, psso, p1, k2 tog, k4, yo, k1, yo, k2 tog*, rep *to*.
Repeat rows 5–14 for pattern.

BEAR TRACKS
bear's paw, umbrella pattern

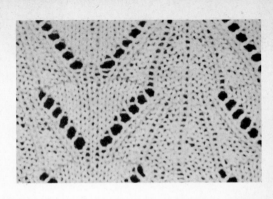

Multiple of 23.
Row 1: *K2, (p4, k1) 3 times, p4, k2*, rep *to*.
Row 2: *P2, k4, (p1, k4) 3 times, p2*, rep *to*.
Row 3: *K1, yo, k1, p2, p2 tog, (k1, p4) twice, k1, p2 tog, p2, k1, yo, k1*, rep *to*.
Row 4: *P1, k1, p1, k3, p1, (k4, p1) twice, k3, p1, k1, p1*, rep *to*.
Row 5: *K2, yo, k1, p3, k1, p2, p2 tog, k1, p2 tog, p2, k1, p3, k1, yo, k2*, rep *to*.
Row 6: *P2, k1, (p1, k3) 4 times, p1, k1, p2*, rep *to*.
Row 7: *K3, yo, k1, p1, p2 tog, (k2, p3) twice, k1, p2 tog, p1, k1, yo, k3*, rep *to*.
Row 8: *P3, k1, p1, k3, p1, (k3, p1) twice, k3, p1, k1, p3*, rep *to*.
Row 9: *K4, yo, k1, p2, k1, p1, p2 tog, k1, p2 tog, p1, k1, p2, k1, yo, k4*, rep *to*.
Row 10: *P4, k1, p1, k2, p1, (k3, p1) twice, k2, p1, k1, p4*, rep *to*.
Row 11: *K5, yo, k1, p2 tog, (k1, p2) twice, k1, p2 tog, k1, yo, k5*, rep *to*.
Row 12: *P5, (k1, p1) twice, (k2, p1) twice, k1, p1, k1, p5*, rep *to*.
Row 13: *K6, yo, k1, p1, k1, (p2 tog, k1) twice, p1, k1, yo, k6*, rep *to*.
Row 14: *P6, k1, p1, k1, (p1, k1) 4 times, p6*, rep *to*.
Repeat these 14 rows for pattern.

SPANISH LACE VARIATION
Spanish lace stitch

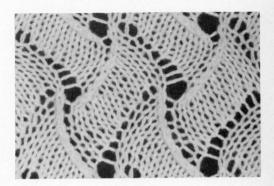

Multiple of 34.
Rows 1, 5, and 9: *K3, k2 tog, k4, yo, p2, (k2, yo, sl 1, k1, psso) 3 times, p2, yo, k4, sl 1, k1, psso, k3*, rep *to*.
Rows 2, 6, and 10: *P2, p2 tog tbl, p4, yo, p1, k2, (p2, yo, p2 tog) 3 times, k2, p1, yo, p4, p2 tog, p2*, rep *to*.
Rows 3, 7, and 11: *K1, k2 tog, k4, yo, k2, p2, (k2, yo, sl 1, k1, psso) 3 times, p2, k2, yo, k4, sl 1, k1, psso, k1*, rep *to*.
Rows 4, 8, and 12: *P2 tog tbl, p4, yo, p3, k2, (p2, yo, p2 tog) 3 times, k2, p3, yo, p4, p2 tog*, rep *to*.
Rows 13, 17, and 21: *Yo, sl 1, k1, psso, k2, yo, sl 1, k1, psso, p2, yo, k4, sl 1, k1, psso, k6, k2 tog, k4, yo, p2, k2, yo, sl 1, k1, psso, k2*, rep *to*. **Rows 14, 18, and 22:** *Yo, p2 tog, p2, yo, p2 tog, k2, p1, yo, p4, p2 tog tbl, p4, yo, p1, k2, p2, yo, p2 tog, p2*, rep *to*. **Rows 15, 19, and 23:** *Yo, sl 1, k1, psso, k2, yo, sl 1, k1, psso, p2, k2, yo, k4, sl 1, k1, psso, k2, k2 tog, k4, yo, k2, p2, k2, yo, sl 1, k1, psso, k2*, rep *to*. **Rows 16, 20, and 24:** *Yo, p2 tog, p2, yo, p2 tog, k2, p3, yo, p4, p2 tog, p2 tog tbl, p4, yo, p3, k2, p2, yo, p2 tog, p2*, rep *to*.
Repeat these 24 rows for pattern.

ALLOVER TRAVELING VINE
scroll pattern, traveling vine

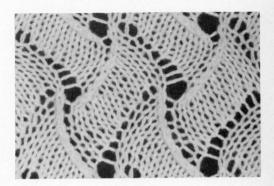

Multiple of 10 + 4.
Row 1: K2, *yo, k8, k2 tog*, rep *to*, k2.
Row 2: K2, *p2 tog, p7, yo, p1*, rep *to*, k2.
Row 3: K4, *yo, k6, k2 tog, k2*, rep *to*.
Row 4: K2, *p2 tog, p5, yo, p3*, rep *to*, k2.
Row 5: K6, *yo, k4, k2 tog, k4*, rep *to*, k2.
Row 6: K2, *p2 tog, p3, yo, p5*, rep *to*, k2.
Row 7: K8, *yo, k2, k2 tog, k6*, rep *to*, yo k2, k2 tog, k2.
Row 8: K2, *p2 tog, p1, yo, p7*, rep *to*, k2.
Row 9: K10, *yo, k2 tog, k8*, rep *to*, yo, k2 tog, k2.
Row 10: K2, yo, p8, p1, sl 1, psso [put the p1 on lh needle, sl the next st over the p1, return to rh needle], *yo, p8, p1, sl 1, psso*, rep *to*, k2.
Row 11: K2, *sl 1, k1, psso, k7, yo, k1*, rep *to*, k2.
Row 12: K2, *p2, yo, p6, p1, sl 1, psso*, rep *to*, k2.
Row 13: K2, *sl 1, k1, psso, k5, yo, k3*, rep *to*, k2.
Row 14: K2, *p4, yo, p4, p1, sl 1, psso*, rep *to*, k2.
Row 15: K2, *sl 1, k1, psso, k3, yo, k5*, rep *to*, k2.
Row 16: K2, *p6, yo, p2, p1, sl 1, psso*, rep *to*, k2.
Row 17: K2, *sl 1, k1, psso, k1, yo, k7*, rep *to*, k2.
Row 18: K2, *p8, yo, p1, sl 1, psso*, rep *to*, k2.
Repeat these 18 rows for pattern.

CROSSED STITCHES

Crossed or twisted stitches (see pp. 41–43) are made by twisting stitches around each other, either by slipping one or more stitches and knitting the stitches beyond them or by putting stitches on a double-pointed needle, holding them in waiting, and knitting them at a later time.

These techniques are the basis for many texture and cable patterns.

CROSSED BROKEN RIB
broken rib, left cross broken rib

Multiple of 7 + 2.
Row 1 (right side): P2, *Cr 2 L, k3, p2*, rep *to*.
Rows 2, 4, 6, and 8: *K2, p5*, rep *to*.
Row 3: P2, *k1, Cr 2 L, k2, p2*, rep *to*.
Row 5: P2, *k2, Cr 2 L, k1, p2*, rep *to*.
Row 7: P2, *k3, Cr 2 L, p2*, rep *to*.
Repeat these 8 rows for pattern.

BEEHIVE STITCH
trellis stitch

Multiple of 6.
Rows 1 and 3: *P2, k2, p2*, rep *to*.
Row 2 and all even-numbered rows: K all k sts and p all
           p sts.
Row 5: *Sl 2 sts to dpn, hold in back, k1, p2 from dpn,
           sl 1 st to dpn, hold in front, p2, k1 from dpn*,
           rep *to*.
Rows 7 and 9: *K1, p4, k1*, rep *to*.
Row 11: *Sl 1 to dpn, hold in front, p2, k1 from dpn, sl
           2 to dpn, hold in back, k1, p2 from dpn*, rep
           to.
Repeat these 12 rows for pattern.

SMALL HONEYCOMB PATTERN
wasp nest stitch, honeycomb stitch

Multiple of 4.
Row 1: *Cr 2 R, Cr 2 L, rep *to*.
Row 2 and 4: P.
Row 3: *Cr 2 L, Cr 2 R*, rep *to*.
Repeat these 4 rows for pattern.

LARGE HONEYCOMB STITCH
large honeycomb, wasp nest large

Multiple of 4.
Row 1: *Yb, sl 1 pwise, Cr 2 L*, rep *to*.
Row 2: *Yf, sl 1 pwise, Cr 2 R*, rep *to*.
Row 3: K.
Row 4: P.
Repeat these 4 rows for pattern, moving 2 stitches
farther over.

OPEN CHAIN STITCH
chain stitch

Multiple of 8 + 4.
Row 1: *P4, Cr 2 L, Cr 2 R*, rep *to*, p4.
Row 2: *K4, p4*, rep *to*, k4.
Rows 3 and 5: *P4, k1, p2, k1*, rep *to*, p4.
Rows 4 and 6: *K4, p1, k2, p1*, rep *to*, k4.
Repeat these 6 rows for pattern.

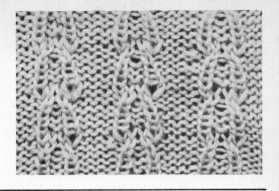

CORDED DIAGONAL STITCH
relief diagonal stitch

Multiple of 6.
Row 1: *P1, Cr 2 R, Cr 2 L, p1*, rep *to*.
Rows 2 and all even-numbered rows: K all k sts and p all p sts.
Row 3: *Cr 2 R, Cr 2 L, p2*, rep *to*.
Continue in pattern, moving 1 stitch to the right on alternate rows.

CORDED OBLIQUE STITCH
oblique fabric stitch

Multiple of 7.
Row 1: *K3, Cr 2 R, Cr 2 L*, rep *to*.
Row 2 and all even-numbered rows: P.
Row 3: *K2, Cr 2 R, Cr 2 L, k1*, rep *to*.
Continue in pattern, moving 1 stitch to the right on odd-numbered rows. End rows 5 and 9 with k1.

SINGLE CORDED RIB
corded rib

Multiple of 5 + 2.
Row 1: *P2, Cr 2 R, k1*, rep *to*, end p2.
Row 2: K2, *p1, sl 2 pwise, k2*, rep *to*.
Row 3: *P2, Cr 2 L, k1*, rep *to*, p2.
Row 4: K2, *p3, k2*, rep *to*.
Repeat these 4 rows for pattern.

TRIPLE CORDED RIB
treble cord stitch

Multiple of 9 + 3.
Row 1: *K3, Cr 2 R 3 times*, rep *to*, k3.
Row 2: P.
Repeat these 2 rows for pattern.

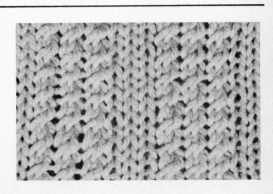

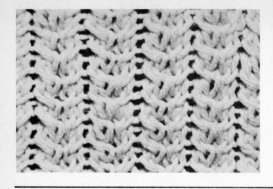

FISH SPINE STITCH
spine stitch, mock gull stitch

Multiple of 4.
Row 1: *Cr 2 R, Cr 2 L*, rep *to*.
Row 2: P.
Repeat these 2 rows for pattern.

VERTICAL CROSSED RIDGE STITCH
ridge stitch

Multiple of 8 + 4.
Row 1: *K4, Cr 2 R, Cr 2 L, rep *to*, k4.
Row 2: P.
Repeat these 2 rows for pattern.

PAIRED RIC RAC RIBS
double ric rac

Multiple of 9 + 5.
Row 1: *P5, Cr 2R, Cr 2 L*, rep *to*, p5.
Rows 2 and 4: K all k sts and p all p sts.
Row 3: *P5, Cr 2 L, Cr 2 R*, rep *to*, p5.
Repeat these 4 rows for pattern.

CORD STITCH
embossed cord, cord rope stitch

Multiple of 6 + 4.
Row 1: P4, *k2, p4*, rep *to*.
Row 2: *K4, Cr 2 (p 2nd st, then k 1st st)*, rep *to*, end k4.
Repeat these 2 rows for pattern.

WOVEN BASKET PATTERN
woven basket stitch, woven stitch

Multiple of 2.
Row 1: *Cr 2 L*, rep *to*.
Row 2: P1, *Cr 2 L*, rep *to*, p1.
Note: Row 2, see directions, p. 42, for *purl* row.
Repeat these 2 rows for pattern.

GRANITE STITCH RIB
granite rib, ribbing

Multiple of 8 + 2.
Row 1: *K2, (Cr 2 R) 3 times*, rep *to*, end k2.
Rows 2 and 4: P.
Row 3: *K2, Cr 3 kwise (k the 3rd st, then the 2nd st,
     then the 3rd st) twice*, rep *to*, end k2.
Repeat these 4 rows for pattern.

SINGLE CABLE RIBBING
single cable

Multiple of 5 + 3.
Row 1: *P3, k2*, rep *to*, end p3.
Rows 2, 3, 4, and 6: K all k sts and p all p sts.
Row 5: *P3, Cr 2 R*, end p3.
Repeat these 6 rows for pattern.

BABY CABLE RIB
basic cable rib

Multiple of 3 + 1.
Row 1: *P1, k2*, rep *to*, end p1.
Rows 2, 3, 4, and 6: K all k sts and p all p sts.
Row 5: *P1, Cr 2 R*, end p1.
Repeat these 6 rows for pattern.

SIMPLE CABLE RIB

Multiple of 7 + 3.
Rows 1 and 3: P3, *k4, p3*, rep *to*.
Rows 2 and 4: K3, *p4, k3*, rep *to*.
Row 5: *P3, sl next 2 sts to dpn, hold in front, k2, k2
     from dpn*, p3.
Repeat rows 2–5 for pattern.

TWISTED RIBBED CABLE
twisted rib, cable twist

Multiple of 8 + 3.
Row 1: *P3, k5*, rep *to*, end p3.
Rows 2, 4, 6, and 8: *K3, p5*, rep *to*, end k3.
Rows 3 and 7: *P3, k1, (sl next st to dpn, hold in back,
     k1, then k st from dpn) twice*, rep *to*, end p3.
Row 5: *P3, (sl next st to dpn, hold in back, k1, then k
     st from dpn) twice, k1*, rep *to*, p3.
Repeat these 8 rows for pattern.

SLIP CROSS CABLE

Multiple of 8 + 3.

Rows 1, 3, and 5: *K3, p5*, rep *to*, end k3.

Row 2: K3, *sl next 4 sts to dpn, hold in back, yf, k1, sl 3 sts from dpn back to lh needle, leaving the 1st sl st on dpn. With yb, k the 3 sts from lh needle, then k the last st from dpn, p3*, rep *to*.

Rows 4 and 6: P3, *k5, p3*, rep *to*.

Repeat these 6 rows for pattern.

WAVY CABLE
snaky cable

Multiple of 7 + 3.

Rows 1, 3, 7, and 9: *P3, k4*, p3.

Row 2 and all even-numbered rows: *K3, p4*, k3.

Row 5: *P3, sl next 2 sts to dpn, hold in back, k2, k2 from dpn*, p3.

Row 11: *P3, sl next 2 sts to dpn, hold in front, k2, k2 from dpn*, p3.

Repeat these 12 rows for pattern.

SIMPLE CABLE CORDED RIB
corded cable rib

Multiple of 9 + 3.

Rows 1 and 3: *P3, k6*, rep *to*, p3.

Rows 2, 4, and 6: *K3, p6*, rep *to*, k3.

Row 5: *P3, sl next 3 sts to dpn, hold in back, k3, k3 sts from dpn*, rep *to*, p3.

Repeat these 6 rows for pattern.

HORSESHOE CABLE RIB
reverse cable rib

Multiple of 11 + 3.

Rows 1 and 3: *P3, k8*, rep *to*, p3.

Rows 2, 4, and 6: *K3, p8*, rep *to*, k3.

Row 5: *P3, sl next 2 sts to dpn, hold in back, k2, k2 sts from dpn, sl next 2 sts to dpn, hold in front, k2, k2 from dpn*, p3.

Repeat these 6 rows for pattern.

PLAITED RIBBED CABLE
plaited cable rib

Multiple of 23 + 5.

Rows 1 and 5: P5, k18*, rep *to*, k5.

Rows 2, 4, 6, and 8: *K5, p18*, rep *to*, k5.

Row 3: *P5, (sl next 3 sts to dpn, hold in back, k3, k3 sts from dpn) 3 times*, rep *to*, p5.

Row 7: *P5, k3, (sl next 3 sts to dpn, hold in front, k3, k3 sts from dpn) twice, k3*, rep *to*, p5.

Repeat these 8 rows for pattern.

INDIAN PILLAR STITCH
Hindu pillar, cluster, muster stitch

Multiple of 4 + 1.
Row 1: K1, *k3 tog, keep sts on lh needle, p them tog, k them tog again, drop sts off needle, k1*, rep *to*.
Row 2 (right side): P.
Repeat these 2 rows for pattern.

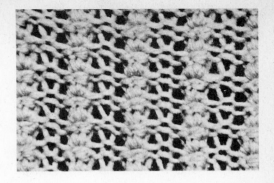

SPIRALED COLUMNS
twisted columns, spiral columns 2

Multiple of 9 + 2.
Row 1: K1, *p3, (k2 tog, do not let the sts slip off needle, k 1st st again, sl both sts off lh needle tog) twice*, end p3, k1.
Rows 2 and 4: K4, *p6, k3*, rep *to*, end k1.
Row 3: K1, *p3, k1, (k2 tog, do not let the sts slip off needle, k the 1st st again, sl both sts off lh needle tog) twice, rep *to*, p3, k1.
Repeat these 4 rows for pattern.

TWISTED SPIRAL COLUMNS
twisted columns, twisted spirals

Multiple of 6 + 2.
Row 1: P2, *k4, p2*, rep *to*.
Row 2: *K2, (p2 tog) twice*, rep *to*, k2.
Row 3: P2, *(k st of preceding row that slants to the right, then k st on lh needle) twice, p2*, rep *to*.
Row 4: *K1, (p2 tog) twice, k1*, rep *to*, k2.
Row 5: P2, *p1, (k st of preceding row that slants to the right, then k st on lh needle) twice, p1*, rep *to*.
Repeat rows 2–5 for pattern.

HERRINGBONE RIBBING
herringbone pattern

Multiple of 14.
Row 1: *K3, p1 (wind yarn twice around needle), p6, p1 (wind yarn twice around needle), k3*, rep *to*.
Row 2 (right side): *P3, sl next st to dpn (dropping the extra loop), hold in front, k3, sl next 3 sts to dpn, hold in back, k next st (dropping the extra loop), k3 from dpn, k3,* rep *to*.
Repeat these 2 rows for pattern.

CABLED DROP STITCH
embossed drop stitch, crossed drop stitch

Multiple of 9.
Row 1: *P4, Cr 2 R, p3*, rep *to*.
Row 2: *K3, p1, lift the horizontal thread before the next st and p it, p1, k4*, rep *to*.
Rows 3, 5, 7, and 9: *P4, k3, p3*, rep *to*.
Rows 4, 6, and 8: *K3, p3, k4*, rep *to*.
Row 10: *K3, p1, let the next st drop 8 rows down, p1, k4*, rep *to*.
Repeat these 10 rows for pattern.

WOVEN CHALICE STITCH
chalice stitch, chalice pattern

Multiple of 8.
Rows 1–4: *K4, p4*, rep *to*.
Row 5: *P4, sl next 2 sts to dpn, hold in front, k2, k2 sts from dpn*, rep *to*.
Rows 6, 7, and 8: *P4, k4*, rep *to*.
Row 9: *sl 2 sts to dpn, hold in front, k2, k2 sts from dpn, p4*, rep *to*.
Repeat rows 2–9 for pattern.

RIPPLE PATTERN
ripple stitch, the ripples

Multiple of 3.
Row 2: *K2 tog, do not let the sts drop from lh needle, reknit the 1st st*, rep *to*.
Rows 2 and 4: P.
Row 3: *K1, k2 tog, do not let the sts drop from lh needle, reknit the 1st st*, rep *to*.
Repeat these 4 rows for pattern.

ALTERNATING PIQUÉ SQUARES
piqué squares, piqué checker

Multiple of 12.
Rows 1, 3, and 5: *K6, (p2, put 2 sts back onto lh needle, take yarn across front to back, replace 2 sts on rh needle) 3 times*, rep *to*.
Row 2 and all even-numbered rows: P.
Rows 7, 9, and 11: *Rep row 1 instructions in parentheses 3 times, k6*, rep *to*.
Repeat these 12 rows for pattern.

WAFFLE PATTERN
waffles pattern, waffle stitch

Multiple of 4 + 2 selvage stitches.
Row 1: Selv st, yo, *sl 1, k1, psso, k2 tog, yo (twice)*, rep *to*, end sl 1 k1, psso, k2 tog, yo, selv st.
Row 2: Selv st, k1, p2, *k 1st yo tbl, then k 2nd yo, p2*, rep *to*, end k yo, selv st.
Row 3: Selv st, *p1, Cr 2 R, p1*, rep *to*, selv st.
Row 4: Selv st, *k1, p2, k1*, rep *to*, selv st.
Row 5: Selv st, *k2 tog, yo (twice), sl 1, k1, psso*, rep *to*, selv st.
Row 6: Selv st, *p1, k 1st yo tbl, then 2nd yo, p1*, rep *to*, selv st.
Row 7: Selv st, k1, *p2, Cr 2 R*, rep *to*, end p2, k1, selv st.
Row 8: Selv st, p1, k2, *p2, k2*, rep *to*, end p1, selv st.
Repeat these 8 rows for pattern.

BIAS STITCH

Multiple of 2.
Row 1 (right side): Selv st, *Cr 1 R*, rep *to*, selv st.
Row 2: Selv st, p1, *Cr 1 R*, p1, selv st.
Repeat these 2 rows for pattern.

WAVE CABLE RIB
wave cable stitch, wavy cables

Multiple of 7.
Rows 1, 5, and 9: K.
Rows 2 and all even-numbered rows: P.
Row 3: *Sl 2 sts to dpn, hold in back, k2, k2 sts from
    dpn, k3*, rep *to*.
Row 7: *K2, sl sts to dpn, hold in front, k2, k2 sts from
    dpn, k1*, rep *to*.
Repeat rows 3–10 for pattern.

ALTERNATE WAVE CABLE RIB
wave cable, ribbon cable

Multiple of 12.
Row 1 and all odd-numbered rows: *K3, p6, k3*, rep
    to.
Row 2: *P3, sl next 3 sts to dpn, hold in back, k3, then
    k3 from dpn, p3*, rep *to*.
Rows 4, 6, 8, 12, 14, and 16: *P3, k6, p3*, rep *to*.
Row 10: *P3, sl next 3 sts to dpn, hold in front, k3, then
    k3 from dpn, p3*, rep *to*.
Repeat these 16 rows for pattern.

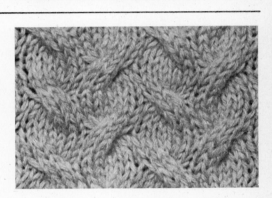

WAVY RIPPLES
ocean waves, sand pattern

Multiple of 12.
Rows 1, 5, and 9: K.
Row 2 and all even-numbered rows: P.
Row 3: *Sl 3 sts to dpn, hold in front, k3, k3 from dpn,
    k6*, rep *to*.
Row 7: *K6, sl 3 sts to dpn, hold in back, k3, k3 from
    dpn*, rep *to*.
Repeat rows 3–10 for pattern.

FALLING CABLE LEAF
sycamore stitch

Multiple of 12 + 4.
Rows 1, 3, and 5: P4, *k2, p4*, rep *to*.
Rows 2 and 4: K4, *p2, k4*, rep *to*.
Row 6: K4, *yf, sl 2 sts pwise, yb, k4*, rep *to*.
Row 7: P4, *sl next 2 sts to dpn, hold in front, p2, yo,
    k2 tog tbl from dpn, sl next 2 sts to dpn, hold
    in back, k 2 tog, yo, p2 from dpn, p4*, rep *to*.
Row 8: K4, *p2, k1 tbl, p2, k1 tbl, p2, k4*, rep *to*.
Repeat these 8 rows for pattern.

ALTERNATING CROSSED RIB
alternating 2 + 2 rib

Multiple of 4 + 2.
Rows 1 and 3: *K2, p2*, rep *to*, k2.
Rows 2, 4, and 12: *P2, k2*, rep *to*, p2.
Row 5: *Cr 2 L, p2*, rep *to*, Cr 2 L.
Rows 6, 8, and 10: *K2, p2*, rep *to*, k2.
Rows 7 and 9: *P2, k2*, rep *to*, p2.
Row 11: *P2, Cr 2 L*, rep *to*, p2.
Repeat these 12 rows for pattern.

CROSSED BABY RIB
crossed rib, crossed cable ribbing

Multiple of 4 + 1.
Rows 1 and 3: *(P1, k1) twice*, rep *to*, end p1.
Rows 2, 4, and 6: *(K1, p1) twice*, rep *to*, end k1.
Row 5: *P1, Cr 3 R (k the 3rd st, p the 2nd st, k the 1st st, let all 3 sts drop from lh needle)*, rep *to*, end p1.
Repeat these 6 rows for pattern.

BRAID STITCH
braid stitch, plaited variation

Multiple of 4.
Row 1: K.
Row 2 and all even-numbered rows: P.
Rows 3, 7, and 11: K2, *sl 2 sts to dpn, hold in back, k2, k2 sts from dpn*, rep *to*, end k2.
Rows 5, 9, and 13: *Sl 2 sts to dpn, hold in front, k2, k2 sts from dpn*, rep *to*.
Repeat rows 3–14 for pattern.

RANDOM OATS
scattered oats, woven oats

Multiple of 4 + 1.
Rows 1 and 5: *K2, sl 1 pwise, k1*, rep *to*, end k1.
Rows 2 and 6: P1, *p1, sl 1 pwise, p2*, rep *to*.
Row 3: *Sl 2 sts to dpn, hold in back, k the sl st from row 1, k2 sts from dpn, k1*, rep *to*, end k1.
Rows 4 and 8: P.
Row 7: *K1, put the sl st of 2 rows before on dpn, hold in front, k2, k st from dpn*, rep *to*.
Repeat these 8 rows for pattern.

DROPPING OATS
falling oats

Multiple of 19 + 6.
Row 1: K6, *(sl 1 pwise, k4, sl 1 pwise, k1) twice, k5*, rep *to*.
Rows 2 and 4: P, but sl the sl sts of the preceding row.
Row 3: K6, *(put the sl st of the preceding row on dpn, hold in front, k2, k st from dpn, sl next 2 sts to dpn, hold in back, k1, k2 from dpn, k1) twice, k5*, rep *to*.
Repeat these 4 rows for pattern.

CABLED OAT RIBS
twisted ribs

Multiple of 10 + 3.
Row 1: *P3, k3, p1, k3*, rep *to*, end p3.
Rows 2 and 6: K3, *p3, k1, p3, k3*, rep *to*.
Row 3: *P3, yb, sl 1 pwise, k2, p1, k2, sl 1 pwise*, rep *to*, end p3.
Row 4: K3, *yf, sl 1 pwise, p2, k1, p2, sl 1 pwise, k3*, rep *to*.
Row 5: *P3, put sl st on dpn, hold in front, k2, k st from dpn, p1, sl next 2 sts to dpn, hold in back, k the sl st, then k the 2 sts from dpn*, rep *to*.
Repeat these 6 rows for pattern.

KNOTTED STITCH PATTERN
knotted stitch I

Multiple of 4.
Rows 1 and 3: K.
Rows 2, 4, and 6: P.
Row 5: *K2, (yo, pass 2nd st on rh needle over 1st st and the yo) twice*, rep *to*.
Repeat these 6 rows for pattern.

ALTERNATING KNOTTED STITCH PATTERN
knotted stitch II

Multiple of 12 + 3.
Rows 1, 3, 5, 9, 11, and 13: K.
Row 2 and all even-numbered rows: P.
Row 7: *K9, (p3 tog, leave sts on lh needle, k them tog, then p them tog again [3 sts on rh needle])*, rep *to*.
Row 15: *K3, rep inst in parentheses in row 7, k6*, rep *to*.
Repeat these 16 rows for pattern.

WAVED RIBBING wavy rib

Multiple of 6.
Rows 1, 3, and 5 (wrong side): *P2, k4*, rep *to*.
Rows 2 and 4: *P4, k2*, rep *to*.
Row 6: *P2, sl 2 sts to dpn, hold in back, k2, p2 from dpn*, rep *to*.
Rows 7, 9, and 11: *K2, p2, k2*, rep *to*.
Rows 8 and 10: *P2, k2, p2*, rep *to*.
Row 12: *Sl 2 sts to dpn, hold in back, k2, p2 from dpn, p2*, rep *to*.
Rows 13, 15, and 17: *K4, p2*, rep *to*.
Rows 14 and 16: *K2, p4*, rep *to*.
Row 18: P4, *sl 2 sts to dpn, hold in back, k2, p2 from dpn, p2*, rep *to*, k2.
Repeat these 18 rows for pattern.

BRAIDED RIB
basketweave rib, plaited ribs

Multiple of 19.
Row 1: *P5, k2, p5, k1, (Cr 2 L) 3 times*, rep *to*.
Row 2: *P1, (Cr 2 R pwise) 3 times, k5, Cr 2 R pwise, K5*, rep *to*.
Repeat these 2 rows for pattern.

KNIT-PURL ZIGZAG fancy zigzag, zigzag stripes
Multiple of 14.
Right Slant
Row 1: *P5, Cr 2 R, k4, Cr2 R, p1*, rep *to*.
Row 2 and all even-numbered rows: K all k sts and p all p sts.
Row 3: *P4, Cr 2 R, k4, Cr 2 R, p2*, rep *to*.
Row 5: *P3, Cr 2 R, k4, Cr 1 R, p3*, rep *to*.
Row 7: *P2, Cr 2 R, k4, Cr 2 R, p4*, rep *to*.
Row 9: *P1, Cr 2 R, k4, Cr 2 R, p5*, rep *to*.
Left Slant
Row 11: *P1, Cr 2 L, k4, Cr 2 L, p5*, rep *to*.
Row 13: *P2, Cr 2 L, k4, Cr 2 L, p4*, rep *to*.
Row 15: *P3, Cr 2 L, k4, Cr 2 L, p3*, rep *to*.
Row 17: *P4, Cr 2 L, k4, Cr 2 L, p2*, rep *to*.
Row 19: *P5, Cr 2 L, k4, Cr 2 L, p1*, rep *to*.
Repeat these 20 rows for pattern.

INVERTED V STRIPES vice versa

Multiple of 28.
Row 1: *K6, Cr 2 R, Cr 2 L, k6, Cr 2 L, k8, Cr 2 R*, rep *to*.
Row 2 and all even-numbered rows: P.
Row 3: *K5, Cr 2 R, k2, Cr 2 L, k6, Cr 2 L, k6, Cr 2 R, k1*, rep *to*.
Row 5: *K4, Cr 2 R, k4, Cr 2 L, k6, Cr 2 L, k4, Cr 2 R, k2*, rep *to*.
Row 7: *K3, Cr 2 R, k6, Cr 2 L, k6, Cr 2 L, k2, Cr 2 R, k3*, rep *to*.
Row 9: *K2, Cr 2 R, k8, Cr 2 L, k6, Cr 2 L, Cr 2 R, k4*, rep *to*.
Repeat these 10 rows for pattern.

FRACTURED V STRIPES
twig pattern

Multiple of 13.
Row 1: *K1, Cr 2 R, k2, Cr 2 R, k1, Cr 2 L, k3*, rep *to*.
Rows 2, 4, 6, and 8: P.
Row 3: *K4, Cr 2 R, k3, Cr 2 L, k2*, rep *to*.
Row 5: *K3, Cr 2 R, k1, Cr 2 L, k2, Cr 2 L, k1*, rep *to*.
Row 7: *K2, Cr 2 R, k3, Cr 2 L, k4*, rep *to*.
Repeat these 8 rows for pattern.

LITTLE TREES
the palms, scattered leaves

Multiple of 14.
Rows 1 and 5: *K2, Cr 2 R, Cr 2 L, k8*, rep *to*.
Row 2 and all even-numbered rows: P.
Row 3: *K1, Cr 2 R, k2, Cr 2 L, k7*, rep *to*.
Row 7: *K3, sl 1, k1, psso and k the st, k9*, rep *to*.
Rows 9 and 19: K.
Rows 11 and 15: *K8, Cr 2 R, Cr 2 L, k2*, rep *to*.
Row 13: *K7, Cr 2 R, k2, Cr 2 L, k1*, rep *to*.
Row 17: *K9, sl 1, k1, psso and k the st, k3*, rep *to*.
Repeat these 20 rows for pattern.

SLIP STITCH DIAMOND PATTERN
slip stitch diamond

Multiple of 14 + 2.
Row 1: *Cr 2 R, k12*, rep *to*, Cr 2 R.
Row 2 and all even-numbered rows: P.
Row 3: K1, *Cr 2 L, k10, Cr 2 R*, rep *to*, k1.
Row 5: *K2, Cr 2 L, k8, Cr 2 R*, rep *to*, k2.
Continue in pattern, working 2 stitches fewer between the crossed stitches until they cross each other, as in row 1.

ALTERNATING PEANUT STITCH
peanut stitch

Multiple of 12 + 4.
Rows 1, 7, and 13: *K1, Cr 2 R pwise, k9*, rep *to*, k1, Cr 2 R, k1.
Rows 2 and 8: *Cr 2 R kwise, Cr 2 L kwise*, rep *to*, p8, Cr 2 R, Cr 2 L.
Rows 3, 5, 9, and 11: *P4, k8*, rep *to*, p4.
Rows 4 and 10: K4, *p8, k4*, rep *to*.
Rows 6 and 12: Cr 2 L, Cr 2 R, *p8, Cr 2 L, Cr 2 R*, rep *to*.
Rows 14 and 28: P.
Rows 15, 21, and 27: *K7, Cr 2 R pwise, k3*, rep *to*, k4.
Rows 17, 19, 23, and 25: *K6, p4, k2*, rep *to*, k4.
Rows 16 and 22: P4, *p2, Cr 2 R, Cr 2 L, p6*, rep *to*.
Rows 18 and 24: P4, *p2, k4, p6*, rep *to*.
Rows 20 and 26: P4, *p2, Cr 2 L, Cr 2 R, p6*, rep *to*.   Repeat these 28 rows for pattern.
Note: In odd-numbered rows, Cr 2 L and Cr 2 R are worked pwise. In even-numbered rows, Cr 2 L and Cr 2 R are worked kwise unless otherwise indicated.

TRIPLE EMBOSSED ZIGZAG STITCH
zigzag relief stitch

Multiple of 20.
Row 1 (wrong side): P to form a foundation row.
Row 2: *K5, (Cr 2 R) 5 times*, k5.
Row 3 and all odd-numbered rows: P.
Row 4: *K4, (Cr 2 R) 5 times, k6*.
Rows 6, 8, and 10: Rep row 3, moving pattern 1 st to the right on each even-numbered row.
Row 12: *(Cr 2 R) 5 times, k10*.
Row 14: *(Cr 2 L) 5 times, k10*.
Rows 16, 18, 20, and 22: Rep row 14, moving pattern 1 st to the right on each even-numbered row.
Repeat rows 2–22 for pattern.

TEXTURED ZIGZAG RIB
zigzag rib, horizontal zigzag stripe

Multiple of 6 + 2 selvage stitches.
Row 1: Selv st, *(Cr 2 L) 2 times, p2*, rep *to*, selv st.
Row 2: Selv st, *k2, (p1, k1) twice*, rep *to*, selv st.
Row 3: Selv st, *p1, (Cr 2 L) twice, p1*, rep *to*, selv st.
Row 4: Selv st, *k1, (k1, p1) twice, k1*, rep *to*, selv st.
Row 5: Selv st, *p2, (Cr 2 L) twice*, rep *to*, selv st.
Row 6: Selv st, *(p1, k1) twice, k2*, rep *to*, selv st.
Rows 7 and 9: Selv st, *yf, sl 3 sts pwise, yb, k1, yf, sl 1 pwise, yb, k1*, rep *to*, selv st.
Rows 8 and 10: Selv st, *p1, yb, sl 1 pwise, yf, p1, yb, sl 3 pwise, yf*, rep *to*, selv st.
Row 11: Selv st, *p2, (Cr 2 R) twice*, rep *to*, selv st.
Row 12: Selv st, *(k1, p1) twice, k2*, rep *to*, selv st.

Row 13: Selv st, *p1, (Cr 2 R) twice, p1*, selv st.   **Row 14:** Selv st, *k1, (k1, p1) twice, k1*, rep *to*, selv st.   **Row 15:** Selv st, *(Cr 2 R) twice, p2*, rep *to*, selv st.   **Row 16:** Selv st, *k3, p1, k1, p1*, rep *to*, selv st.   **Rows 17 and 19:** Selv st, *k1, yf, sl 1 pwise, yb, k1, yf, sl 3 pwise, yb*, rep *to*, selv st.   **Rows 18 and 20:** Selv st, *yb, sl 3 pwise, yf, p1, yb, sl 1 pwise, yf, p1*, rep *to*, selv st.
Repeat these 20 rows for pattern.

BOW TWIST *little bow twist, bowknots*

Multiple of 16.
Rows 1 and 15 (right side): P.
Rows 2 and 16: K.
Rows 3, 5, 9, and 13: P5, *k1, p3, k2, p11*, rep *to*, k1, p3, k1, p5.
Rows 4, 6, 8, 10, 12, and 14: K5, *p1, k3, p1, k11*, rep *to*, p1, k3, p1, k6.
Rows 7 and 11: P5, *sl next 4 sts to dpn, hold in front, k1, sl the 3 p sts from dpn back to lh needle and p these 3 sts, k the last st from dpn*, p11, end p5.
Rows 17, 19, 23, and 27: P13, *k1, p3, k1, p13*, rep *to*.
Rows 18, 20, 22, 24, 26, and 28: K13, *p1, k3, p2, k13*, rep *to*.
Rows 21 and 25: P13, rep *to* of row 7, end p13.
Repeat these 28 rows for pattern.

CABLE CROSS WITH WIDE RIB
crossed rib II, flat ribbed cable

Multiple of 10.
Rows 1: *K3, p1, k2, p1, k3*, rep *to*.
Rows 2 and 4: K all k sts and p all p sts.
Row 3: *K3, p1, Cr 2 L, p1, k3*, rep *to*.
Repeat these 4 rows for pattern.

PLAITED LATTICE STITCH

Multiple of 6.
Row 1: *K4, p2*, rep *to*.
Row 2 and all even-numbered rows: K all k sts and p all p sts.
Row 3: *Sl 2 sts to dpn, hold in back, k2, k2 from dpn, p2*, rep *to*.
Row 5: P2, *k2, sl 2 sts to dpn, hold in back, k2, p2 from dpn*, rep *to*, k4.
Row 7: *P2, sl 2 sts to dpn, hold in front, k2, k2 from dpn*, rep *to*.
Row 9: *K4, sl 2 sts to dpn, hold in front, p2, k2 from dpn, k2*, rep *to*, p2.
Repeat rows 3–10 for pattern.

BELL PATTERN
the bells

Multiple of 8.
Rows 1, 3, and 5: *K4, p4*, rep *to*.
Row 2 and all even-numbered rows: K all k sts and p all p sts.
Row 7: *Cr 2 L pwise, Cr 2 R pwise, k4*, rep *to*.
Rows 9, 11, and 13: *P4, k4*, rep *to*.
Row 15: *K4, Cr 2 L, Cr 2 R*, rep *to*.
Repeat these 16 rows for pattern.

RIB CABLE TWIST
corded rib

Multiple of 6.
Row 1: *P2, Cr 2 R, k2*, rep *to*.
Rows 2, 4, and 6: *P4, k2*, rep *to*.
Row 3: *P2, k1, Cr 2 L, k1*, rep *to*.
Row 5: *P2, k2, Cr 2 L*, rep *to*.
Repeat these 6 rows for pattern.

LOZENGE DIAMOND PATTERN
lozenge pattern IV

Multiple of 6 + 2.
Row 1: *Cr 2 R, k4*, rep *to*, Cr 2 R.
Row 2 and all even-numbered rows: P.
Row 3: K1, *Cr 2 L, k2, Cr 2 R*, rep *to*, k1.
Row 5: K2, *Cr 2 L, Cr 2 R, k2*, rep *to*.
Row 7: K2, *k1, Cr 2 R, k3*, rep *to*.
Row 9: K2, *Cr 2 R, Cr 2 L, k2*, rep *to*.
Row 11: K1, *Cr 2 R, k2, Cr 2 L*, rep *to*, k1.
Repeat these 12 rows for pattern.

EMBOSSED BRAIDED FROGGING
braided frogging, banded frogging insert

Multiple of 6 + 3.
Rows 1, 3, 27, and 29: K.
Rows 2 and 28: P.
Row 4: P3, *p1, (k1, p1, k1 in next st), p4*, rep *to*.
Rows 5, 7, 9, and 11: *K4, p3, k1*, rep *to*, k3.
Rows 6, 8, and 10: P3, *(p1, k1) twice, p4*, rep *to*.
Rows 12 and 18: P3, *p1, sl 2 sts to dpn, hold in back, k next st, p 2nd st from dpn, then k 1st st, sl both sts off dpn tog, p4*, rep *to*.
Row 13: *K3, sl next st to dpn, hold in front, p next st, k st from dpn, k1, k 2nd st on lh needle, p 1st st, sl both sts off tog*, rep *to*, k3.
Row 14: K1, p1, *k 2nd st on lh needle, then p 1st st, sl both sts off tog, p3, sl next st to dpn, hold in front, p next st, k st from dpn, p1*, rep *to*, k1.

Row 15: *Cr 3 (sl 2 sts to dpn, hold in back, k next st, p 2nd st from dpn, then k 1st st, sl both sts off tog), k5*, rep *to*, end Cr 3. **Row 16:** P2, *sl 1st st to dpn, hold in front, p next st, k st from dpn, p3, k 2nd st on lh needle, p 1st st, sl both sts off tog, p1*, rep *to*, p1. **Row 17:** K3, *k 2nd st on lh needle, p 1st st, sl both sts off tog, k1, sl next st to dpn, hold in front, p next st, k st from dpn, k3*, rep *to*. **Rows 19, 21, 23, and 25:** *K4, p3, k1*, rep *to*, k3. **Rows 20, 22, and 24:** P3, *(p1, k1) twice, p4*, rep *to*. **Row 26:** P3, *p1, p3 tog, p4*, rep *to*.

TUNISIAN KNITTING STITCHES

TUNISIAN KNITTING (horizontal)

Multiple of 2.
Row 1 (wrong side): *Sl 1 kwise, yo*, rep *to*. Hold last yo when turning for 2nd row.
Row 2: *K2 tog tbl [sl st and yo of preceding row]*, rep *to*. Push the sts tog with your fingers as you work the 2nd row.
Repeat these 2 rows for pattern.

TUNISIAN KNITTING (vertical)

Multiple of 2.
Row 1 (wrong side): *Yo, sl 1 kwise*, rep *to*.
Row 2: *K2 tog tbl [yo and sl st of preceding row]*, rep *to*.
Repeat these 2 rows for pattern.

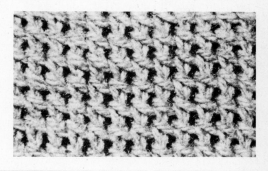

MOCK TUNISIAN KNITTING (horizontal)

Multiple of 2.
Row 1 (wrong side): *Yo, sl 1 pwise, k1 [carry yarn across the sl st]*, rep *to*.
Row 2: *K1, k2 tog tbl [yo and sl st of preceding row]*, rep *to*.
Row 3: *K1, yo, sl 1 pwise*, rep *to*.
Row 4: *K2 tog tbl [yo and sl st of preceding row], k1*, rep *to*.
Repeat these 4 rows for pattern.

MOCK TUNISIAN KNITTING (vertical)

Multiple of 2.
Row 1 (wrong side): *Yo, sl 1 pwise, k1*, rep *to*.
Row 2: *K1, k2 tog tbl [sl st and yo of preceding row]*, rep *to*.
Repeat these 2 rows for pattern.

PULLED-LOOP STITCHES

RIGHT BIAS RINGLET ringlet stitch

Multiple of 4 + 2.
Row 1: *K1, p1*, rep *to*.
Row 2 and all even-numbered rows: K all k sts and p all p sts.
Rows 3 and 7: *Put rh needle under the horizontal thread between the edge stitch and 1st st. Pull a loop through onto rh needle, k1, p1, k1, pass the loop over the last 3 sts, p1*, rep *to*, end k1, p1.
Row 5: K1, p1, *make a loop (as in row 3), k1, p1, k1, pass the loop over the last 3 sts, p1*, rep *to*.
Repeat rows 5–8 for pattern.

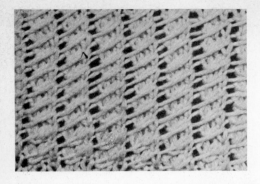

COUCHING STITCH
blister couching

Multiple of 3 + 1.
Row 1: K1, *put rh needle between 2nd and 3rd sts, pull a loop and hold it on rh needle, k3*, rep *to*.
Row 2: P1, *p2, p2 tog*, rep *to*.
Repeat these 2 rows for pattern.

COUCHING ROW PATTERN
comma stitch

Multiple of 4 + 1.
Row 1: K.
Row 2: P.
Row 3: *K4, sl 3 sts to lh needle, insert rh needle between 3rd and 4th sts, pulling a loop through onto rh needle, sl the 3 sts to rh needle*, rep *to*, k1.
Row 4: *P3, p tog next st and the loop from the preceding row*, rep *to*, p1.
Repeat these 4 rows for pattern.

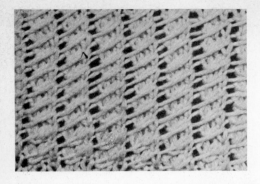

EYELET DAISY PATTERN
daisy stitch

Multiple of 10.
Rows 1, 3, 7, and 9: K.
Rows 2, 4, 8, and 10: P.
Row 5: *Place needle into 3rd st from beg in *row 1*, pull loop through and leave on rh needle, k2. Make another loop into the same st, k3, make a 3rd loop into the same st, k5*, rep *to*.
Row 6: *P5, p tog the loop and the next st, p1, p tog the 2nd loop and the next st, p1, p tog the 3rd loop and the next st*, rep *to*.
Note: Start the first and every other repeat: K5 sts before 1st daisy of row 5.
Repeat rows 5–10 for pattern.

STAGGERED BUTTERFLIES
bowknot, little butterfly

Multiple of 10 + 2.
Rows 1, 3, and 5 (right side): K1, *k5, yf, sl the next 5 sts pwise*, rep *to*, k1.
Rows 2, 4, 8, and 10: K1, *p10*, rep *to*, k1.
Row 6: K1, p2, *put rh needle under the 3 loose threads on wrong side of work, pull up loop, p the next st, sl the loop st over the p st, p9*, rep *to*, end p7, k1.
Rows 7, 9, and 11: K1, *yf, sl the next 5 sts pwise, k5*, rep *to*, end k1.
Row 12: K1, p7, rep *to* as in row 6, end last rep with p2, k1.
Repeat these 12 rows for pattern.

TASSEL PATTERN STITCH

Multiple of 6 + 1.
Rows 1 and 3: *K4, p2*, rep *to*, end k1.
Rows 2 and 4: P1, *k2, p4*, rep *to*.
Row 5: *Put rh needle between 4th and 5th sts, pull loop through, k1, p2, k3*, rep *to*, end k1.
Row 6: P1, *p3, k2, p2 tog*, rep *to*.
Rows 7 and 9: K1, *p2, k4*, rep *to*.
Rows 8 and 10: *P4, k2*, rep *to*, end p1.
Row 11: K3, *rep row 5, *to*, *end k1, p2, k1.
Row 12: P3, rep row 6, *to*.
Repeat these 12 rows for pattern.

STACKS OF WHEAT
wheat stitch, alternating wheat stacks

Multiple of 6 + 2.
Row 1: K1, p1, *k4, p2*, rep *to*, k4, p1, k1.
Row 2: K2, *p4, k2*, rep *to*.
Row 3: K1, p1, *yb, place rh needle between 4th and 5th
sts, pull loop through, k the 4 sts, next sl the
loop over the 4 k sts, p2*, rep *to*, p1, k1.
Row 4: K2, *p4, k2*, rep *to*.
Row 5: K3, *p2, k4*, rep *to*, p2, k3.
Rows 6 and 8: K1, p2, *k2, p4*, rep *to*, k2, p2, k1.
Row 7: K1, yb, *place rh needle between 2nd and 3rd
sts, pull loop through, k the 2 sts, next sl the
loop over the 2 sts, p2, yb, place rh needle
between 4th and 5th sts on lh needle, pull loop
through, k4, next sl the loop over the 4 k sts*,
p2, end k1.
Repeat these 8 rows for pattern.

MOCK CASHMERE STITCH
lattice stitch

Multiple of 8 + 7.
Row 1: K1, p1, *p3, k5*, rep *to*, p4, k1.
Rows 2, 4, and 6: P1, k4, *p5, (yo) twice, k3*, rep *to*,
k1, p1.
Rows 3, 5, and 7: K1, p1, *p3, drop yo sts, with rh
needle take next st off lh needle, pull up to
form a loop, hold in front, k4, pick up loop and
put on rh needle as a purl st*, rep *to*, p4, k1.
Row 8: P1, k4, *p5, k3*, rep *to*, k1, p1.
Row 9: K1, *k5, p3*, rep *to*, k6.
Rows 10, 12, and 14: P6, *(yo) twice, k3, p5*, rep *to*,
(yo) twice, p1.
Rows 11, 13, and 15: K1, *drop yo sts, take next st off lh
needle, pull up to form a loop, hold in front,
k4, pick up a loop and put on rh needle [see
row 3], p3*, rep *to*, drop yo, pull next st to
form a loop, k4, put loop on needle as before,
k1.
Row 16: P6, *k3, p5*, rep *to*, p1.
Repeat these 16 rows for pattern.

BORDERED LEAF BUDS
leaf stitch, fans

Multiple of 10 + 1 + 2 selvage stitches.
Rows 1, 3, 5, 7, 9, 13, 15, 17, 19, and 21: P.
Row 2: Selv st, *k3, k2 tog, yo, k1, yo, sl 1, k1, psso,
k2*, rep *to*, end k1, selv st.
Row 4: Selv st, *k2, k2 tog, yo, k3, yo, sl 1, k1, psso,
k1*, rep *to*, end k1, selv st.
Row 6: Selv st, *k1, k2 tog, yo, k5, yo, sl 1, k1, psso*,
rep *to*, end k1, selv st.
Rows 8, 12, 20, and 24: K.
Row 10: Selv st, k6, *insert rh needle in 1st space made
by the yo of row 6, pull a loop of yarn through
to the front, leave on rh needle; repeat in each
of the 5 remaining spaces until you have 6
loops on the rh needle, k10*, rep *to*, end k5,
selv st.
Row 11: Selv st, p5, *p tog the 6 loops and the next st,
p9*, rep *to*, end p5, selv st.
Row 14: Selv st, *k1, yo, sl 1, k1, psso, k5, k2 tog, yo*,
rep *to*, end k1, selv st.
Row 16: Selv st, *k2, yo, sl 1, k1, psso, k3, k2 tog, yo,
k1*, rep *to*, end k2, selv st.
Row 18: Selv st, *k3, yo, sl 1, k1, psso, k1, k2 tog, yo,
k2*, rep *to*, end k1, selv st.

Row 22: Selv st, k1, pull a loop through in each of the next 3 yo spaces [as in row 10], *k10, pull a loop in
each of the next 6 yo spaces as before*, rep *to*, end make 3 loops, selv st.
Row 23: Selv st, p tog the 3 loops and the next st, *p9, p tog the 6 loops and the next st*, rep *to*, end p tog
3 loops and the next st, selv st.
Repeat these 24 rows for pattern.

LAYETTE PATTERN STITCHES

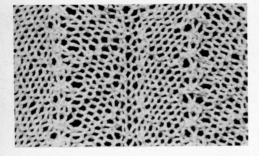

LAYETTE PATTERN I
chevron layette I

Multiple of 13.
Row 1: K.
Rows 2 and 4: *Inc 1 [k into front and back of st], k4, sl 1, k2 tog, psso, k4, inc 1*, rep *to*.
Row 3: P.
Repeat these 4 rows for pattern.

LAYETTE PATTERN II
chevron layette II

Multiple of 10 + 9.
Rows 1, 2, 3, and 7: K.
Rows 4 and 6: *Yo, k3, sl 1, k2 tog, psso, k3, yo, k1*, rep *to*, end yo.
Row 5: P.
Repeat rows 4–7 for pattern.

LAYETTE PATTERN III
chevron layette III

Multiple of 7 + 2 selvage stitches.
Row 1: Selv st, *k2, sl 1, k2 tog, psso, k2, yo*, rep *to*, selv st.
Row 2: Selv st, *p6, yo*, rep *to*, selv st.
Repeat these 2 rows for pattern.

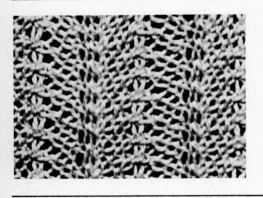

LAYETTE PATTERN IV
chevron layette IV

Multiple of 8.
Row 1: *K1, inc 1 [simple raised inc, p. 32], k2, k2 tog tbl, put this st back on lh needle and pass the next st over it. Put back on rh needle, k2, inc 1*, rep *to*.
Row 2: P.
Repeat these 2 rows for pattern.

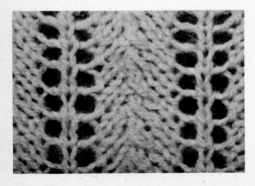

LAYETTE PATTERN V
chevron layette V

Multiple of 8 + 1.
Row 1: *K1, yo, k2, sl 1, k2 tog, psso, k2, yo*, rep *to*, k1.
Rows 2 and 4: P.
Row 3: *K1, yo, k2, k3 tog pwise, k2, yo*, rep *to*, k1.
Repeat these 4 rows for pattern.

LAYETTE PATTERN VI
chevron layette VI

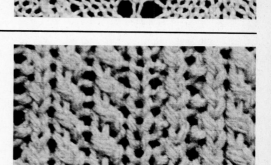

Multiple of 13 + 1.
Row 1: *K1, yo, k4, k2 tog, sl 1, k1, psso, k4, yo*, rep
　　　to, end k1.
Row 2: P.
Repeat these 2 rows for pattern.

LAYETTE PATTERN VII
chevron layette VII

Multiple of 9.
Rows 1 and 2: K.
Row 3: *(K2 tog, yo) twice, k1, (yo, k2 tog tbl) twice*,
　　　rep *to*.
Row 4: P.
Repeat rows 3 and 4 for pattern.

LAYETTE PATTERN VIII
layette stitch

Multiple of 4 + 3.
Rows 1 and 3 (right side): P1, *k3, p1*, rep *to*, end k2.
Rows 2 and 6: P2, *k1, p3*, rep *to*, end k1.
Row 4: P2 tog, *yo, k1, yo, p3 tog*, rep *to*, end yo, k1.
Rows 5 and 7: K2, *p1, k3*, rep *to*, end p1.
Row 8: K1, yo, *p3, tog, yo, k1, yo*, rep *to*, end p2
　　　tog.
Repeat these 8 rows for pattern.

DOUBLE PIQUÉ PATTERN

Multiple of 2.
Row 1: *K1, p1*, rep *to*.
Rows 2 and 4: P.
Row 3: *P1, k1*, rep *to*.
Repeat these 4 rows for pattern.

KNOTTED RIBBING
knot rib stitch

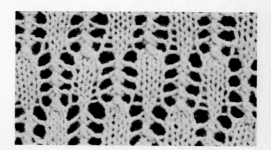

Multiple of 2.
Rows 1 and 2: *K1, p1*, rep *to*.
Row 3: *K twice into k st [k once into front loop, once
　　　into back loop], p1*, rep *to*.
Row 4: *K1, p2 tog*, rep *to*.
Repeat these 4 rows for pattern.

ALTERNATING INSET OPENWORK
inset openwork stitch

Multiple of 6 + 2 selvage stitches.
Rows 1, 3, 5, and 7: Selv st, *yo, sl 1, k2 tog, psso, yo,
　　　k3*, rep *to*, selv st.
Row 2 and all even-numbered rows: P.
Rows 9, 11, 13, and 15: Selv st, *k3, yo, sl 1, k2 tog,
　　　psso, yo*, rep *to*, selv st.
Repeat these 16 rows for pattern.

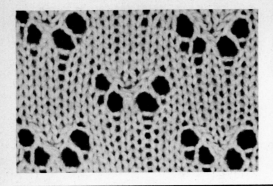

OPENWORK BUTTERFLY
openwork V

Multiple of 12 + 2 selvage stitches.
Rows 1 and 7: K.
Row 2 and all even-numbered rows: P.
Row 3: Selv st, *k7, yo, sl 1, k1, psso, k1, k2 tog, yo*, rep *to*, selv st.
Row 5: Selv st, *k8, yo, sl 1, k2 tog, psso, yo, k1*, rep *to*, selv st.
Row 9: Selv st, *k1, yo, sl 1, k1, psso, k1, k2 tog, yo, k6*, rep *to*, selv st.
Row 11: Selv st, *k2, yo, sl 1, k2 tog, psso, yo, k7*, rep *to*, selv st.
Repeat these 12 rows for pattern.

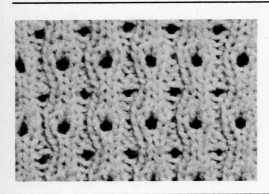

LITTLE LACE RIBS
the lacy ribs, laced ribbing

Multiple of 5 + 2 + 2 selvage stitches.
Row 1: Selv st, p2, *yo, k2 tog tbl, k1, p2*, rep *to*, selv st.
Row 2: Selv st, k2, *yo, k2 tog tbl, p1, k2*, rep *to*, selv st.
Repeat these 2 rows for pattern.

LAYETTE RINGLET
chain stitch

Multiple of 4.
Row 1: *K2, p2*, rep *to*.
Row 2: *K2, p1, yo, p1*, rep *to*.
Rows 3 and 8: *K3, p2*, rep *to*.
Rows 4 and 7: *K2, p3*, rep *to*.
Row 5: *K1, k2 tog, p2*, rep *to*.
Row 6: *K1, yo, k1, p2*, rep *to*.
Row 9: *K2, p1, p2 tog*, rep *to*.
Repeat rows 2–9 for pattern.

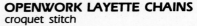

OPENWORK LAYETTE CHAINS
croquet stitch

Multiple of 11 + 2 + 2 selvage stitches.
Row 1: Selv st, *yo, k2 tog, yo, sl 1, k1, psso, k3, k2 tog, yo, k2*, rep *to*, end yo, k2 tog, selv st.
Rows 2, 4, 6, and 8: Selv st, p2, *yo, p2 tog, p9*, rep *to*, selv st.
Row 3: Selv st, *yo, k2 tog, yo, sl 1, k1, psso, k1, k2 tog, k1, yo, k2*, rep *to*, end yo, k2 tog, selv st.
Row 5: Selv st, *yo, k2 tog, k1, k2 tog, yo, k1, yo, sl 1, k1, psso, k3*, rep *to*, end yo, k2 tog, selv st.
Row 7: Selv st, *yo, k2 tog, sl 1, k1, psso, k1, yo, k1, yo, k1, sl 1, k1, psso, k2*, rep *to*, end yo, k2 tog, selv st.
Repeat these 8 rows for pattern.

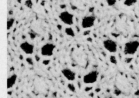

HALO RINGS
rosery stitch

Multiple of 8 + 1 + 2 selvage stitches.
Rows 1 and 3: Selv st, k1, *yo, k2, sl 1, k2 tog, psso, k2, yo, k1*, rep *to*, selv st.
Rows 2, 4, 6, and 8: P.
Rows 5 and 7: Selv st, k2 tog, *k2, yo, k1, yo, k2, sl 1, k2 tog, psso*, rep *to*, end sl 1, k1, psso, selv st.
Repeat these 8 rows for pattern.

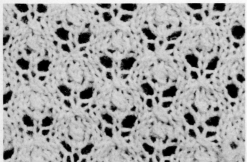

BULKY KNITTED STITCHES

The bulky or giant stitches are produced by knitting with a bulky yarn on large needles. These stitch patterns work up quickly. Because of the heavy-weight yarn, they are used primarily for outerwear and blankets.

BULKY ALTERNATING VERTICAL GRANITE STITCH

Multiple of 4.
Rows 1, 3, and 5: *Yf, sl 2 pwise, yo, k2*.
Rows 2, 4, and 6: *P2, k2 tog tbl, k1*.
Rows 7, 9, and 11: *K2, yf, sl 1 pwise, yo, yf, sl 1 pwise, yb*.
Rows 8, 10, and 12: *K1, k2 tog tbl, p2*.
Repeat these 12 rows for pattern.

BULKY GARTER STITCH AND BULKY WOVEN BASKET PATTERN

These can be knitted to create a square or rectangular pattern. See garter stitch, p. 49; woven basket pattern, p. 116.

BULKY TASSEL PATTERN

Multiple of 6 + 1.
Rows 1 and 3: *K4, p2*, end k1.
Rows 2 and 4: P1, *k2, p4*.
Row 5: *Put rh needle between 4th and 5th sts, pull loop through, k1, p2, k3*, end k1.
Row 6: P1, *p3, k2, p2 tog*.
Rows 7 and 9: K1, *p2, k4*.
Rows 8 and 10: *P4, k2*, end p1.
Row 11: K3, work row 5 *to*, end k1, p2, k1.
Row 12: P3, work row 6 *to*.
Repeat these 12 rows for pattern.

BULKY HONEYCOMB VARIATION
large honeycomb, calisson stitch

Multiple of 6.
Row 1: *P2, k2, p2*, rep *to*.
Row 2 and all even-numbered rows: K all k sts and p all p sts.
Row 3: *P1, Cr 2 R, Cr 2 L, p1*, rep *to*.
Row 5: *Cr 2 R, k2, Cr 2 L*, rep *to*.
Row 7: K.
Row 9: *Cr 2 L, k2, Cr 2 R*, rep *to*.
Row 11: *P1, Cr 2L, Cr 2 R, p1*, rep *to*.
Repeat these 12 rows for pattern.

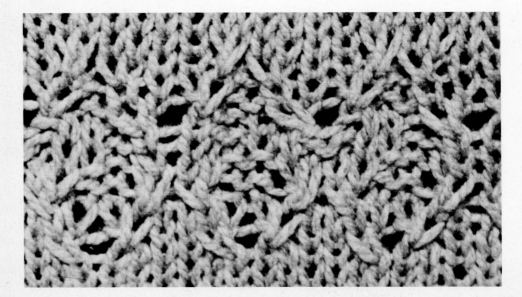

ROUND KNITTING

Most pattern stitches can be knit in the round, on circular or dp needles. Remember that all the rows (rounds) are worked with the right side facing the knitter.

STOCKINETTE STITCH

On the right side you see the knit stitches. Every round is knitted.

GARTER STITCH

Round 1: K.
Round 2: P.
Repeat these 2 rounds for pattern.

RIBBING

To work ribbing on two needles, the knit stitches of the previous row are purled on the next row. On dp or circular needles only the instructions for the first row are followed. For 2 + 2 ribbing follow the instructions for row 1: *K2, p2*, rep *to* for each round.

SEED OR MOSS STITCH

Round 1: *K1, p1*, rep *to*.
Round 2: *P1, k1*, rep *to*.
Remember to work a knit stitch over each purl stitch and a purl stitch over each knit stitch.

DIAGONAL STRIPE PATTERN
barley sugar pattern

Multiple of 11.
Round 1: *Sl 1, k1, psso, k6, yo, k3*, rep *to*.
Round 2: K.
Repeat these 2 rounds for pattern.

DIAGONAL LACE PATTERN
spiral stitch, lacy spiral stitch

Multiple of 12.
Round 1: *P3, yo, k4, k2 tog k3*, rep *to*.
Round 2: *P3, k1, yo, k4, k2 tog, k2*, rep *to*.
Round 3: *P3, k2, yo, k4, k2 tog, k1*, rep *to*.
Round 4: *P3, k3, yo, k4, k2 tog*, rep *to*.
Repeat these 4 rounds for pattern.

STEPPED DIAGONAL PATTERN reed pipe

Multiple of 17.
Round 1: *Yo, k2 tbl, (p3, k2 tbl) twice, sl 1 k1, psso, k3*, rep *to*.
Round 2: *Yo, p1, (k2 tbl, p3) twice, k1 tbl, sl 1, k1, psso, k3*, rep *to*.
Round 3: *Yo, p2, (k2 tbl, p3) twice, sl 1, k1, psso, k3*, rep *to*.
Round 4: *Yo, (p3, k2 tbl) twice, p2, sl 1, k1, psso, k3*, rep *to*.
Round 5: *Yo, k1 tbl, (p3, k2 tbl) twice, p1, sl 1, k1, psso, k3*, rep *to*.
Round 6: *Yo, k2 tbl, (p3, k2 tbl) twice, sl 1, k1, psso, k3*, rep *to*.
Round 7: *Yo, p1, (k2 tbl, p3) twice, k1 tbl, sl 1, k1, psso, k3*, rep *to*.
Repeat these 7 rounds for pattern.

TWISTED 1 + 1 RIBBING

Multiple of 2.
All rounds: *K1 tbl, p1*, rep *to*.

BELLS PATTERN
Canterbury bells, sails stitch

Multiple of 6.
Round 1: *P2, k1 tbl, p2, inc 7 [k into front and back of next st 3 times and into the front again]*, rep *to*.
Round 2: *P2, k1 tbl, p2, k7 [k into the back loop of each inc st of previous row]*, rep *to*.
Round 3: *P2, k1 tbl, p2, k5, k2 tog*, rep *to*.
Round 4: *P2, k1 tbl, p2, k4, k2 tog*, rep *to*.
Round 5: *P2, k1 tbl, p2, k3, k2 tog*, rep *to*.
Round 6: *P2, k1 tbl, p2, k2, k2 tog*, rep *to*.
Round 7: *P2, k1 tbl, p2, k1, k2 tog*, rep *to*.
Round 8: *P2, k1 tbl, p2, k2 tog*, rep *to*.
Round 9: *P2, k1 tbl, p3*, rep *to*.
Repeat these 9 rounds for pattern.

JACQUARD PATTERNS

Most jacquard patterns are easy to work in the round. Since all the stitches are knitted, the chart is always read from right to left. Carry the contrasting yarn loosely at the back of the work.

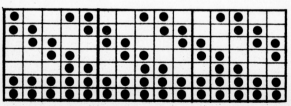

SIMPLE EYELET ALPHABET

A garment knitted in plain garter or stockinette stitch can be decorated and personalized by the addition of initials or a name.

Every letter in this unique alphabet is 20 rows high and 17 stitches wide, including 4 border stitches on the side of each letter.

To combine letters for a monogram or name, omit the 4 border stitches at the left side of each letter, where it is joined to another letter in the instructions.

In the sample "J G" shown in the photograph, the 4 stitches were omitted from the left side of the G. The sample also shows a garter stitch border placed evenly around the stockinette stitch background of the initials for a raised effect.

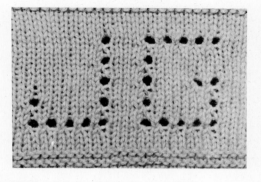

A

Rows 1, 5, and 13: K4, k2 tog, k6, k2 tog, k3.
Rows 2, 6, and 14: P4, yo, p7, p4.
Rows 3, 7, 11, 15, and 19: K.
Rows 4, 8, 12, 16, and 20: P.
Rows 9 and 17: K4, (k2 tog) 5 times, k3.
Rows 10 and 18: P3, (p1, yo) 5 times, p4.

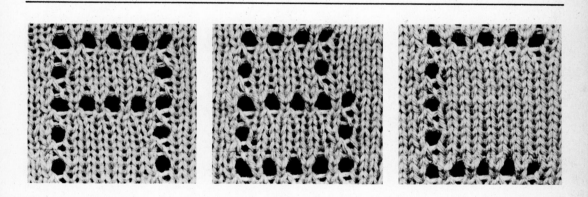

B

Rows 1 and 9: K4, (k2 tog) 5 times, k3.
Rows 2 and 10: P3, (p1, yo) 5 times, p4.
Rows 3, 7, 11, 15, and 19: K.
Rows 4, 8, 12, 16, and 20: P.
Row 5: K4, k2 tog, k6, k2 tog, k3.
Row 6: P4, yo, p7, yo, p4.
Row 13: K6, k2 tog, k4, k2 tog, k3.
Row 14: P4, yo, p5, yo, p6.
Row 17: K6, (k2 tog) 4 times, k3.
Row 18: P3, (p1, yo) 4 times, p6.

C

Rows 1 and 17: K4, (k2 tog) 5 times, k3.
Rows 2 and 18: P3, (p1, yo) 5 times, p4.
Rows 3, 7, 11, 15, and 19: K.
Rows 4, 8, 12, 16, and 20: P.
Rows 5, 9, and 13: K12, k2 tog, k3.
Rows 6, 10, and 14: P4, yo, p12.

D

Rows 1 and 17: K6, (k2 tog) 4 times, k3.
Rows 2 and 18: P3, (p1, yo) 4 times, p6.
Rows 3, 7, 11, 15, and 19: K.
Rows 4, 8, 12, 16, and 20: P.
Rows 5, 9, and 13: K4, k2 tog, k6, k2 tog, k3.
Rows 6, 10, and 14: P4, yo, p7, yo, p4.

E

Rows 1 and 17: K4, (k2 tog) 5 times, k3.
Rows 2 and 18: P3, (p1, yo) 5 times, p4.
Rows 3, 7, 11, 15, and 19: K.
Rows 4, 8, 12, 16, and 20: P.
Rows 5 and 13: K12, k2 tog, k3.
Rows 6 and 14: P4, yo, p12.
Row 9: K8, (k2 tog) 3 times, k3.
Row 10: P3, (p1, yo) 3 times, p8.

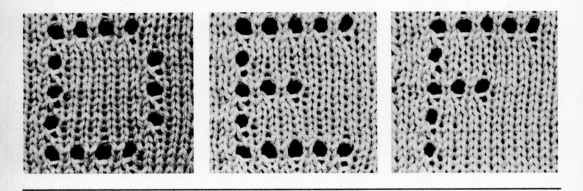

F

Rows 1, 5, and 13: K12, k2 tog, k3.
Rows 2, 6, and 14: P4, yo, p12.
Rows 3, 7, 11, 15, and 19: K.
Rows 4, 8, 12, 16, and 20: P.
Row 9: K8, (k2 tog) 3 times, k3.
Row 10: P3, (p1, yo) 3 times, p8.
Row 17: K4, (k2 tog) 5 times, k3.
Row 18: P3, (p1, yo) 5 times, p4.

G

Rows 1 and 17: K4, (k2 tog) 5 times, k3.
Rows 2 and 18: P3, (p1, yo) 5 times, p4.
Rows 3, 7, 11, 15, and 19: K.
Rows 4, 8, 12, 16, and 20: P.
Row 5: K4, k2 tog, k6, k2 tog, k3.
Row 6: P4, yo, p7, yo, p4.
Row 9: K4, (k2 tog) twice, k4, k2 tog, k3.
Row 10: P4, yo, p4, (p1, yo) twice, p4.
Row 13: K12, k2 tog, k3.
Row 14: P4, yo, p12.

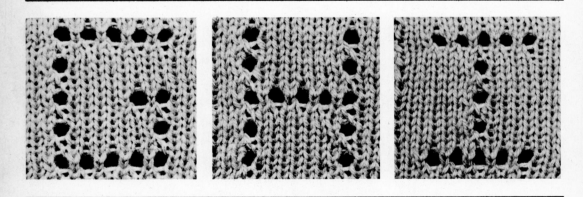

H

Rows 1, 5, 13, and 17: K4, k2 tog, k6, k2 tog, k3.
Rows 2, 6, 14, and 18: P4, yo, p7, yo, p4.
Rows 3, 7, 11, 15, and 19: K.
Rows 4, 8, 12, 16, and 20: P.
Row 9: K4, (k2 tog) 5 times, k3.
Row 10: P3, (p1, yo) 5 times, p4.

I

Rows 1 and 17: K4, (k2 tog) 5 times, k3.
Rows 2 and 18: P3, (p1, yo) 5 times, p4.
Rows 3, 7, 11, 15, and 19: K.
Rows 4, 8, 12, 16, and 20: P.
Rows 5, 9, and 13: K8, k2 tog, k7.
Rows 6, 10, and 14: P8, yo, p8.

J

Row 1: K4, (k2 tog) 5 times, k3.
Row 2: P3, (p1, yo) 5 times, p4.
Rows 3, 7, 11, 15, and 19: K.
Rows 4, 8, 12, 16, and 20: P.
Row 5: K4, k2 tog, k6, k2 tog, k3.
Row 6: P4, yo, p7, yo, p4.
Rows 9, 13, and 17: K4, k2 tog, k11.
Rows 10, 14, and 18: P12, yo, p4.

K

Rows 1 and 17: K4, k2 tog, k6, k2 tog, k3.
Rows 2 and 18: P4, yo, p7, yo, p4.
Rows 3, 7, 11, 15, and 19: K.
Rows 4, 8, 12, 16, and 20: P.
Rows 5 and 13: K6, k2 tog, k4, k2 tog, k3.
Rows 6 and 14: P4, yo, p5, yo, p6.
Row 9: K8, (k2 tog) 3 times, k3.
Row 10: P3, (p1, yo) 3 times, p8.

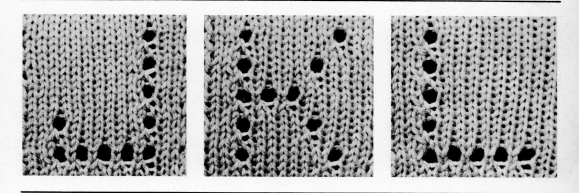

L

Row 1: K4, (k2 tog) 5 times, k3.
Row 2: P3, (p1, yo) 5 times, p4.
Rows 3, 7, 11, 15, and 19: K.
Rows 4, 8, 12, 16, and 20: P.
Rows 5, 9, 13, and 17: K12, k2 tog, k3.
Rows 6, 10, 14, and 18: P4, yo, p12.

M

Rows 1, 5, and 17: K4, k2 tog, k6, k2 tog, k3.
Rows 2, 6, and 18: P4, yo, p7, yo, p4.
Rows 3, 7, 11, 15, and 19: K.
Rows 4, 8, 12, 16, and 20: P.
Row 9: K4, (k2 tog, k2) twice, k2 tog, k3.
Row 10: P4, (yo, p3) twice, yo, p4.
Row 13: K4, (k2 tog) twice, k2, (k2 tog) twice, k3.
Row 14: P4, yo, p1, yo, p3, yo, p1, yo, p4.

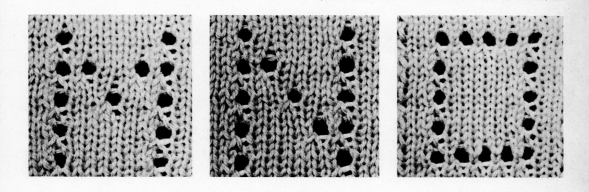

N

Rows 1 and 17: K4, k2 tog, k6, k2 tog, k3.
Rows 2 and 18: P3, yo, p7, yo, p4.
Rows 3, 7, 11, 15, and 19: K.
Rows 4, 8, 12, 16, and 20: P.
Row 5: K4, (k2 tog) twice, k4, k2 tog, k3.
Row 6: P4, yo, p4, (p1, yo) twice, p4.
Row 9: K4, (k2 tog, k2) twice, k2 tog, k3.
Row 10: P4, (yo, p3) twice, yo, p4.
Row 13: K4, K2 tog, k4, (k2 tog) twice, k3.
Row 14: P4, (yo, p1) twice, p4, yo, p4.

O

Rows 1 and 17: K4, (k2 tog) 5 times, k3.
Rows 2 and 18: P3, (p1, yo) 5 times, p4.
Rows 3, 7, 11, 15, and 19: K.
Rows 4, 8, 12, 16, and 20: P.
Rows 5, 9, and 13: K4, k2 tog, k6, k2 tog, k3.
Rows 6, 10, and 14: P4, yo, p7, yo, p4.

P

Rows 1 and 5: K12, k2 tog, k3.
Rows 2 and 6: P4, yo, p12.
Rows 3, 7, 11, 15, and 19: K.
Rows 4, 8, 12, 16, and 20: P.
Rows 9 and 17: K4, (k2 tog) 5 times, k3.
Rows 10 and 18: P3, (p1, yo) 5 times, p4.
Row 13: K4, k2 tog, k6, k2 tog, k3.
Row 14: P4, yo, p7, yo, p4.

Q

Row 1: K4, (k2 tog) 5 times, k3.
Row 2: P3, (p1, yo) 5 times, p4.
Rows 3, 7, 11, 15, and 19: K.
Rows 4, 8, 12, 16, and 20: P.
Rows 5, 9, and 13: K6, k2 tog, k4, k2 tog, k3.
Rows 6, 10, and 14: P4, yo, p5, yo, p6.
Row 17: K6, (k2 tog) 4 times, k3.
Row 18: P3, (p1, yo) 4 times, p6.

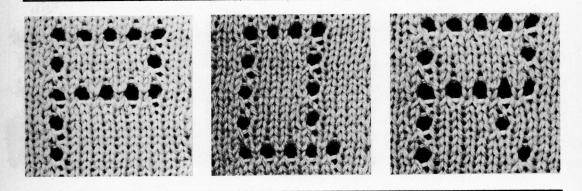

R

Rows 1 and 13: K4, k2 tog, k6, k2 tog, k3.
Rows 2 and 14: P4, yo, p7, yo, p4.
Rows 3, 7, 11, 15, and 19: K.
Rows 4, 8, 12, 16, and 20: P.
Row 5: K6, k2 tog, k4, k2 tog, k3.
Row 6: P4, yo, p5, yo, p6.
Rows 9 and 17: K4, (k2 tog) 5 times, k3.
Rows 10 and 18: P3, (p1, yo) 5 times, p4.

S

Rows 1, 9, and 17: K4, (k2 tog) 5 times, k3.
Rows 2, 10, and 18: P3, (p1, yo) 5 times, p4.
Rows 3, 7, 11, 15, and 19: K.
Rows 4, 8, 12, 16, and 20: P.
Row 5: K4, k2 tog, k11.
Row 6: P12, yo, p4.
Row 13: K12, k2 tog, k3.
Row 14: P4, yo, p12.

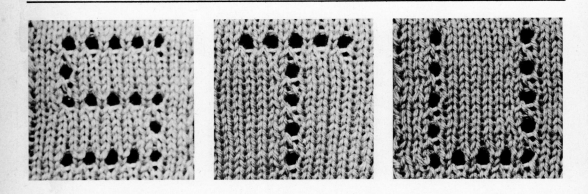

T

Rows 1, 5, 9, and 13: K8, k2 tog, k7.
Rows 2, 6, 10, and 14: P8, yo, p8.
Rows 3, 7, 11, 15, and 19: K.
Rows 4, 8, 12, 16, and 20: P.
Row 17: K4, (k2 tog) 5 times, k3.
Row 18: P3, (p1, yo) 5 times, p4.

U

Row 1: K4, (k2 tog) 5 times, k3.
Row 2: P3, (p1, yo) 5 times, k3.
Rows 3, 7, 11, 15, and 19: K.
Rows 4, 8, 12, 16, and 20: P.
Rows 5, 9, 13, and 17: K4, k2 tog, k6, k2 tog, k3.
Rows 6, 10, 14, and 18: P4, yo, p7, yo, p4.

V

Row 1: K8, k2 tog, k7.
Row 2: P8, yo, p8.
Rows 3, 7, 11, 15, and 19: K.
Rows 4, 8, 12, 16, and 20: P.
Rows 5 and 9: K6, k2 tog, k2, k2 tog, k5.
Rows 6 and 10: P6, yo, p3, yo, p6.
Rows 13 and 17: K4, k2 tog, k6, k2 tog, k3.
Rows 14 and 18: P4, yo, p7, yo, p4.

W

Row 1: K6, k2 tog, k2, k2 tog, k5.
Row 2: P6, yo, p3, yo, p6.
Rows 3, 7, 11, 15, and 19: K.
Rows 4, 8, 12, 16, and 20: P.
Rows 5, 9, 13, and 17: K4, (k2 tog, k2) twice, k2 tog, k3.
Rows 6, 10, 14, and 18: P4, (yo, p3) twice, yo, p4.

X

Rows 1 and 17: K4, k2 tog, k6, k2 tog, k3.
Rows 2 and 18: P4, yo, p7, yo, p4.
Rows 3, 7, 11, 15, and 19: K.
Rows 4, 8, 12, 16, and 20: P.
Rows 5 and 13: K6, k2 tog, k5.
Rows 6 and 14: P6, yo, p3, yo, p6.
Row 9: K8, k2 tog, k7.
Row 10: P8, yo, p8.

Y

Rows 1 and 5: K8, k2 tog, k7.
Rows 2 and 6: P8, yo, p8.
Rows 3, 7, 11, 15, and 19: K.
Rows 4, 8, 12, 16, and 20: P.
Row 9: K4, (k2 tog) 5 times, k3.
Row 10: P3, (p1, yo) 5 times, p4.
Rows 13 and 17: K4, k2 tog, k6, k2 tog, k3.
Rows 14 and 18: P4, yo, p7, yo, p4.

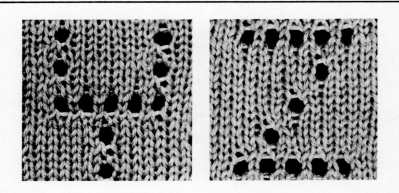

Z

Rows 1 and 17: K4, (k2 tog) 5 times, k3.
Rows 2 and 18: P3, (p1, yo) 5 times, p4.
Rows 3, 7, 11, 15, and 19: K.
Rows 4, 8, 12, 16, and 20: P.
Row 5: K10, k2 tog, k5.
Row 6: P6, yo, p10.
Row 9: K8, k2 tog, k7.
Row 10: P8, yo, p8.
Row 13: K6, k2 tog, k9.
Row 14: P10, yo, p6.

CABLES

Cables are a combination of stitches crossed over each other to the left or right. A variety of decorative effects can be obtained by varying the direction and number of crossings. The cable is known as the basic pattern in Aran knitting.

Classic single cables are formed on any even number of stitches. They are worked in stockinette stitch on a purl background.

To form a cable cross, slip half the number of stitches onto a cable or double-pointed needle. If you want the cable to be crossed to the *left*, hold the cable needle at the front of your work.

This is sometimes referred to as "cable front." To cross the cable to the *right*, hold the stitches on the cable needle at the back of your work. This is often called a "cable back." Knit the second half of the stitches (still on the lh needle), then knit the stitches that are being held on the cable or dp needle. It is important to take care not to twist these stitches. The cable pattern is determined by repeating these crossings in a regular sequence, every second, fourth, sixth, etc. row. Most cable patterns are worked on a background of reversed stockinette stitch or enclosed in a vertical band between other patterns with a few purl stitches worked on each side of the cable.

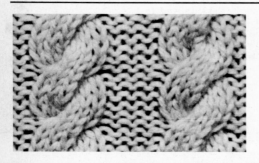

SIMPLE CABLE REPEAT

Multiple of 16.
Rows 1, 3, and 5 (wrong side): *K4, p8, k4*, rep *to*.
Rows 2 and 4: *P4, k8, p4*, rep *to*.
Row 6: *P4, sl 4 sts to dpn, hold in back, k4, k4 from dpn, p4*, rep *to*.
Repeat these 6 rows for pattern.

SINGLE CABLE RIB
simple cable rib

Multiple of 5 + 3.
Row 1: *P3, k2*, rep *to*, end p3.
Rows 2, 3, 4, and 6: K all k sts and p all p sts.
Row 5: *P3, Cr 2 R [k the 2nd st, then the 1st]*, rep *to*, end p3.
Repeat these 6 rows for pattern.

SINGLE CABLE 6 + 6
classic cable

Multiple of 10.
Rows 1, 3, and 5 (wrong side): *K2, p6, k2*, rep *to*.
Rows 2 and 6: *P2, k6, p2*, rep *to*.
Row 4: *P2, sl next 3 sts to dpn and hold in front, k3, k3 sts from dpn, p2*, rep *to*.
Repeat these 6 rows for pattern.

SINGLE CABLE 6 + 8
classic cable

Multiple of 10.
Rows 1, 3, 5, and 7 (wrong side): *K2, p6, k2*, rep *to*.
Rows 2, 6, and 8: *P2, k6, p2*, rep *to*.
Row 4: *P2, sl next 3 sts to dpn and hold in front, k3, k3
     sts from dpn, p2*, rep *to*.
Repeat these 8 rows for pattern.

HORSESHOE CABLE
double cable

Multiple of 16.
Rows 1, 3, 5, and 7 (wrong side): *K2, p12, k2*, rep *to*.
Row 2: *P2, sl next 3 sts to dpn, hold in back, k3, k3
     from dpn, sl next 3 sts to dpn and hold in
     front, k3, k3 from dpn, p2*, rep *to*.
Rows 4, 6, and 8: *P2, k12, p2*, rep *to*.
Repeat these 8 rows for pattern.

REVERSE HORSESHOE CABLE
reverse double cable

Follow directions for horseshoe cable, reversing order by
substituting "hold in front" for "hold in back" and vice
versa in row 2.

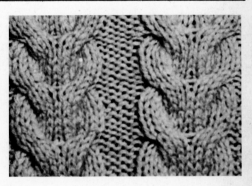

PLAIT CABLE
plaited cable

Multiple of 15.
Rows 1 and 5 (right side): *P3, k9, p3*, rep *to*.
Rows 2, 4, 6, and 8: *K3, p9, k3*, rep *to*.
Row 3: *P3, sl next 3 sts to dpn, hold in front, k3, k3
     from dpn, k3, p3*, rep *to*.
Row 7: *P3, k3, sl next 3 sts to dpn, hold in back, k3, k3
     from dpn, p3*, rep *to*.
Repeat these 8 rows for pattern.

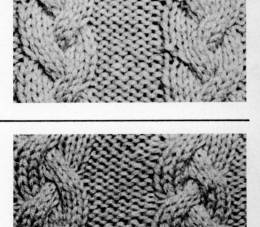

REVERSE PLAIT CABLE
reverse plaited, branch cable

Follow directions for plait cable, reversing order by
substituting "hold in front" for "hold in back" and vice
versa in rows 3 and 7. All other directions remain the
same.

UNEVEN CABLE
chain cable, eccentric cable

Multiple of 14.
Rows 1, 5, and 7 (right side): *P4, k6, p4*, rep *to*.
Rows 2, 4, 6, 8, 10, and 26: *K4, p6, k4*, rep *to*.
Rows 3 and 9: *P4, sl next 3 sts to dpn, hold in back, k3, k3 from dpn, p4*, rep *to*.
Row 11: *P3, sl next st to dpn, hold in back, k3, p1 from dpn, sl next 3 sts to dpn, hold in front, p1, k3 from dpn, p3*, rep *to*.
Rows 12, 14, 16, 18, 20, 22, and 24: *K3, p3, k2, p3, k3*, rep *to*.
Rows 13, 15, 17, 19, 21, and 23: *P3, k3, k2, p3, k3*, rep *to*.
Row 25: *P3, sl next 3 sts on dpn, hold in front, p1, k3 from dpn, sl next st to dpn, hold in back, k3, p1 from dpn, p3*, rep *to*.
Repeat rows 3–26 for pattern.

PINCHED CABLE
wavy cable

Multiple of 15.
Rows 1, 3, 7, 9, 11, 13, 15, 17, and 19: *P3, k9, p3*, rep *to*.
Row 2 and all even-numbered rows: *K3, p9, k3*, rep *to*.
Row 5: *P3, sl next 3 sts to dpn, hold in back, sl next 3 sts to a 2nd dpn, hold in front, k next 3 sts, k3 from 2nd dpn, k3 from 1st dpn, p3*, rep *to*.
Row 21: *P3, sl next 3 sts to dpn, hold in back, sl next 3 sts to 2nd dpn, hold in back, k3, k3 from 2nd dpn, k3 from 1st dpn, p3*, rep *to*.
Repeat these 21 rows for pattern. The crossings alternate every 16 rows.

WOVEN CABLES
interwoven cables, open cableweave

Multiple of 29.
Row 1: K1, p1, k3, *p4, k6*, rep *to* (once), p3, k1.
Row 2 and all even-numbered rows: P all p sts and k all k sts.
Row 3: K1, p1, k3, *p4, sl next 3 sts to dpn, hold in front, k3, then k3 from dpn*, rep *to* (once), p3, k1.
Row 5: K1, p1, *sl next 3 sts to dpn, hold in front, p2, then k3 from dpn, sl next 2 sts to dpn, hold in back, k3, then p2 from dpn*, rep *to* (once), sl next 3 sts to dpn, hold in front, p2, then k3 from dpn, p1, k1.
Row 7: K1, p3, *sl next 3 sts to dpn, hold in back, k3, then k3 from dpn, p4*, rep *to* (once), k3, p1, k1.
Row 9: K1, p1, *sl next 2 sts to dpn, hold in back, k3, then p2 from dpn, sl next 3 sts to dpn, hold in front, p2, k3 from dpn*, rep *to* (once), sl next 2 sts to dpn, hold in back, k3, then p2 from dpn, p1, k1.
Repeat rows 3–10 for pattern.

HORSESHOE CABLE WITH MOSS STITCH
double cable with moss stitch

Multiple of 28.
Rows 1 and 5: (P1, k1) 3 times, p1, k14, (p1, k1) 3 times, p1.
Rows 2 and 6: (K1, p1) 3 times, k1, p14, (k1, p1) 3 times, k1.
Row 3: (K1, p1) 4 times, k12, (p1, k1) 4 times.
Row 4: (P1, k1) 4 times, p12, (k1, p1) 4 times.
Row 7: (K1, p1) 4 times, sl 3 sts to dpn, hold in front, k3, k3 from dpn, sl 3 sts to dpn, hold in back, k3, k3 from dpn, (p1, k1) 4 times.
Row 8: (P1, k1) 3 times, p1, p12, (k1, p1) 3 times, k1.
Repeat these 8 rows for pattern.

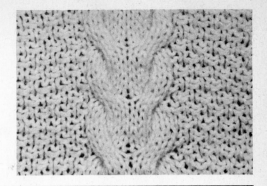

CHAIN CABLE
ring cable, double ribbon stitch

Multiple of 14.
Rows 1, 3, 5, and 7: *K3, p8, k3*, rep *to*.
Row 2: *P3, sl next 2 sts to dpn, hold in back, k2, k2 from dpn, slip next 2 sts to dpn, hold in front, k2, k2 from dpn, p3*, rep *to*.
Rows 4 and 8: *P3, k8, p3*, rep *to*.
Row 6: *P3, sl next 2 sts to dpn, hold in front, k2, k2 from dpn, p3*, rep *to*.
Repeat these 8 rows for pattern.

ALTERNATE CHAIN CABLE
alternate ring, round and elongated chain

Multiple of 14.
Rows 1, 3, and 5: *K5, p4, k5*, rep *to*.
Rows 2 and 4: *P5, k4, p5*, rep *to*.
Row 6: *P3, sl next 2 sts to dpn, hold in back, k2, p2 from dpn, sl next 2 sts to dpn, hold in front, p2, k2 from dpn, p3*, rep *to*.
Rows 7, 9, and 11: *K3, p2, k4, p2, k3*, rep *to*.
Rows 8 and 10: *P3, k2, p4, k2, p3*, rep *to*.
Row 12: *P3, sl next 2 sts to dpn, hold in front, p2, k2 from dpn, sl next 2 sts to dpn, hold in back, k2, p2 from dpn, p3*, rep *to*.
Repeat these 12 rows for pattern.

COMPLEX PLAITED CABLES
plait, plaited cables

Multiple of 24.
Rows 1 and 5: K.
Rows 2, 4, and 6: P.
Row 3: *(Sl 3 to dpn, hold in back, k3, k3 from dpn) 3 times*, rep *to*.
Row 7: *K3, (sl next 3 sts to dpn, hold in front, k3, k3 from dpn) twice, k3*, rep *to*.
Row 8: P.
Repeat these 8 rows for pattern.

CORN CABLE
corn stitch, gull stitch, wishbone cable

Multiple of 13.
Row 1: *P2, k9, p2*, rep *to*.
Rows 2 and 4: *K2, p9, k2*, rep *to*.
Row 3: *P2, sl next 3 sts to dpn, hold in back, k1, k3 from dpn, k1, sl 1 st to dpn, hold in front, k3, k1 from dpn, p2*, rep *to*.
Repeat these 4 rows for pattern.
Note: For single cable line, omit *to*.

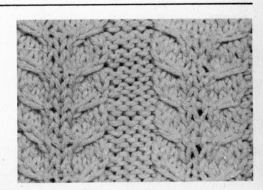

HONEYCOMB CABLES
multiple chain cables, fancy stitch

Multiple of 8 + 4.
Rows 1 and 5: K.
Rows 2, 4, 6, and 8: P.
Row 3: K2, *sl 2 sts to dpn, hold in front, k2, k2 from dpn, sl 2 sts to dpn, hold in back, k2, k2 from dpn*, rep *to*, end k2.
Row 7: K2, *sl 2 sts to dpn, hold in back, k2, k2 from dpn, sl 2 sts to dpn, hold in front, k2, k2 from dpn*, rep *to*, end k2.
Repeat these 8 rows for pattern.

TUCKED CABLES
leaf cable, triple gull stitch, fancy strip

Multiple of 8 + 2.
Rows 1, 3, and 11: *P2, k6*, rep *to*, end p2.
Row 2 and all even-numbered rows: *K2, p6*, rep *to*, end k2.
Rows 5, 7, and 9: *P2, sl 2 to dpn, hold in back, k1, k2 from dpn, sl 1 to dpn, hold in front, k2, k1 from dpn*, rep *to*, end p2.
Repeat these 12 rows for pattern.

FILLED DIAMOND CABLE
diamond cable, diamond-moss cable

Multiple of 16.
Row 1: P6, k4, p6.
Row 2: K6, p4, k6.
Row 3: P5, Cross 3 Right [C 3 R: sl next st to dpn, hold in back, k2, k1 from dpn], Cross 3 Left [C 3 L: sl 2 sts to dpn, hold in front, p1, k2 from dpn], p5.
Row 4: K5, p2, k1, p1 [Irish moss stitch—diamond center, hereafter referred to as IM], p2, k5.
Row 5: P4, C 3 R, p1, k1, C 3 L, p4.
Row 6: K4, p2, (k1, p1) twice for IM, p2, k4.
Row 7: P3, C 3 R, (k1, p1) twice for IM, C 3 L, p3.
Row 8: K3, p2, (k1, p1) 3 times for IM, p2, k3.
Row 9: P2, C 3 R, (k1, p1) 3 times for IM, C 3 L, p2.
Row 10: K2, p2, (k1, p1) 4 times for IM, p2, k2.
Row 11: P1, C 3 R, (k1, p1) 4 times for IM, C 3 L, p1.
Row 12: K1, p2, (k1, p1) 5 times for IM, p2, k1.
Row 13: C 3 R, (k1, p1) 5 times for IM, C 3 L.
Row 14: P2, (k1, p1) 6 times for IM, p2.
Row 15: C 3 L, (k1, p1) 5 times for IM, C 3 R (p the stitch that passes behind).
Row 16: K1, p2, (k1, p1) 5 times for IM, p2, k1.
Row 17: P1, C 3 L, (k1, p1) 4 times for IM, C 3 R, p1.
Row 18: K2, p2, (k1, p1) 4 times for IM, p2, k2.
Row 19: P2, C 3 L, (k1, p1) 3 times for IM, C 3 R, p2.
Row 20: K3, p2, (k1, p1) 3 times for IM, p2, k3.
Row 21: P3, C 3 L, (k1, p1) twice for IM, C 3 R, p3.
Row 22: K4, p2, (k1, p1) twice for IM, p2, k4.
Row 23: P4, C3 L, (k1, p1) for IM, C 3 R, p4.
Row 24: K5, p2, (k1, p1) for IM, p2, k5.
Row 25: P5, C3 L, C 3 R, p5.
Repeat rows 2–25 for pattern.

SIMPLE ZIGZAG
single zigzag

Multiple of 8 + 4.
Row 1: P8, back cross [BC: sl 1 to dpn, hold in back, k1, p1 from dpn], p2.
Row 2 and all even-numbered rows through row 26: K all the k sts and p all p sts.
Row 3: P7, BC, p3.
Row 5: P6, BC, p4.
Row 7: P5, BC, p5.
Row 9: P4, BC, p6.
Row 11: P3, BC, p7.
Row 13: P2, BC, p8.
Row 15: P2, front cross [FC: sl 1 to dpn, hold in front, p1, k1 from dpn], p8.
Row 17: P3, FC, p7.
Row 19: P4, FC, p6.
Row 21: P5, FC, p5.
Row 23: P6, FC, p4.
Row 25: P7, FC, p3.
Row 27: P8, FC, p2.
Row 28: K2, p1, k9.
Repeat these 28 rows for pattern.

KNOTTED CABLE
knotted cords

Multiple of 10 + 2.
Rows 1 and 3: *P2, k2, p2, k4*, rep *to*, end p2.
Row 2 and all even-numbered rows: K all k sts and p all p sts.
Rows 5 and 7: *P1, k4, p2, k2, p1*, rep *to*, end p1, k1.
Row 9: *P1, sl 2 sts to dpn, hold in back, k next 2 sts, k the 2 sts from dpn, p2, k2, p1*, rep *to*, end p1, k1.
Rows 11, 15, and 19: Rep row 2.
Row 13: *P2, k2, p2, k4*, rep *to*, end p2.
Row 17: *P2, k2, p2, sl 2 sts to dpn, hold in back, k next 2 sts, k the 2 sts from dpn*, rep *to*, end p2.
Repeat rows 5–20 for pattern.

DOUBLE CABLE HEARTS
hearts, cabled hearts

Multiple of 12 + 4.
Row 1: K2, *p4, k4, p4, k2*.
Row 2 and all even-numbered rows: K all k sts and p all p sts.
Row 3: K2, *p4, sl 2 sts to dpn, hold in front, k the next 2 sts, k2 sts from dpn, p4*, end k2.
Row 5: K2, *p3, sl next st to dpn, hold in back, k next 2 sts, p the st from the dpn, sl next 2 sts to dpn, hold in front, p the next st, k the 2 sts from dpn, p3*, end k2.
Row 7: K2, *p2, sl next st to dpn, hold in back, k the next 2 sts, p the st from the dpn, p2, sl next 2 sts to dpn, hold in front, p the next st, k2 sts from dpn, p2*, end k2.
Row 9: K2, *p1, sl 1st st to dpn, hold in back, k next 2 sts, p the st from the dpn, p4, sl next 2 sts to dpn, hold in front, p the next st, k the 2 sts from dpn, p1*, end k2.
Repeat these 10 rows for pattern.

ENTWINED LOZENGE PATTERN
entwined lozenges

Multiple of 16.
Row 1: K2, p4, k4, p4, k2.
Row 2 and all even-numbered rows: K all k sts and p all p sts.
Rows 3 and 19: K2, p4, Cr 4 R [sl 2 sts to dpn, hold in back, k2, k2 from dpn], p4, k2.
Row 5: Cr 2 L [sl 2 sts to dpn, hold in front, p1, k2 sts from dpn], p2, Cr 2 R [sl 1 st to dpn, hold in back, k2, p1 from dpn], Cr 2 L, p2, Cr 2 R.
Row 7: P1, Cr 2 L, Cr 2 R, p2, Cr 2 L, Cr 2 R, p1.
Rows 9 and 13: P2, Cr 4 R, p4, Cr 4 R, p2.
Row 11: P2, k4, p4, k4, p2.
Row 15: P1, Cr 2 R, Cr 2 L, p2, Cr 2 R, Cr 2 L, p1.
Row 17: (Cr 2 R, p2, Cr 2 L) twice.
Repeat these 20 rows for pattern.

BORDERED ENTWINED LOZENGES
entwined lozenges

Multiple of 20.
Row 1: (K4, p4) twice, k4.
Row 2: (P4, k4) twice, p4.
Rows 3 and 19: K4, p4, Cr 4 R [sl 2 sts to dpn, hold in back, k2, k2 from dpn], p4, k4.
Rows 4 and 20: (P4, k4) twice, p4.
Row 5: K2, Cr 2 L [sl 2 sts to dpn, hold in front, p1, k2 sts from dpn], p2, Cr 2 R [sl 1 st to dpn, hold in back, k2, p1 from dpn], Cr 2 L, p2, Cr 2 R, k2.
Row 6: P2, k1, (p2, k2) 3 times, p2, k1, p2.
Row 7: K2, p1, Cr 2 L, Cr 2 R, p2, Cr 2 L, Cr 2 R, p1, k2.
Row 8: P2, k2, p4, k4, p4, k2, p2.
Rows 9 and 13: K2, p2, Cr 4 R, p4, Cr 4 R, p2, k2.
Rows 10 and 14: P2, k2, p4, k4, p4, k2, p2.
Row 11: K2, p2, k4, p4, k4, p2, k2.
Row 12: P2, k2, p4, k4, p4, k2, p2.
Row 15: K2, p1, Cr 2 R, Cr 2 L, p2, Cr 2 R, Cr 2 L, p1, k2.
Row 16: P2, k1, (p2, k2) 3 times, p2, k1, p2.
Row 17: K2, Cr 2 R, p2, Cr 2 L, Cr 2 R, p2, Cr 2 L, k2.
Row 18: (P4, k4) twice, p4.
Repeat these 20 rows for pattern.

TRIPLE ZIGZAG
twist zigzag

Multiple of 9 + 3.
Row 1: K3, *Cr 2 L [insert rh needle behind first st, k the 2nd st tbl, k the 1st st, let both sts drop from lh needle] 3 times, k3*.
Row 2 and all even-numbered rows: P.
Row 3: K4, *(Cr 2 L) 3 times, k3*, end k2.
Row 5: (Cr 2 L) once, *k3, (Cr 2 L) 3 times,* end k1.
Row 7: K1, (Cr 2 L) once*, k3, (rep *to*) 3 times*.
Row 9: K1, Cr 2 R [K the 2nd st on lh needle, k the 1st st, let both sts slip off lh needle];* k3, (Cr 2 R) 3 times*.
Row 11: Cr 2 R, *k3, (Cr 2 R) 3 times*, k1.
Row 13: K4, *(Cr 2 R) 3 times, k3*, k2.
Row 15: K3, *(Cr 2 R) 3 times, k3*, k3.
Repeat these 16 rows for pattern.

INTERLACED PATTERN

This simple technique produces a very spectacular allover pattern (also called entrelacs, or intertwined trellis). You can knit in one color, bicolored, or even multicolored yarns. Observe the following basic rules for best results:

1. Use stockinette stitch to emphasize the interlaced appearance of the pattern. Complicated stitches will distract from the pattern's multidirectional technique.

2. The basis for the pattern is the triangle. By adjusting the number of stitches in the base of each triangle, you can adapt this knitting pattern to most garment instructions. The formula is: no. of sts ÷ by no. of sts in the base of 1 triangle = number of triangles.

3. Always begin with a row of triangles.

4. The rectangles are formed by the picked-up stitches (width) and the knitted stitches (length) and joined by decreases in the stitches left unworked. Always work the rows of rectangles in consecutive order.

5. End by making another row of triangles to fill in the spaces formed on the last set of rectangles.

The procedure is worked as follows:

1 Start with a basic triangle of 12 sts. With color A, cast on 48 sts on a set of double-pointed needles.

2 *P2, turn, k the 2 sts just worked, turn, p3, turn, k3, turn, p4, turn, k4, turn, p5, turn, k5; continue in this way until there are 12 sts on needle (leave these 12 sts on dpn)*; with next dpn, rep *to* until 4 triangles are made. These are called the base triangles.

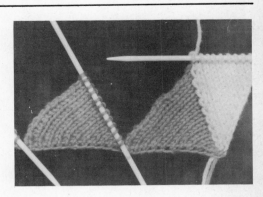

3 Change to color B. *K2, turn, p2, turn, inc 1 in 1st st, sl 1, k1, psso, turn, p3, turn, inc 1 in 1st st, k1, sl l, k1, psso, turn, p4, inc 1 in 1st st, k2, sl 1, k1, psso, turn, p5, turn; continue, adding 1 extra st between the inc and sl st, until all the sts in color A of the 1st triangle have been used. You now have 12 sts of color B on dpn. Leave these sts on this needle.

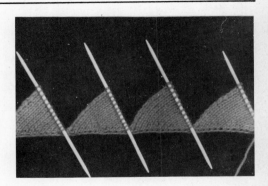

4 Continuing with color B and another dpn, *pick up and k12 sts along lh edge of 1st triangle;

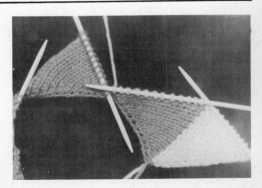

p these 12 sts, turn k11, sl 1, k1, psso (the sl st is the last st of the 12 sts, the k st is the 1st st of the next triangle), turn, p12, turn, k11, sl 1, k1, psso, turn, p12; continue until all the sts of the 2nd triangle have been used*. Rep *to*, picking up 12 sts from the lh edge of each triangle until all 4 triangles have been worked.

5   Continuing to work with B, pick up and k12 on lh edge of the last triangle, turn, p2 tog, p10, turn, k11, turn, p2 tog, p9, turn, k10, turn, p2 tog, p8, turn, k9; continue until there is 1 st remaining.

6   Using color A and the last st as your 1st st, pick up and p11 sts from the straight edge of the triangle just worked; turn, *k12, turn, p11, p2 tog (use the last st on the needle and the 1st st of the next triangle), turn, k12, turn, p11, p2 tog (as before); continue until all the color B sts have been used*. With color A, pick up and p12 sts from the side of the next triangle. Rep *to* for each triangle.

7   Using color B, rep from *to* in step 3. When you have completed the last desired row of color B rectangles, complete the pattern with color A as follows: *Pick up and p11 sts on the side of the last triangle, turn, k12, turn, p2 tog, p9, p2 tog (use last st on needle and 1st st of next triangle), turn, k11, turn, p2 tog, p8, p2 tog, turn, k10, turn; continue until 1 st is left*, rep *to* to the end of the last triangle.

JACQUARD AND MULTICOLORED PATTERNS, DUPLICATE STITCH

There are two techniques used to work jacquard patterns in knitting. The Fair Isle or knitted jacquard method is adaptable to many variations, such as double-sided knitting, reversible jacquard, and multicolored patterns.

The second method is the Swiss darning or embroidered jacquard, which is embroidered on the surface of a finished piece. Both methods are always worked in stockinette stitch with two or more colors.

KNITTED JACQUARD

The *crossed yarn* method is used when the design consists of separate large motifs or patterns to be worked in several colors. First, wind a separate bobbin for each color and each motif. This will keep the colors separate and avoid tangles. The colors will not be carried across the back of the work or create unnecessary bulk or thickness. When changing colors, cross or twist the yarns around each other by taking the new color from under the yarn worked for the last stitch.

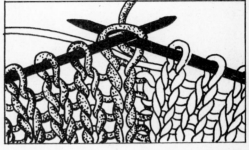

If the twisting technique is not carefully followed, the different colors will not be evenly joined and holes will form on the face of the knitted work. The yarn can be carried across 2 or 3 stitches when working a pattern by passing the colored yarn across the back (wrong side) loosely, always remembering to twist the yarn being used at the beginning of each color change.

WEAVING METHOD

When small, closely spaced motifs are knitted on a basic plain background, the weaving method is used. In this technique, it is very important to carefully regulate the tension of the yarn as it is being carried across the back of the work so that the shape of the motif is not distorted by pulling too tight. It is also important to avoid loose tension or carrying the yarn across too many stitches. A long span of yarn can catch on buttons or jewelry when the garment is worn.

To work this method, put the right-hand needle under the yarn color to be carried before you work the next stitch. Be careful to knit only the working color through the stitch, leaving the carried yarn at the back.

When working on the purl side, keep the yarn being used in front and pass the right-hand needle one time under and one time over the yarn before purling a stitch.

This technique works up very easily in round or circular knitting, as all the rounds are worked on the knit side.

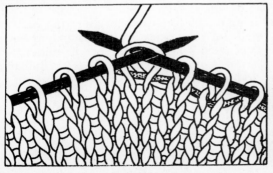

Knit Side

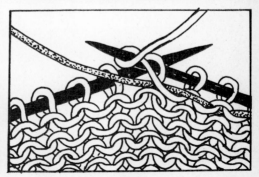

Purl Side

EMBROIDERED JACQUARD

This is a form of surface embroidery worked on a finished stockinette background. The stitch used for embroidered jacquard is a surface reproduction of stockinette stitch, called duplicate stitch. This method is used to add one stitch or a row of stitiches to the knitted or weaving methods. A single motif or monogram can be easily put anywhere on the finished knitted garment. The duplicate stitch can also be used to save a stained garment by placing a motif or initial over the damaged spot.*

To Work Duplicate Stitch:

Step 1 Thread a tapestry or yarn needle with the chosen color of yarn.

Step 2 Place the needle from the back coming out the front at the base of the first stitch to be worked.

Step 3 *Insert the needle from right to left under the two threads of the stitch directly above the stitch being worked. Pull the yarn gently through the two threads.

Step 4 Insert the needle back into the base of the first stitch and bring it back to the front at the base of the next stitch*. Repeat *to* for each stitch.

Step 5 To work the last stitch in a row, put the needle into the base of the stitch being worked and come up at the base of the stitch to be worked on the row above.

Step 6 To continue working from right to left, turn the work upside down and repeat *to* (step 3), placing the needle under two strands of the stitch directly *below* the stitch to be covered.

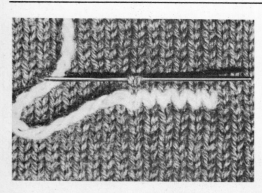

*Alphabet used with permission from *New Ideas for Needlepointers* by Marion Broome Pakula (Crown Publishers, 1976).

Jacquard from a Chart

Jacquard designs for any of the methods described are usually shown on a chart on graph paper. Always remember, 1 square equals 1 stitch. Each line of squares equals 1 row of stitches. Each symbol represents a color of yarn, and a blank square is the background color of the work unless otherwise specified.

The design is read from right to left on the knit side and from left to right on the purl side. The design chart is always read from the bottom to the top.

In round or circular knitting the chart is always read from the right to the left.

Standard graph paper will produce a workable chart for knitting. However, since knitted stitches are not square, KnittingGraph paper will produce a more accurate and proportional representation of your design.

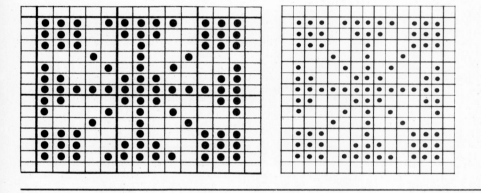

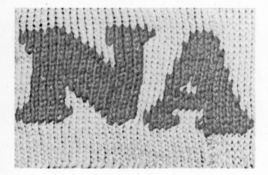

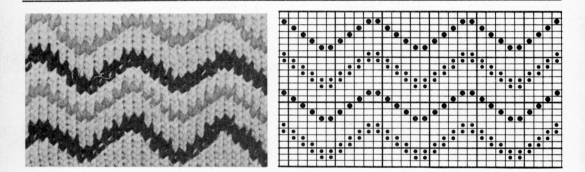

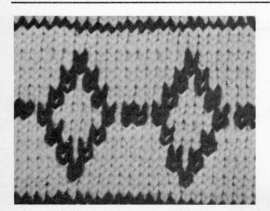

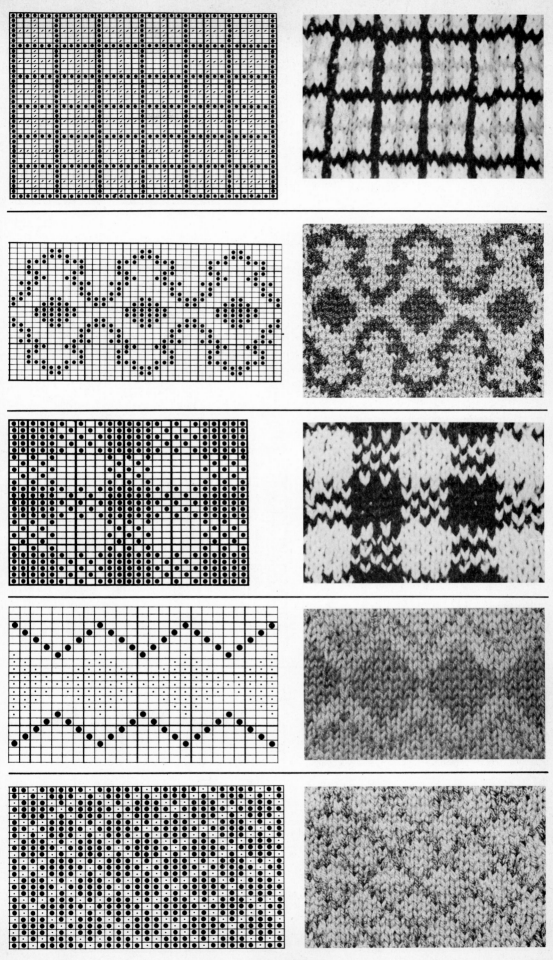

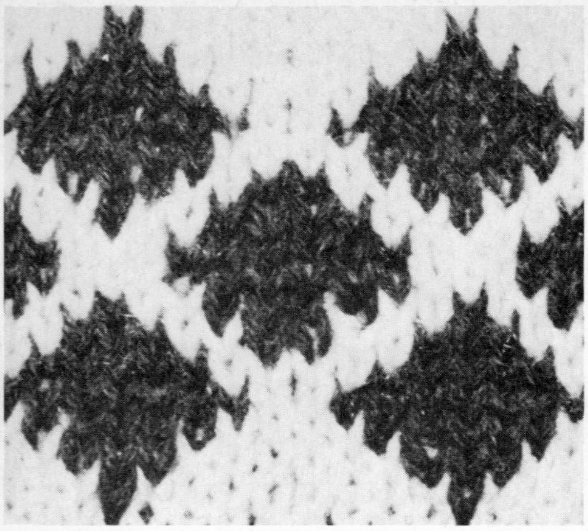
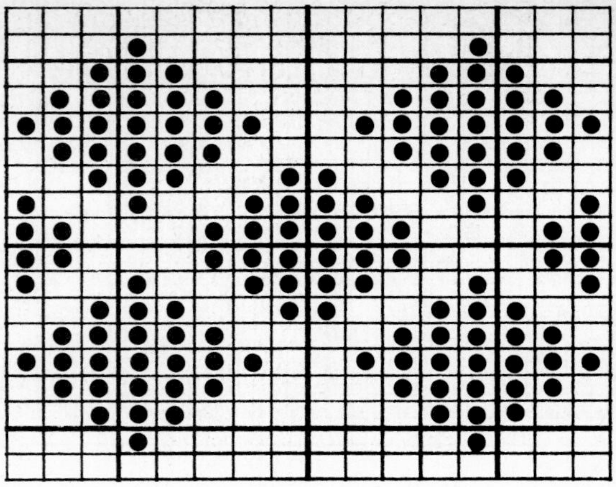
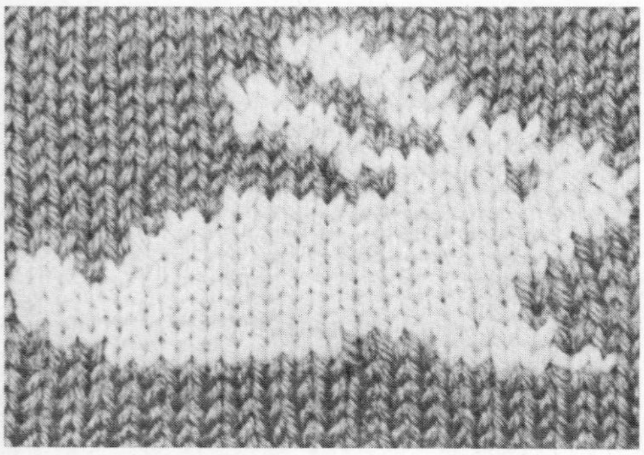
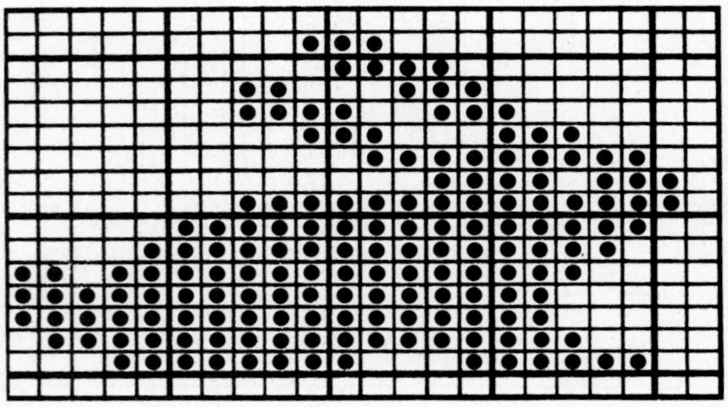
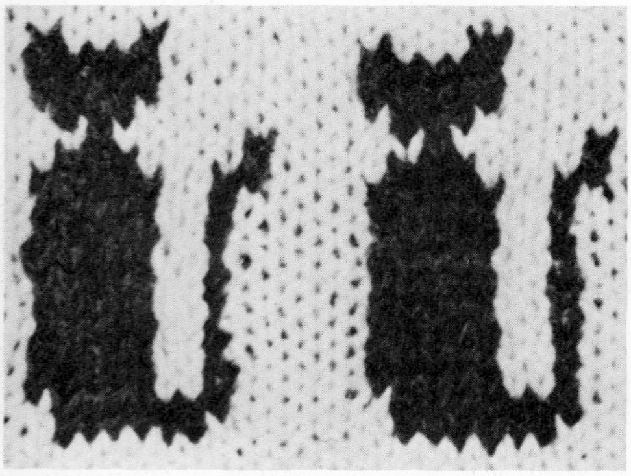
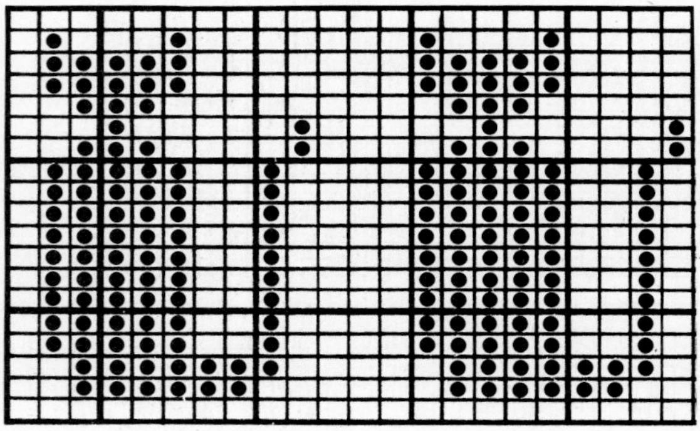
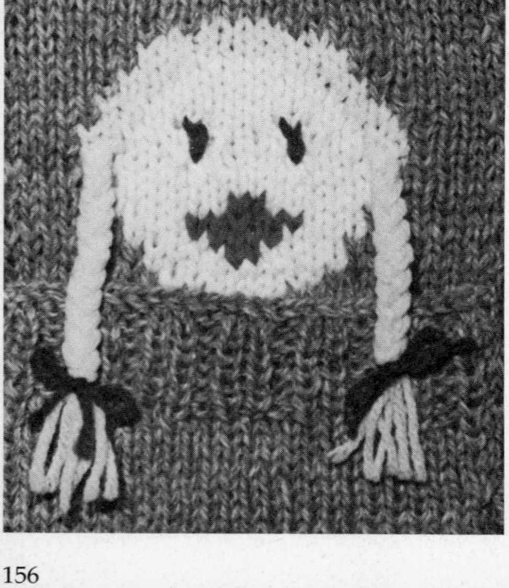
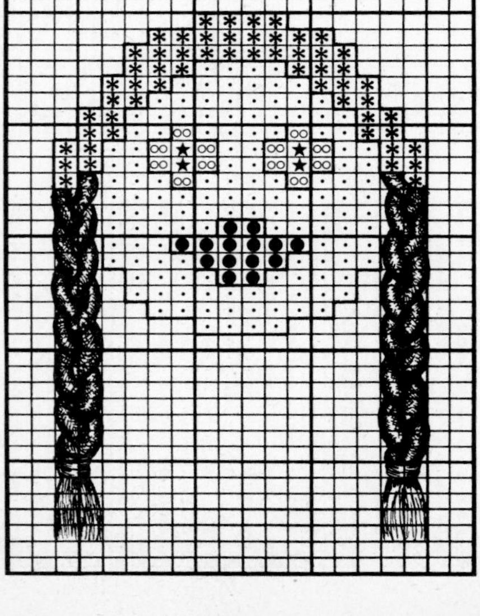

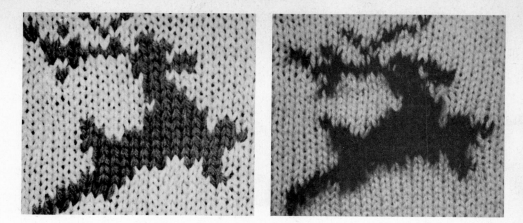

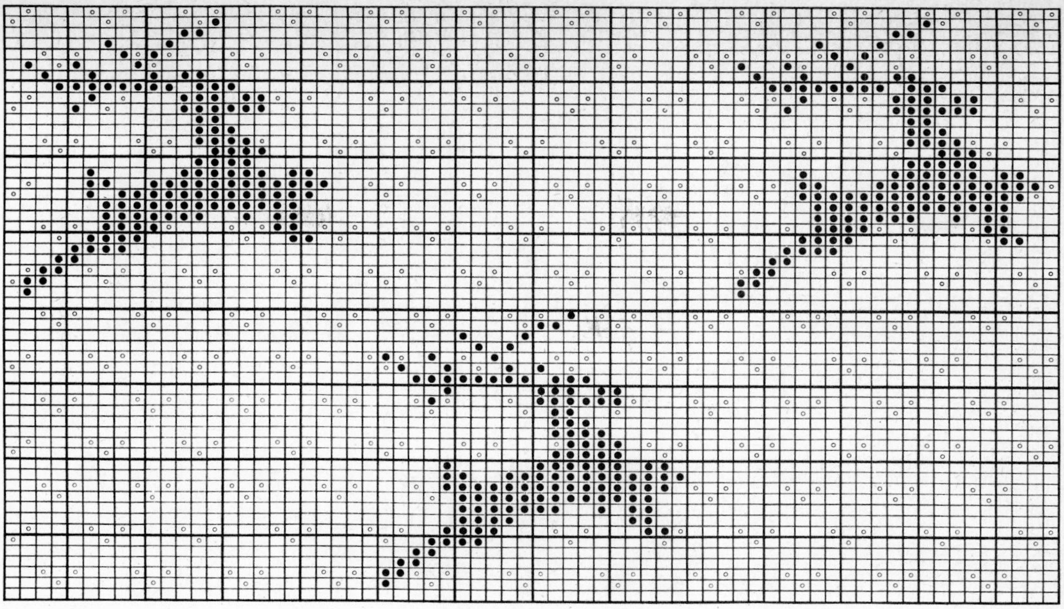

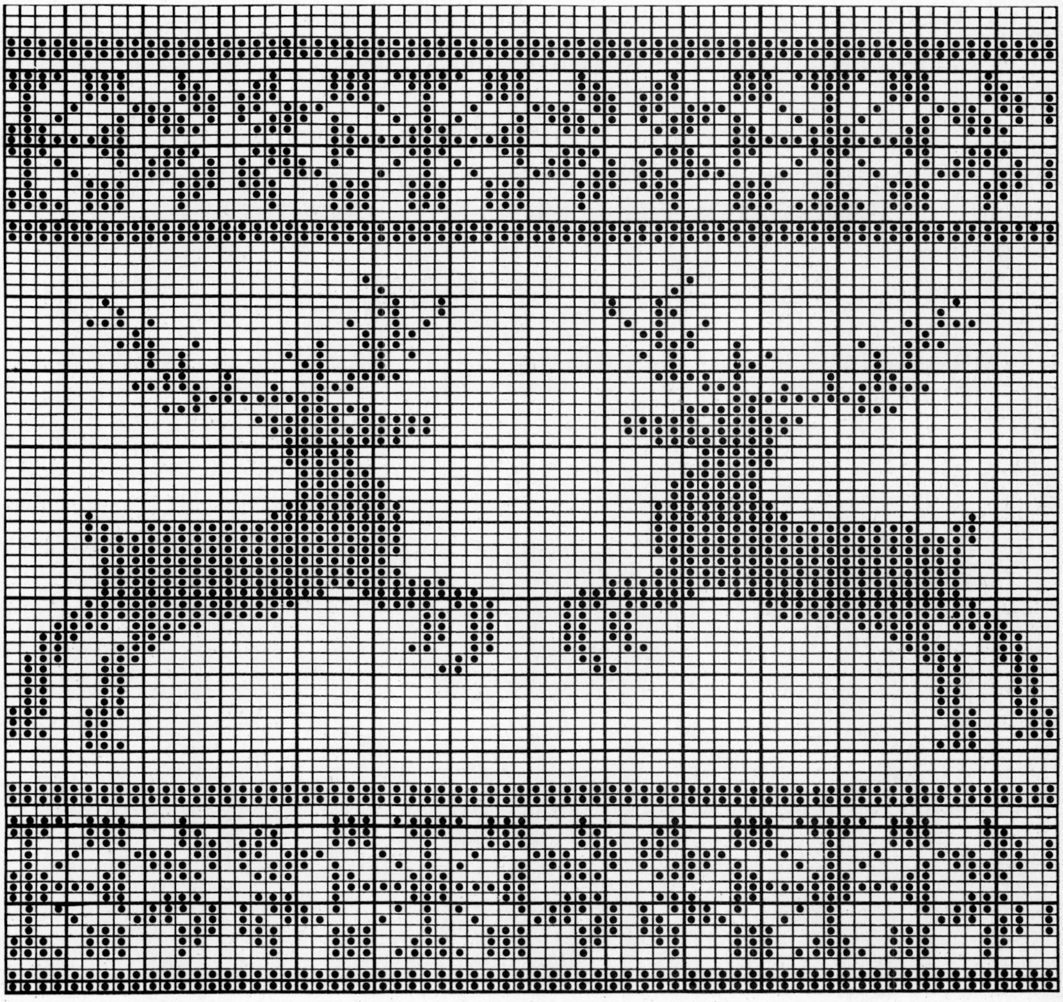

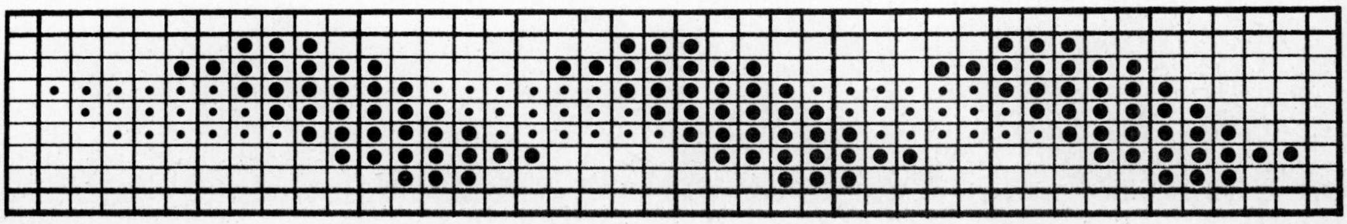

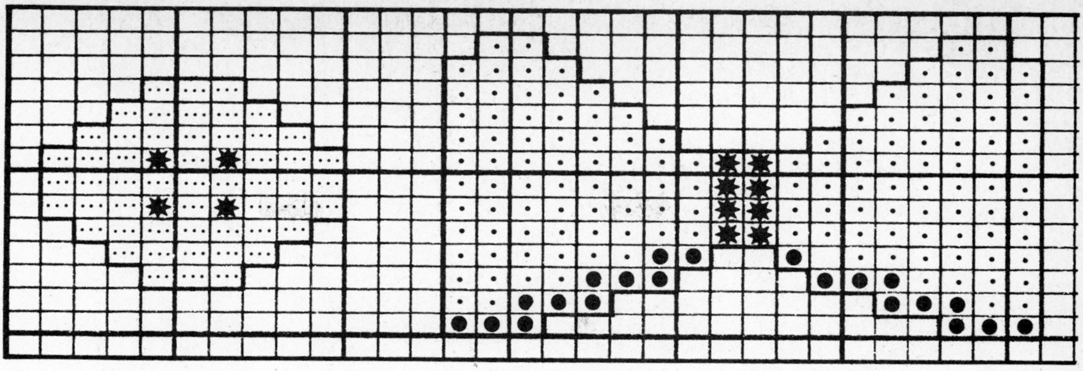

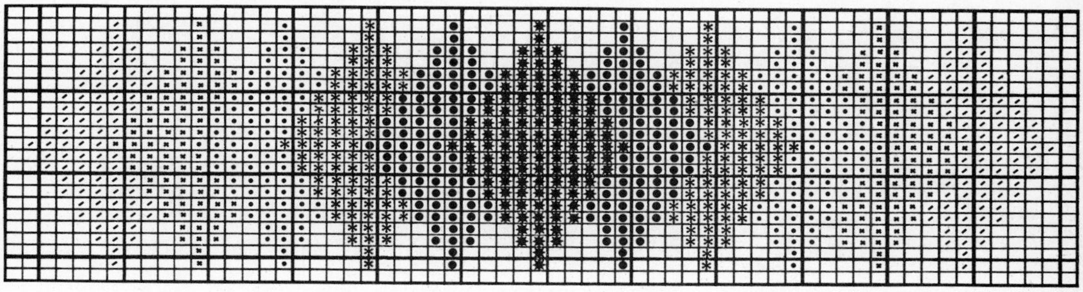

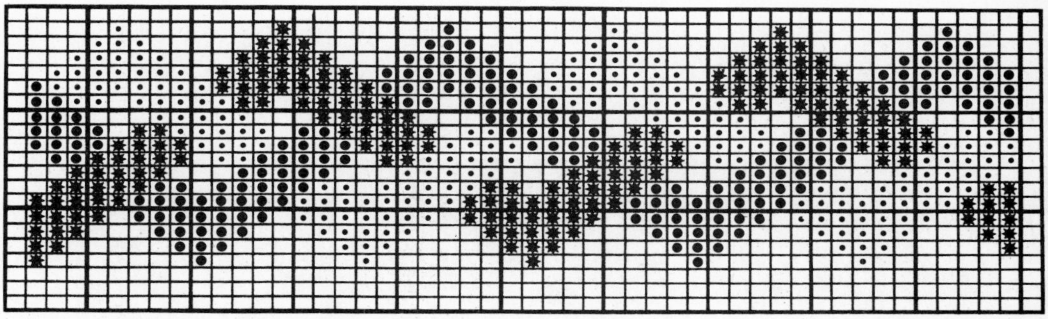

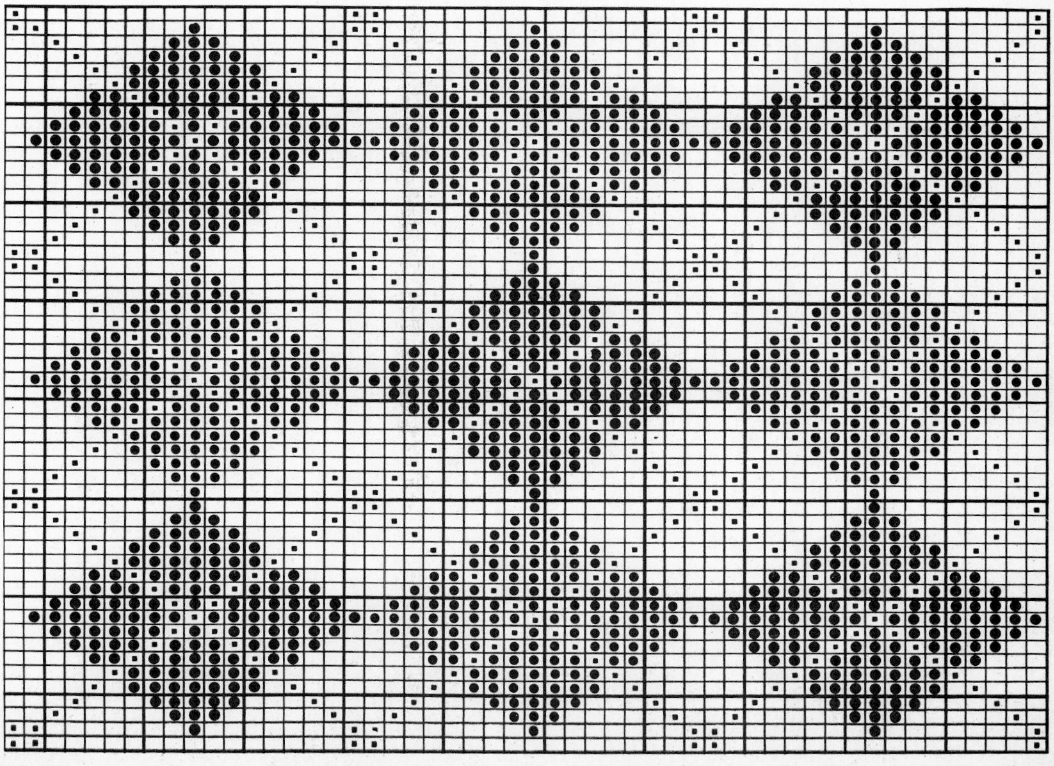

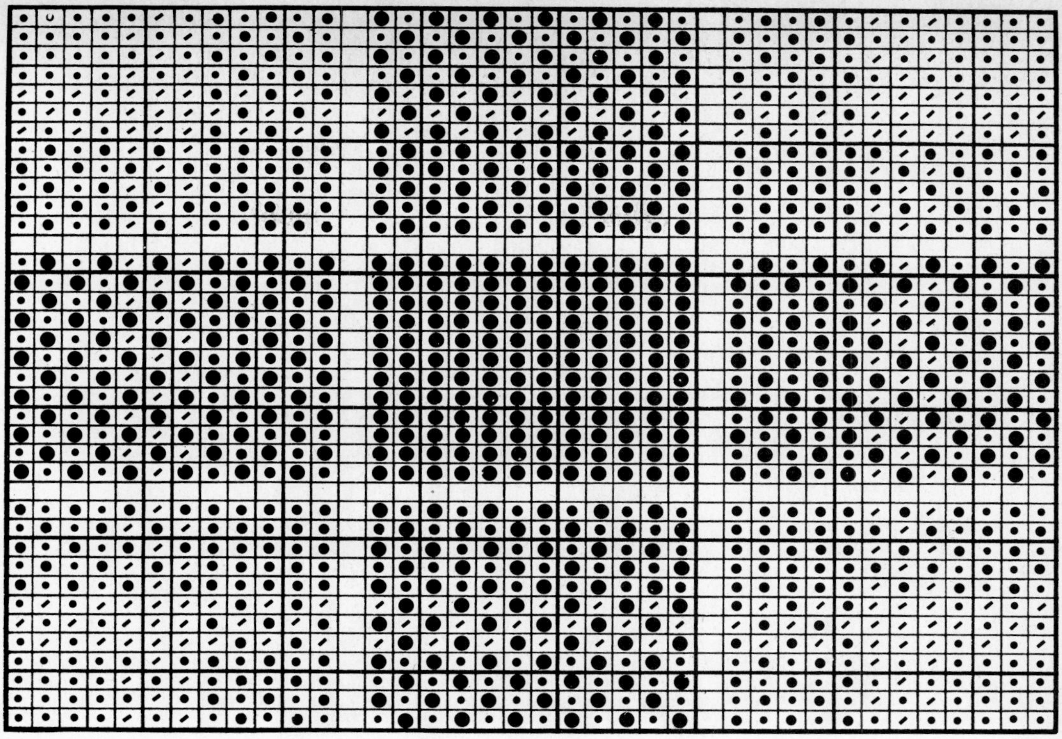

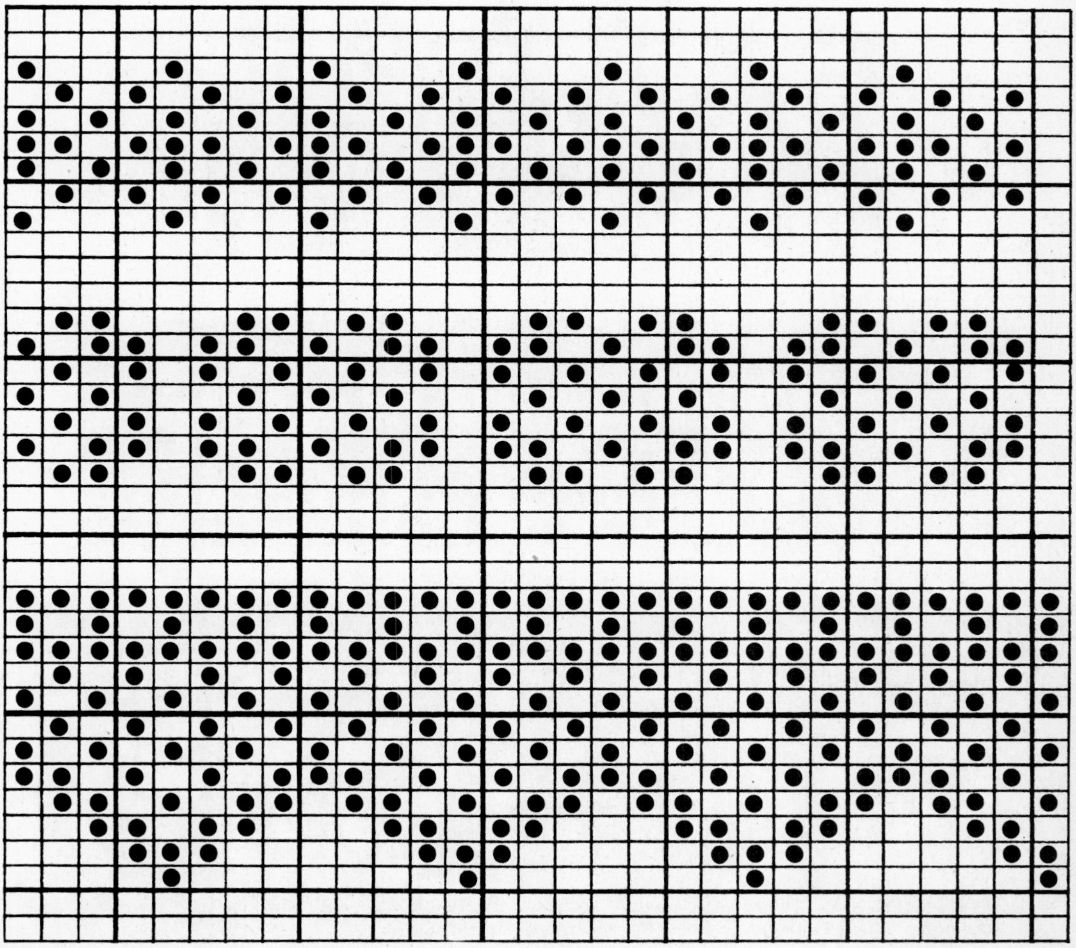

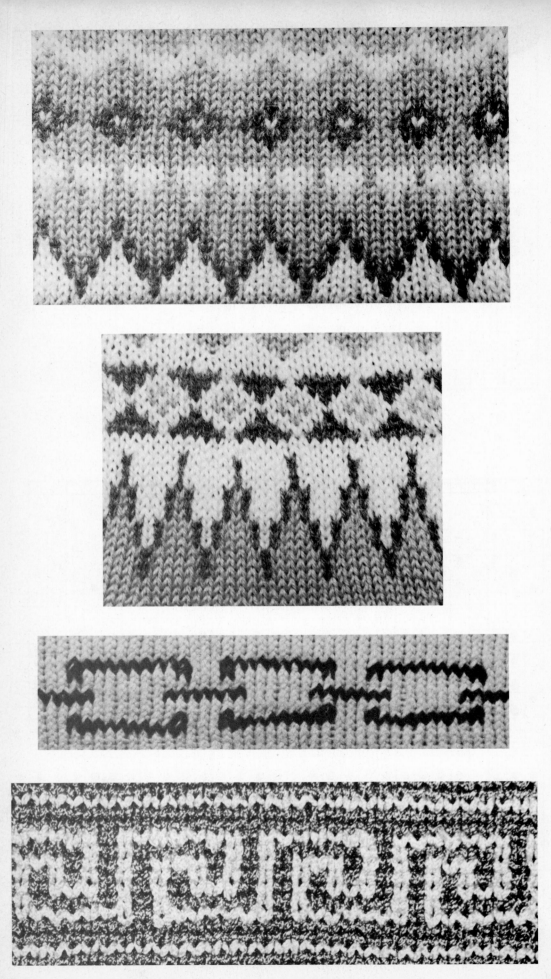

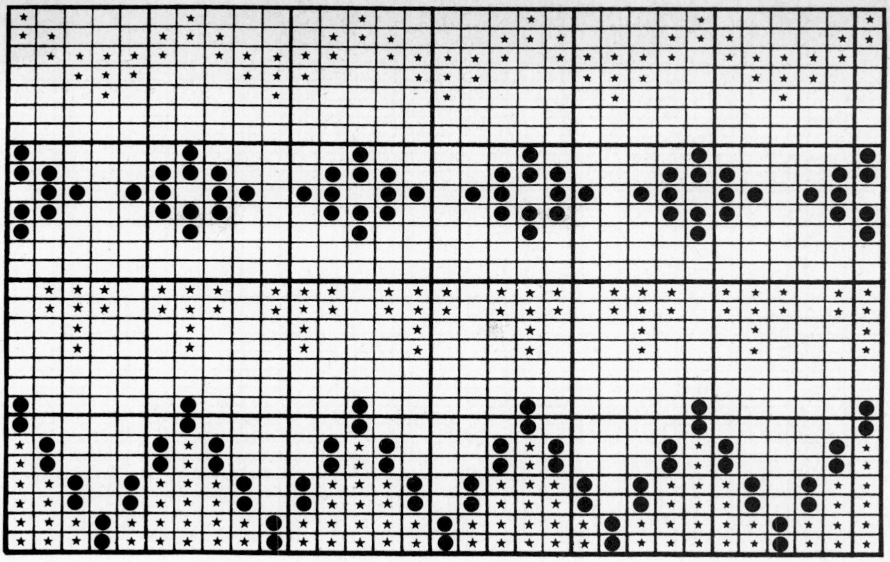

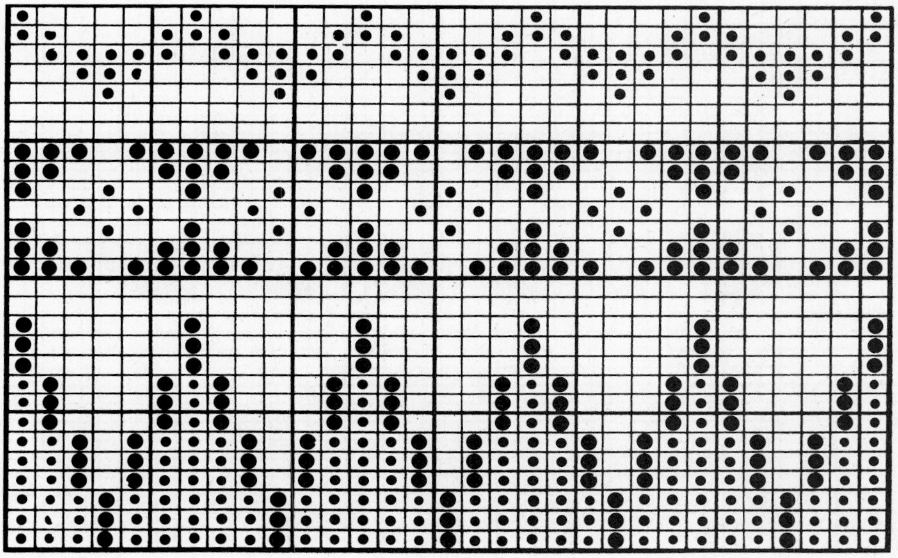

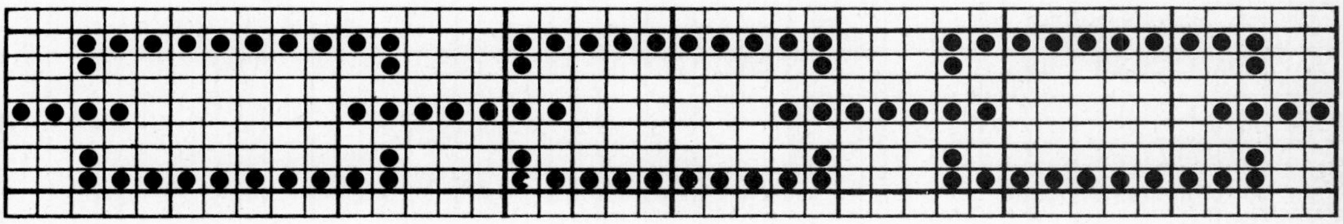

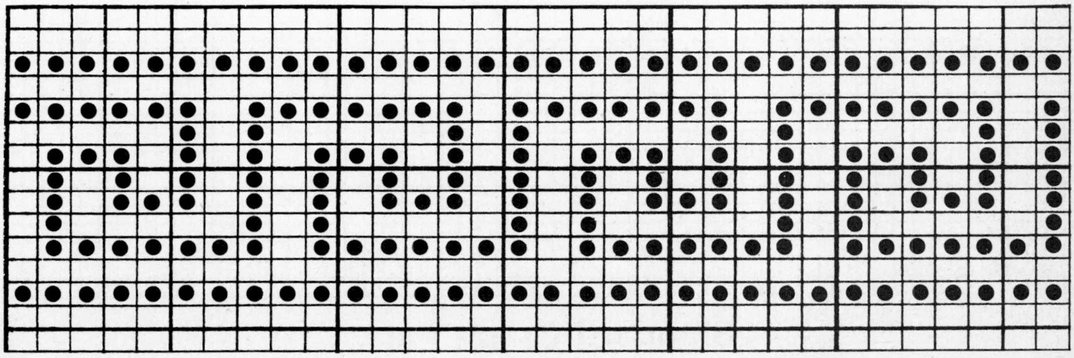

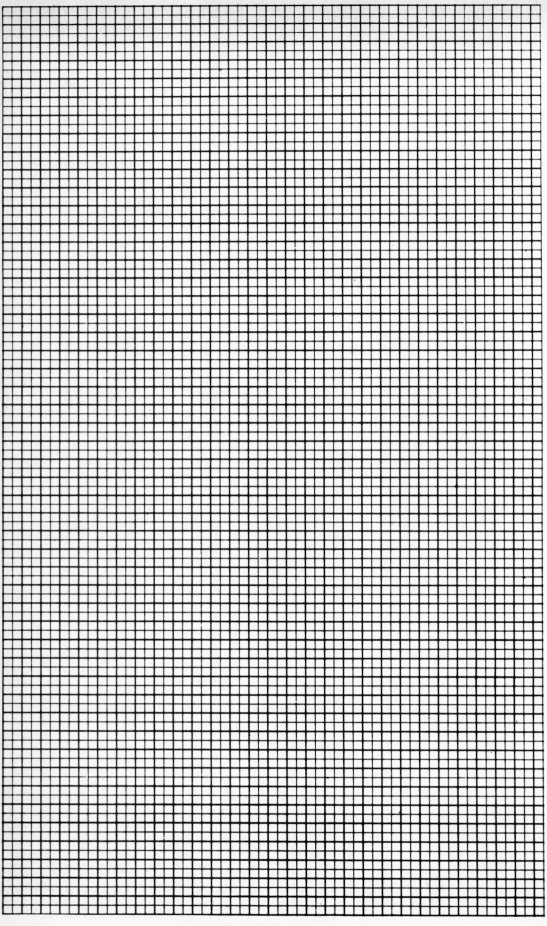

Standard Graph Paper

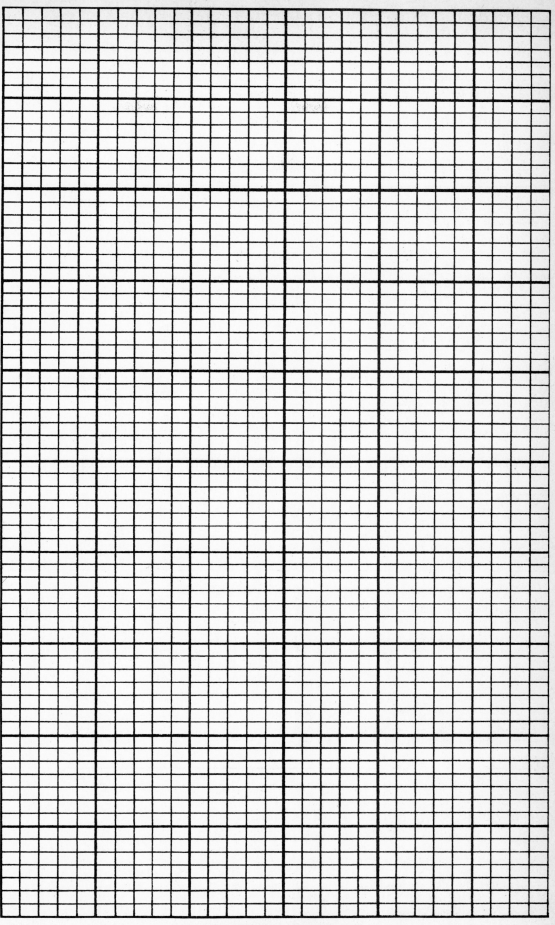

KnittingGraph Paper

Multicolored Stitches

The following patterns belong in the jacquard category but are worked from written directions, not a chart. Some of the patterns are worked in stockinette stitch, but many require techniques more advanced than knit and purl. Color changes are indicated by (light), (medium), and (dark).

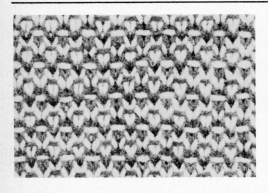

TWO-COLOR HALF-LINEN STITCH
bicolor half-linen stitch

Multiple of 2.
Row 1: (Dark) *k1, yf, sl 1 pwise, yb*, rep *to*.
Row 2: (Dark) P.
Row 3: (Light) k1, *k1, yf, sl 1 pwise, yb*, rep *to*, k1.
Row 4: (Light) P.
Repeat these 4 rows for pattern.

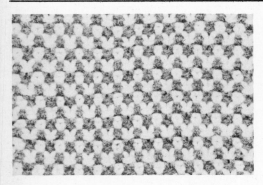

TWO-COLOR LINEN STITCH
bicolor linen stitch

Multiple of 2.
Row 1: (Dark) *yf, sl 1 pwise, yb, k1*, rep *to*.
Row 2: (Dark) *yb, sl 1 pwise, yf, p1*, rep *to*.
Row 3: (Light) rep row 1.
Row 4: (Light) rep row 2.
Repeat these 4 rows for pattern.

PARTRIDGE EYE
eye of partridge, bicolored partridge

Multiple of 2.
Row 1: (Dark) *sl 1 pwise, k1*, rep *to*.
Row 2: (Dark) p.
Row 3: (Light) *k1, sl 1 pwise*, rep *to*.
Row 4: (Light) p.
Repeat these 4 rows for pattern.

TWO-COLOR CROSSED STITCH
crossed bicolor stitch

Multiple of 2 + 1.
Rows 1, 2, 5, and 6: (Dark) k.
Row 3: (Light) *k1, sl 1 pwise*, rep *to*, k1.
Row 4: (Light) *k1, yf, sl 1 pwise, yb*, rep *to*, k1.
Row 7: (Light) *sl 1 pwise, k1*, rep *to*, sl 1.
Row 8: (Light) *sl 1 pwise, yb, k1, yf*, rep *to*, sl 1.
Repeat these 8 rows for pattern.

BEE STITCH
bicolored bee

Multiple of 2.
Rows 1, 2, and 6: (Dark) k.
Row 3: (Light) *k1-b, k1*, rep *to*.
Row 4: (Light) k.
Row 5: (Dark) rep row 3.
Repeat rows 3–6 for pattern.

TWEEDED MOSS STITCH
moss tweed stitch

Multiple of 2.
Row 1: (Dark) *k1, sl 1 pwise*, rep *to*.
Row 2: (Light) *sl 1 pwise, k1*, rep *to*.
Row 3: (Dark) *sl 1 pwise, yb, k1, yf*, rep *to*.
Row 4: (Light) *k1, yf, sl 1 pwise, yb*, rep *to*.
Row 5: (Dark) rep row 2.
Row 6: (Light) rep row 1.
Row 7: (Dark) rep row 4.
Row 8: (Light) rep row 3.
Repeat these 8 rows for pattern.

FEZ PATTERN
lampshades

Multiple of 4.
Rows 1 and 3: (Dark) k.
Rows 2 and 4: (Dark) p.
Row 5: (Light) *k3, put rh needle in next st in the 1st row of dark color, pull a loop of yarn through to the right side, k1 and pass loop over this st*, rep *to*.
Rows 6 and 8: (Light) p.
Row 7: (Light) k.
Row 9: (Dark) k1, *k1 below into row 5, k1, pass loop over this st, k3*, rep *to*, end k2.
Repeat rows 2–9 for pattern.

TWO-COLOR SEED STITCH
bicolor moss stitch

Multiple of 2.
Row 1: (Dark) k1, *k1, sl 1 pwise*, rep *to*, k1.
Row 2: (Dark) k1, *yf, sl 1 pwise, yb, k1*, rep *to*, k1.
Row 3: (Light) k1, *sl 1 pwise, k1*, rep *to*, k1.
Row 4: (Light) k1, *k1, yf, sl 1 pwise, yb*, rep *to*, k1.
Repeat these 4 rows for pattern.

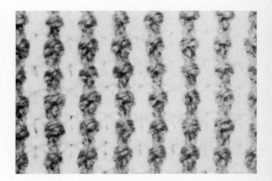

TWO-COLOR SAND STITCH
bicolor sand stitch

Multiple of 2 + 1.
Row 1: (Light) k.
Row 2: (Light) p.
Row 3: (Dark) k1, *sl 1 pwise, k1*, rep *to*.
Row 4: (Dark) *k1, yf, sl 1 pwise, yb*, rep *to*, k1.
Repeat these 4 rows for pattern.

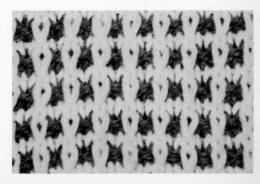

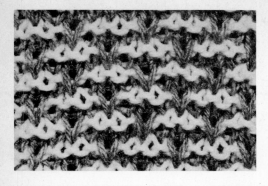

TWO-COLOR HURDLE STITCH
hurdle bicolor

Multiple of 4 + 3. Use 2 dpn.
Row 1: (Dark) *k3, yo, k1*, k3; return to start of row.
Row 2: (Light) *k3, drop yo sts of preceding row, sl pwise*, k3.
Row 3: (Light) *k3, yf, sl 1 pwise, yb*, end k3; return to start of row.
Row 4: (Dark) p2, *yo, p4*, yo, p1.
Row 5: (Light) k1, *drop the yo sts, sl 1 pwise, k3*, drop yo st, sl 1 pwise, k1.
Row 6: (Light) k1, *yf, sl 1 pwise, yb, k3*, yf, sl 1 pwise, yb, k1.
Repeat these 6 rows for pattern.

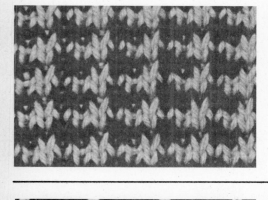

PLAID LADDERS
bicolored ladders

Multiple of 6 + 5.
Row 1: (Light) k2, *sl 1 pwise, k5*, sl 1, k2.
Row 2: (Light) p2, *sl 1 pwise, p5*, sl 1 pwise, p2.
Row 3: (Dark) *k5, sl 1 pwise*, k5.
Row 4: (Dark) *k5, yf, sl 1 pwise, yb*, k5.
Repeat these 4 rows for pattern.

MOCK HOUNDSTOOTH CHECK
mock houndstooth

Multiple of 3.
Row 1: (Dark) *sl 1 pwise, k2*, rep *to*.
Row 2: (Dark) p.
Row 3: (Light) *k2, sl 1 pwise*, rep *to*.
Row 4: (Light) p.
Repeat these 4 rows for pattern.

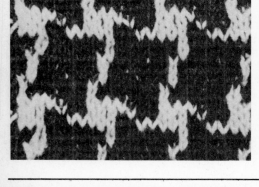

HOUNDSTOOTH CHECK VARIATION II
houndstooth check I

Multiple of 7.
Rows 1 and 3: K, 3 dk, *1 lt, 6 dk*, 1 lt, 3 dk.
Rows 2 and 10: P, working colors same as preceding row.
Row 4: P, 4 dk, *1 lt, 6 dk*, 1 lt, 2 dk.
Row 5: K, working colors same as preceding row.
Row 6: P, *5 lt, 2 dk*.
Row 7: K, *1 lt, 1 dk, 3 lt, 2 dk*.
Row 8: P, 2 dk, *4 lt, 3 dk*, 4 lt, 1 dk.
Row 9: K, 4 dk, *1 lt, 6 dk*, 1 lt, 2 dk.
Repeat these 10 rows for pattern.

HOUNDSTOOTH CHECK VARIATION III
houndstooth check II

Multiple of 4.
Row 1: K, 2 lt, *1 dk, 3 lt*, 1 dk, 1 lt.
Row 2: P, *1 lt, 3 dk*.
Row 3: K, *1 lt, 3 dk*.
Row 4: P, 2 lt, *1 dk, 3 lt*, 1 dk, 1 lt.
Repeat these 4 rows for pattern.

THREE-COLOR LINEN STITCH
tricolor linen stitch

Multiple of 2.
Row 1: (Medium) *yf, sl 1 pwise, yb k1*.
Row 2: (Light) *yb, sl 1 pwise, yf, p1*.
Row 3: (Dark) rep row 1.
Row 4: (Medium) rep row 2.
Row 5: (Light, rep row 1.
Row 6: (Dark) rep row 2.
Repeat these 6 rows for pattern.

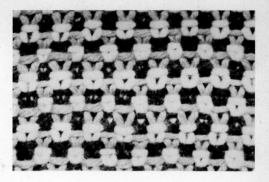

CHECKED STOCKINETTE STITCH
check stocking stitch

Multiple of 4.
Row 1: K, *2 dk, 2 lt*, rep *to*.
Row 2: P, *2 lt, 2 dk*, rep *to*.
Row 3: K, *2 lt, 2 dk*, rep *to*.
Row 4: P, *2 dk, 2 lt*, rep *to*.
Repeat these 4 rows for pattern.

FLEUR-DE-LIS
fleur-de-lys

Multiple of 6 + 3.
Rows 1 and 3: K, *1 lt, 5 dk*, 1 lt.
Row 2: P, 2 lt, *3 dk, 3 lt*, 1 dk.
Rows 4 and 6: P, 3 dk, *1 lt, 5 dk.*.
Row 5: K, 1 lt, *3 dk, 3 lt*, 2 dk.
Repeat these 6 rows for pattern.

DIAMOND PATTERN
diamond jacquard, diamond diamonds

Multiple of 8 + 7.
Row 1: K, 3 lt, *1 dk, 7 lt*, 1 dk, 3 lt.
Row 2 and all even-numbered rows: Work colors as
  preceding row.
Rows 3 and 15: K, 2 lt, *3 dk, 5 lt*, 3 dk, 2 lt.
Rows 5 and 13: K, 1 lt, *5 dk, 3 lt*, 5 dk, 1 lt.
Rows 7 and 11: K, *7 dk, 1 lt*, 7 dk.
Row 9: K, dk.
Repeat these 16 rows for pattern.

STAGGERED DIAMONDS

Multiple of 8 + 1.
Row 1: K, *1 lt, 7 dk*, 1 lt.
Rows 2 and 6: P, *2 lt, 5 dk, 1 lt*, 1 lt.
Rows 3, 5, and 7: K in color of preceding row.
Row 4: P, *3 lt, 3 dk, 2 lt*, 1 lt.
Row 8: P, 1 lt, *7 dk, 1 lt*.
Row 9: Work pattern 4 sts to the left following from row
  1, (k4 dk, *1 lt, 7 dk*, etc.)

TWO-COLOR RIBBING
bicolor ribs

Multiple of 4. Carry all yarn on the wrong side.
Row 1: *P2 lt, k2 dk*, rep *to*.
Row 2: *P2 dk, k2 lt*, rep *to*.
Repeat these 2 rows for pattern.

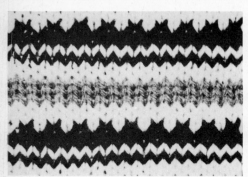

PATTERNED ROWS
multicolor rows

Multiple of 2.
Rows 1 and 3: (Medium) k.
Row 2: (Medium) p.
Row 4: (Light) p.
Row 5: (Light) k.
Row 6: (Dark) p.
Row 7: (Light) k.
Row 8: (Dark) p.
Row 9: (Dark) k.
Row 10: *P1 dk, p1 lt*, rep *to*.
Row 11: (Light) k.
Row 12: (Light) p.
Repeat these 12 rows for pattern.

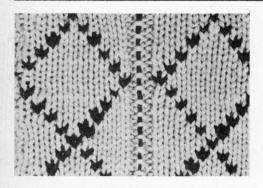

VERTICAL DIAMOND OUTLINE
fancy lozenges

Multiple of 14.
Row 1: *P1 lt, k1 lt, p1 lt, k1 dk, k9 lt, k1 dk*.
Row 2 and all even-numbered rows: (Light) *p11, k3*.
Row 3: * (P1 lt, k1 lt) twice, k1 dk, k7 lt, k1 dk, k1 lt.
Row 5: *(P1 lt, k1 lt) twice, k1 lt, k1 dk, k5 lt, k1 dk, k2 lt.
Continue in pattern, decreasing 2 stitches between the dark stitches every alternate row.
   Using a separate strand of yarn in the dark color after the pattern is complete, draw a strand of the yarn through the center of the 3-stitch bands, as shown.

PLAID PATTERN
ribbons

Multiple of 23.
Use a bobbin for each color, Remember to twist yarn as you change colors, to avoid making holes.
Rows 1, 3, and 5: K, 5 white, 1 dk, 2 lt, 1 dk, 2 med, 1 dk, 2 med, 1 dk, 2 lt, 1 dk, 5 white.
Rows 2, 4, and 8: (Rep colors of preceding row) p.
Rows 6, 12, and 18: (Dark) p.
Row 7: K, 5 lt, 1 dk, 2 lt, 1 dk, 2 med, 1 dk, 2 med, 1 dk, 2 lt, 1 dk, 5 lt.
Rows 9 and 15: (Dark) k.
Row 10: P, 5 med, 1 dk, 2 lt, 1 dk, 2 med, 1 dk, 2 med, 1 dk, 2 lt, 1 dk, 5 lt.
Row 11: (Rep colors of preceding row) k.
Row 13: (Rep colors of row 10) k.
Row 14: (Rep colors of preceding row) p.
Row 16: (Rep colors of row 7) p.
Row 17: (Rep colors of preceding row) k.
Rows 19, 21, and 23: (Rep colors of row 1) k.
Rows 20 and 22: (Rep colors of preceding row) p.
Repeat these 23 rows for pattern.

DIAMOND LINED BORDER
colored border

Multiple of 6 + 1.
Rows 1 and 7: K, *1 dk, 2 lt*, 1 dk.
Rows 2 and 6: P, 1 lt, *1 dk, 3 lt, 1 dk, 1 lt*.
Rows 3 and 5: K, *2 lt, (1 dk, 1 lt) twice*, 1 lt.
Row 4: P, *1 dk, 2 lt*, 1 dk.
Row 8: (Light) p.
Row 9: (Dark) k.
Row 10: (Dark) p.
Repeat these 10 rows for pattern.

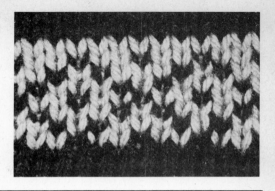

ZIGZAG BORDER PATTERN
sawtooth pattern

Multiple of 4.
Row 1: K, *1 lt, 3 dk*.
Row 2: P, 1 lt, *1 dk, 3 lt*, 1 dk, 2 lt.
Row 3: (Light) k.
Row 4: P, *3 lt, 1 dk*.
Row 5: K, 2 dk, *1 lt, 3 dk*, 1 lt, 1 dk.
Knit 5 rows of stockinette stitch in background color,
then repeat rows 1–5 for pattern.

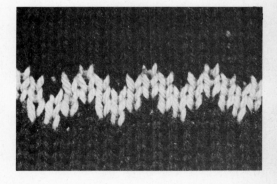

TWO-COLOR PLAIT CABLES
bicolor four cables

Multiple of 18 + 6.
Rows 1 and 3: K, 3 lt, (3 dk, 3 med) twice, 6 dk, 3 lt.
Rows 2, 4, 6, and 8: P, working colors as preceding row.
Row 5: K, 3 lt, 3 dk, (put 3 med sts on dpn, hold in
front, k3 dk, k3 sts from dpn in med) twice, 3
dk, 3 lt.
Row 7: K, 3 lt, 3 dk, (3 dk, 3 med) twice, 3 dk, 3 lt.
Row 9: K, 3 lt, put 3 dk sts on dpn, hold in back, k3 dk,
k3 sts from dpn in med, put 3 med sts on dpn,
hold in back, k3 dk sts, k3 med sts from dpn,
put next 3 sts on dpn, hold in back, k3 dk from
dpn in dk, k3 lt.
Repeat rows 2–9 for pattern.

TWO-COLOR PLAITED STITCH
plaited two-color, bicolor plait

Multiple of 4.
Row 1: *K2 dk, k2 lt*.
Row 2 and all even-numbered rows: P with colors of
preceding row.
Rows 3, 7, and 11: *Sl the 2 dk sts to dpn, hold in back,
k the next 2 sts with lt, k the sts from dpn with
dk.*
Rows 5, 9, and 13: K2 dk, *sl next 2 dk sts to dpn, hold
in front, k next 2 sts with lt, k the sts from dpn
in dk, end k2 lt.
Repeat rows 2–14 for pattern.

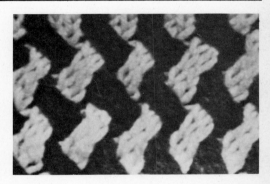

STOCKINETTE WITH V
bicolor stocking stitch

Multiple of 6 + 3.
Row 1: K, 4 dk, *1 lt, 5 dk*, 1 lt, 4 dk.
Row 2: P, *3 dk, 1 lt, 1 dk, 1 lt*, 3 dk.
Rows 3 and 5: (Dark) k.
Rows 4 and 6: (Dark) p.
Repeat these 6 rows for pattern.

TWO-COLOR DIAGONAL STRIPE
the bicolor diagonals

Multiple of 12.
Row 1: (Light) *k6, p6*.
Row 2: (Light) p1, *k6, p6*, end k6, p5.
Row 3: (Dark) k4, *p6, k6*, end p6, k2.
Row 4: (Dark) p3, *k6, p6*, end k6, p3.
Row 5: (Light) k2, *p6, k6*, end p6, k4.
Row 6: (Light) p5, *k6, p6*, end k6, p1.
Row 7: (Dark) *p6, k6*.
Row 8: (Dark) k1, *p6, k6*, end p6, k5.
Row 9: (Light) p4, *k6, p6*, end k6, p2.
Row 10: (Light) k3, *p6, k6*, end k6, k3.
Row 11: (Dark) P2, *k6, p6*, end k6, p4.
Row 12: (Dark) k5, *p6, k6*, end p6, k1.
Repeat these 12 rows for pattern.

GARTER MULTICOLORED RIBBONS
zigzag stitch, woven rib

Multiple of 4.
Rows 1 and 11: (White) p.
Rows 2 and 12: (Color A) *k3, sl 1 pwise*.
Rows 3 and 13: (A) *yf, sl 1, yb, k3*.
Rows 4 and 14: (White) k.
Rows 5 and 15: (White) p.
Rows 6 and 8: (Color B) k1, *sl 1, k3*, k2.
Rows 7 and 9: (B) k2, *yf, sl 1, yb, k3*, k1.
Rows 10 and 20: (White) k.
Rows 16 to 19: (Color C) rep rows 6–9.
Repeat rows 1–20 for pattern.

ALTERNATING BICOLOR CROSSED STITCH
crossed stitch

Multiple of 3 + 1.
Row 1: (Light) k.
Row 2: (Light) p1, *1 inset inc, p2*, p1.
Row 3: (Light) *k3, pass 1st of these 3 sts over the other 2*.
Row 4: (Dark) *p2, 1 inset inc*, p2.
Row 5: (Dark) k1, *k3, pass 1st of these 3 sts over the other 2*, k1.
Repeat rows 2–5 for pattern.

GARTER BRICK WALL
bicolor knitted stitch

Multiple of 6 + 1.
Row 1: (Dark) k.
Row 2: (Dark) p.
Row 3: (Light) k3, *sl 1, k5*, end sl 1, k3.
Rows 4 and 6: (Light) k3, *yf, slip sl st of preceding row, yb, k5*, end sl 1, k3.
Row 5: (Light) p3, *slip sl st of preceding row, p5*, end sl 1, p3.
Row 7: (Dark) k.
Row 8: (Dark) p.
Row 9: (Light) *sl 1, k5*, end sl 1.
Rows 10 and 12: (Light), *yf, slip sl st of preceding row, yb, k5*, end sl 1, k3.
Row 11: (Light) *sl 1, p5*, end sl 1.
Repeat these 12 rows for pattern.

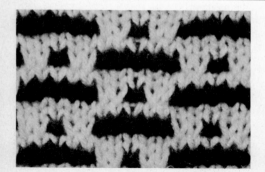

MORSE CODE
dots and dashes

Multiple of 10 + 1.
Row 1: (Light) p.
Row 2: (Dark) *k1, yb, sl 2, k5, sl 2*, end k1.
Row 3: (Dark) *k1, yf, sl 2, k5, sl 2*, end k1.
Row 4: (Light) k.
Row 5: (Light) p.
Row 6: (Dark) k3, *yb, sl 2, k1, yb, sl 2, k5*, end k3.
Row 7: (Dark) k3, *yf, sl 2, k1, yf, sl 2, k5*, end k3.
Row 8: (Light) rep row 4.
Repeat these 8 rows for pattern.

ENCLOSED BEANS
coffee beans

Multiple of 10 + 1.
Row 1: (Light) k4, *sl 1, k2 tog, psso, k7*, end sl 1, k2 tog, psso, k4.
Rows 2, 4, 8, 10, 12, and 16: (Light) p.
Row 3: (Light) k2, *k2 tog, k1, sl 1, k1, psso, k3*, end k2.
Row 5: (Dark) sl 3, *(k1, p1, k1, p1, k1) in next st, sl 5 sts*, end sl 3.
Row 6: (Dark) yf, sl 3, *k5, yf, sl 5*, end k5, sl 3.
Rows 7 and 15: (Light) k.
Row 9: (Light) sl 1, k1, psso, *k7, sl 1, k2 tog, psso*, end k2 tog.
Row 11: (Light) k1, *sl 1, k1, psso, k3, k2 tog, k1*.
Row 13: (Dark) (k1, p1, k1) in next st, *sl 5 sts, (k1, p1, k1, p1, k1) in next st*, end sl 5 sts, (k1, p1, k1) in next st.
Row 14: (Dark) rep row 6, but slip the lt sts and k the dk sts.
Repeat these 16 rows for pattern.

BICOLOR CHEVRON STRIPE
chevron stripe, zebra chevron

Multiple of 24 + 2 selvage stitches.
Row 1: (Dark) selv st, *yb, sl 1 kwise, k2*, selv st.
Row 2: (Dark) selv st, *p2, yf, sl 1*, selv st.
Row 3: (Light) selv st, *k1, sl 1, (k2, sl 2) 3 times, k3, (sl 1, k2) 3 times, sl 1*, selv st.
Row 4: (Light) selv st, *sl 1, (p2, sl 1) 3 times, p3, (sl 1, p2) 3 times, sl 1, p1*, selv st.
Row 5: (Dark) selv st, *k2, (sl 1, k2) 3 times, sl 1, k1, sl 1, (k2, sl 1) 3 times, k1*, selv st.
Row 6: (Dark) selv st, *p1, (sl 1, p2) 3 times, sl 1, p1, sl 1, (p2, sl 1) 3 times, p2*, selv st.
Row 7: (Light) rep row 1.
Row 8: (Light) rep row 2.
Row 9: (Dark) rep row 3.
Row 10: (Dark) rep row 4.
Row 11: (Light) rep row 5.
Row 12: (Light) rep row 6.
Repeat rows 1–12 for pattern.

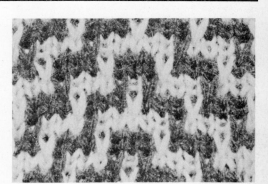

ORIENTAL CHEVRON
rippled chevron, waves and ripples

Multiple of 16 + 1 plus 2 selvage stitches.
Row 1: (Dark) selv st, yb, sl 1, *k3, sl 1*, selv st.
Row 2: (Dark) selv st, yf, sl 1, *p3, sl 1*, selv st.
Row 3: (Light) selv st, k3, *yb, sl 1, k3, sl 1, k1, sl 1, k3, sl 1, k5*, end k3, selv st.
Row 4: (Light) selv st, p3, *yf, sl 1, p3, sl 1, p1, sl 1, p3, sl 1, p5*, end p3, selv st.
Row 5: (Dark) selv st, k2, *yb, sl 1, k3*, end k2, selv st.
Row 6: (Dark) selv st, p2, *yf, sl 1, p3*, end sl 1, p2, selv st.
Row 7: (Light) selv st, k1, *yb, sl 1, k3, sl 1, k5, sl 1, k3, sl 1, k1*, selv st.
Row 8: (Light) selv st, p1, *yf, sl 1, p3, sl 1, p5, sl 1, p3, sl 1, p1*, selv st.
Repeat these 8 rows for pattern.

RIPPLES
Ruth's Ripple

Multiple of 4.
Rows 1: (Color A) k3, *yb, sl 1, k3*, rep *to*, end sl 1, k1.
Rows 2, 4, 6, and 8: (Rep col of previous row) p the p sts and, with yf, sl the sl sts.
Row 3: (Color B) k4, *yb, sl 1, k3*, rep *to*, end yb, sl 1, k4.
Row 5: (A) k1, *yb, sl 1, k3*, rep *to*, end sl 1, k3.
Row 7: (B) k2, *yb, sl 1, k3*, rep *to*, end yb, sl 1, k2.
Repeat these 8 rows for pattern.

TRICOLOR FLEUR-DE-LIS
the fleur-de-lis

Multiple of 4.
Rows 1 and 2: (Dark) k.
Row 3: (Medium) *k3, yb, sl 1 pwise*, rep *to*.
Row 4: (Medium) *yf, sl pwise the sl st of preceding row, yb, k3*, rep *to*.
Row 5: (Light) k1, *yb, sl 1 pwise, k3*, rep *to*, end sl 1, k2.
Row 6: (Light) k2, *yf, sl 1 pwise, yb, k3*, rep *to*, end sl 1, k1.
Row 7: (Dark) rep row 3.
Row 8: (Dark) rep row 4.
Row 9: (Medium) rep row 5.
Row 10: (Medium) rep row 6.
Row 11: (Light) rep row 3.
Row 12: (Light) rep row 4.
Row 13: (Dark) rep row 5.
Row 14: (Dark) rep row 6.
Repeat rows 3–14 for pattern.

TRICOLOR CHECK PATTERN
the tricolor checks

Multiple of 6 + 2 selvage stitches.
Row 1: (Light) selv st, *sl 3 sts pwise, k3*, selv st.
Row 2: (Light) selv st, *k3, yf, sl 3*, selv st.
Row 3: (Dark) selv st, *k3, sl 3 sts*, selv st.
Row 4: (Dark) selv st, *yf, sl 3 sts, k3*, selv st.
Row 5: (Medium) selv st, *sl 3 sts, k3*, selv st.
Row 6: (Medium) selv st, *k3, yf, sl 3 sts*, selv st.
Row 7: (Light) selv st, *k3, sl 3 sts*, selv st.
Row 8: (Light) rep row 4.
Row 9: (Dark) rep row 5.
Row 10: (Dark) rep row 6.
Row 11: (Medium) rep row 7.
Row 12: (Medium) rep row 4.
Repeat these 12 rows for pattern.

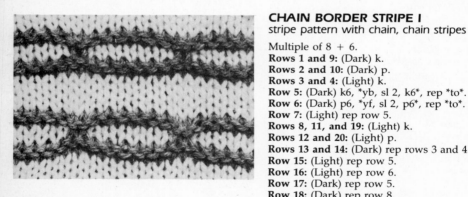

CHAIN BORDER STRIPE I
stripe pattern with chain, chain stripes

Multiple of 8 + 6.
Rows 1 and 9: (Dark) k.
Rows 2 and 10: (Dark) p.
Rows 3 and 4: (Light) k.
Row 5: (Dark) k6, *yb, sl 2, k6*, rep *to*.
Row 6: (Dark) p6, *yf, sl 2, p6*, rep *to*.
Row 7: (Light) rep row 5.
Rows 8, 11, and 19: (Light) k.
Rows 12 and 20: (Light) p.
Rows 13 and 14: (Dark) rep rows 3 and 4.
Row 15: (Light) rep row 5.
Row 16: (Light) rep row 6.
Row 17: (Dark) rep row 5.
Row 18: (Dark) rep row 8.
Repeat these 20 rows for pattern.

CHAIN BORDER STRIPE II
chain stripes

Multiple of 8 + 6.
Row 1: (Light) k.
Row 2: (Light) p.
Rows 3 and 4: (Dark) k.
Row 5: (Light) k6, *yb, sl 2, k6*, rep *to*.
Row 6: (Light) p6, *yf, sl 2, p6*, rep *to*.
Row 7: (Dark) rep row 5.
Row 8: (Dark) k. These 8 rows form the border pattern.
Repeat rows 1–8 for allover pattern.

ALTERNATING CHAIN BORDER STRIPE
chain stripes

Multiple of 8 + 6.
Rows 1 and 9: (Light) k.
Rows 2 and 10: (Light), p.
Rows 3, 4, 11, and 12: (Dark) k.
Row 5: (Light) k6, *yb, sl 2, k6*, rep *to*.
Row 6: (Light), p6, *yf, sl 2, p6*, rep *to*.
Row 7: (Dark) rep row 5.
Rows 8 and 16: (Dark) k.
Row 13: (Light) k2, *yb, sl 2, k6*, end sl 2, k2.
Row 14: (Light) p2, *yf, sl 2, p6*, end sl 2, p2.
Row 15: (Dark), rep row 13.
Repeat these 16 rows for pattern.

ALTERNATING TRICOLOR CHAIN STRIPE

Multiple of 8 + 6.
Rows 1 and 9: (Dark) k.
Rows 2 and 10: (Dark) p.
Rows 3, 4, and 8: (Light) k.
Row 5: (Dark) k6, *yb, sl 2, k6*, rep *to*.
Row 6: (Dark) p6, *yf, sl 2, p6*, rep *to*.
Row 7: (Light) rep row 5.
Rows 11, 12, and 16: (Medium) k.
Row 13: (Dark) k2, *yb, sl 2, k6*, rep *to*, end sl 2, k2.
Row 14: (Dark) p2, *yf, sl 2, p6*, rep *to*, end sl 2, p2.
Row 15: (Medium) rep row 13.
Rows 17 to 24: Rep rows 1–8.
Repeat these 24 rows for pattern.

GARTER STRIPES AND DOTS
stripes and spots, windowpane stripes

Any odd multiple of stitches. Cast on with dark color, k
   one row.
Row 1: (Light) k1, *yb, sl 1, k1*, rep *to*.
Row 2: (Light) p1, *yf, sl 1, p1*, rep *to*.
Rows 3, 4, 7 and 8: (Dark) knit.
Rows 5 and 6: (Light) knit.
Repeat these 8 rows for pattern.

BRICK WITH EYELETS

Multiple of 12 + 2 selvage stitches.
Row 1: (Color A) selv st, *k1, k1 tbl, k5, k1 tbl, k4*, rep
   to, selv st.
Rows 2 and 8: (A) p.
Row 3: (Color B) selv st, *k4, yb, sl 1 pwise, k5, yb, sl 1
   pwise, k1*, rep *to*, selv st.
Row 4: (B) selv st, *p1, yf, sl 1 pwise, p5, yf, sl 1 pwise,
   p4*, rep *to*, selv st.
Row 5: (B) selv st, *(yo, sl 1 kwise, k2 tog, psso, yo, k1,
   yb, sl 1 pwise, k1) twice*, rep *to*, selv st.
Row 6: (B) selv st, *p1, yf, sl 1 pwise, p5, yf, sl 1 pwise,
   p4*, rep *to*, selv st.
Row 7: (A) selv st, *k4, k1 tbl, k5, k1 tbl, k1*, rep *to*,
   selv st.
Row 9: (B) selv st, *k1, yb, sl 1 pwise, k5, yb, sl 1 pwise,
   k4*, rep *to*, selv st.
Row 10: (B) selv st, *p4, yf, sl 1 pwise, p5, yf, sl 1
   pwise, p1*, rep *to*, selv st.
Row 11: (B) selv st, *(k1, yb, sl 1 kwise, k1, yo, sl 1
   kwise, k2 tog, psso, yo) twice*, rep *to*, selv st.
Row 12: (B) selv st, *p4, yf, sl 1 pwise, p5, sl 1 pwise,
   p1*, rep *to*, selv st.
Repeat these 12 rows for pattern.

PATCHWORK

Patchwork is generally thought of in terms of quilting, in which small pieces of fabric are sewn together to form a larger piece of fabric. These small pieces of fabric are usually shaped as squares, rectangles, diamonds, hexagons, or circles.

In knitting, the same concept of putting small shapes together to form a larger piece is used, but the additional choice of stitches, patterns, and colors adds to the diversity of the art. The patches are assembled by sewing (whipstitch) or crochet.

ARAN PATCHWORK SQUARE
Irish square

Any Aran or cable pattern may be combined in this manner to knit an original Aran-type patchwork square.
Cast on 79 sts. Work a foundation row on the wrong side: (K1, p8, k1) 4 times, k1, (p2, k2) 9 times, p1, k1.
On the next row work pattern 1 on 39 sts and pattern 2 on 40 sts. Continue in pattern until 40 pattern rows are complete.

Pattern 1: Work on 39 sts.
Row 1: P1, k1, (p2, k2) 9 times, p1.
Rows 2 and 8: K1, (p2, k2) 9 times, p1, k1.
Row 3: P1 Cr 2 L [sl next st to dpn, hold in front, p next st, k st from dpn], Cr 2 R [pass needle in front of 1st st, k 2nd st, p 1st st and slip both off needle], (Cr 2 L, Cr 2 R) 8 times, Cr 2 L.
Rows 4 and 6: P1, (k2, p2) 9 times, k2.
Row 5: (P2, k2) 9 times, p2, k1.

Row 7: P1, (Cr 2 R, Cr 2 L) 9 times, Cr 2 R.
Repeat these 8 rows for pattern.

Pattern 2: Work on 40 sts.
Rows 1 and 3: (P1, k8, p1) 4 times.
Rows 2, 4, and 6: (K1, p8, k1) 4 times.
Row 5: *P1, sl next 2 sts to dpn, hold in back, k2, k2 from dpn, sl next 2 sts to dpn, hold in front, k2, k2 from dpn, p1*, rep *to* 3 times.
Repeat these 6 rows for pattern.

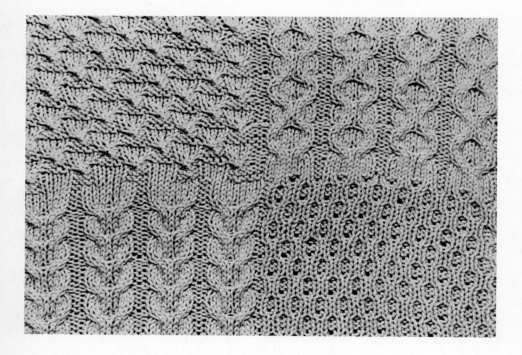

To work the second half of the patchwork square, k1 st for a selvage stitch on every row, then 40 sts for pattern 3 and 38 sts for pattern 4. Work 41 rows and bind off.

Pattern 3: Work on 40 sts.
Rows 1, 3, 5, 9, and 11: (P1, k8, p1) 4 times.
Row 2 and all even-numbered rows: (K1, p8, k1) 4 times.
Row 7: (P1, sl next 2 sts to dpn, hold in back, k2, k2 from dpn, sl next 2 sts to dpn, hold in front, k2, k2 from dpn, p1) 4 times.
Row 13: (P1, sl next 2 sts to dpn, hold in front, k2, k2 from dpn, sl next 2 sts to dpn, hold in back, k2, k2 from dpn, p1) 4 times.
Repeat rows 3–14 for pattern.

Pattern 4: Work on 38 sts.
Rows 1 and 3: P5, (k4, p4) 4 times, p1.
Row 2, 4, 6, and 8: K all k sts and p all p sts.
Row 5: P1, (sl 2 sts to dpn, hold in front, k2, k2 from dpn, p4) 4 times, sl 2 sts to dpn, hold in front, k2, k2 sts from dpn, p1.
Row 7: P1, (k4, p4) 4 times, k4, p1.
Row 9: P5, (sl 2 st to dpn, hold in front, k2, k2 from dpn, p4) 4 times, p1.
Repeat rows 2–9 for pattern.

RAISED LEAF PATTERN
four-leaf square

Use 5 dpn. Cast on 16 sts. Divide onto 4 needles, using the 5th to work the rounds.

Rounds 1 and 2: K.

Round 3: *P1, yo, (k1, yo) twice, k1, yo*, rep *to* 3 times.

Note: On the following rounds, work all *to* sts 4 times on each round, once on each needle.

Round 4: *P1, yo, p1, k2, yo, k1, yo, k2, p1, yo*.
Round 5: *P1, yo, p2, k3, yo, k1, yo, k3, p2, yo*.
Round 6: *P1, yo, p3, k4, yo, k1, yo, k4, p3, yo*.
Round 7: *P1, yo, p4, k5, yo, k1, yo, k5, p4, yo*.
Round 8: *P1, yo, p5, k6, yo, k1, yo, k6, p5, yo*.
Round 9: *P1, yo, p6, k7, yo, k1, yo, k7, p6, yo*.
Round 10: *P1, yo, p7, k2 tog tbl, k13, k2 tog, p7, yo*.
Round 11: *P1, yo, p8, k15, p8, yo*.
Round 12: *P1, yo, p9, k2 tog tbl, k11, k2 tog, p9, yo*.
Round 13: *P1, yo, p10, k13, p10, yo*.
Round 14: *P1, yo, p11, k2 tog tbl, k9, k2 tog, p11, yo*.

Rounds 15 to 23: Continue in pattern, decreasing at the end of each leaf on every other round, 4 times more. At the same time, continue to work the yo before and after the corner sts on each round.

Round 24: *P1, yo, p24, k3 tog tbl, p21, yo*.

Rounds 25 to 27: On these 3 rounds continue to work yo sts as before. P all sts on each side.

Round 28: *P1, yo, k24, k2 tog, k25, yo*.
Round 29: *P1, yo, (k2 tog, yo) 25 times, k2 tog, yo*.
Round 30: *P1, yo, k53, yo*.

Rounds 31 and 32: Continue to work yo sts at corners as before; p all sts on each side [60 sts on each needle].

Round 33: *P1, yo, p28, p2 tog, p29, yo*.
Round 34: *P1, yo, (k2 tog, yo) 29 times, k2 tog, yo*.
Round 35: K this round, continuing to work the yo sts at the corners.

Rounds 36, 37, and 38: P these 3 rounds, continuing to work the yo sts at the corners.

Bind off evenly on 4 sides. Using the same yarn and a tapestry needle, sew a cross stitch in the center hole.

ARAN KNITTING

Aran knitting originated on the Isle of Aran, a fishing community off the coast of Ireland. Folklore indicates that individual families designed combinations of different motifs or patterns for sweaters. Each member of the family then wore the sweater design, in the same manner as a family crest. It is said that these sweaters were used to identify fishermen who died or were hurt at sea.

The traditional yarn used to knit an Aran sweater is a natural-color heavy wool, oiled with lanolin to make it waterproof.

Some Aran patterns have been handed down from generation to generation and are as popular today as when the fishermen wore them. The true Aran sweater pattern is a combination of patterns and cables on a purl ground. The design begins with a center panel, with vertical pattern strips repeated on each side. These strips are separated by a few knit or purl stitches for better definition. The standard combinations include moss stitch, cables in many variations, zigzags, popcorns, and diamond repeats. You are limited only by your imagination in creating an Aran original.

KNITTING MACHINES

The knitting machine cannot be separated from hand knitting, any more than you can separate the sewing machine from sewing. It is another wonderful tool to be added to the list of aids available to the knitter.

Most people think of the knitting machine as part of the future for the hand knitter. The future is now; the knitting machine has arrived.

The first knitting machines that produced a stitch similar to those we know today was invented in the eighteenth century. After World War II, the first knitting machines imported into the United States were single-bed machines that offered little more than stockinette stitch. A few attachments gave the machine knit-and-purl capability. The manufacturers stressed the concept of speed, and the public was intrigued with the idea of knitting a sweater in a few hours. Unfortunately, the price was high, and the machine was viewed as an industrial item adapted in size for home use. The knitting machine was not ready for the average knitter, and the public was not technically oriented toward the knitting machine.

We have changed. In our age, complex computers have become part of our daily lives. Our children play with them before they learn to read and use them in elementary school. We find them in use from the office to the supermarket and even balance the family checkbook with a calculator. We have learned how to use the machine to enhance our lives.

The knitting machine has changed along with us. The creative side of knitting has joined forces with the current generation of knitting machines. You can now create lace and Fair Isle patterns, cable and tuck stitches, single and double knits, ribbing, multi-colored patterns, and with punch cards or computers even complex charted designs. With the turn of a dial and the press of a button you can truly be a creative machine knitter.

Knitter with basic knitting machine

Two colors threaded in knitting machine

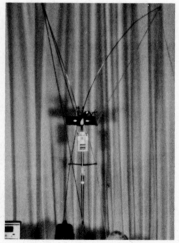

Closeup of Lock

Closeup of computer on knitting machine

Closeup of knitting machine with accessories

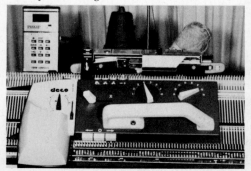

The latest knitting and craft magazines include knitting-machine directions in every issue. Yarn companies and, of course, knitting-machine manufacturers make directions available for every type of garment and accessory. Instructions are now in print for any desired item, from socks to bedspreads and afghans.

As a confirmed hand knitter, I met with many people involved with knitting machines. First on my research tour were the people who make and sell the machines. Their enthusiasm was contagious. The product is now capable and exciting; the possibilities are infinite. The most convincing salesperson was a seventy-year-old woman I met who took a twenty-year-old machine from under her bed, put it on the kitchen table, and ran off a simple shell sweater for me while I drank a cup of coffee.

I chose a machine to show for this book that could do everything offered to the hand-machine knitter by adding accessories as desired.

The knitting machine consists of a few basic parts. The *bed* contains a row of parallel needles with latched hooks that hold the yarn in place. These hooks are slipped into an up or down position to make contact with the yarn. The machine shown in the photographs has a built-in second bed that enables the machine to automatically work ribbing, tubular, and double knit stitches. Many manufacturers offer an optional second bed that will make the single-bed machine function as a *double-bed* unit. The *carriage* is pushed back and forth across the bed of needles on rails or tracks. Each *pass* or trip across the needles knits a complete row of stitches. The carriage also carries the yarn in one or more *eyelets*. Stitch sizing and other dials control the *cams* and several mechanical parts located inside the carriage. They determine the function to be performed by the machine such as a knit stitch, a missed stitch, or a tuck stitch that allows the yarn to go into the hook without knitting. Combinations of these functions will create an infinite number of stitches and patterns. Some machines can be fitted with a motorized carriage.

The *mast* or yarn holder feeds the yarn to the eyelet in the carriage under tension.

An optional charting system is available for most machines with an electronic scanner, perforated punch card, or sheet system. They are made with many precharted patterns or blank for original designing.

The most sophisticated machines now also offer a computer to calculate automatically instructions for the individual measurements and to stitch the pattern style programmed by the knitter. You can start with the simple basic single- or double-bed machine and work up to the computer that gives you all the instructions automatically as you knit.

You must take some time to learn and experiment with your machine. It is worth the effort.

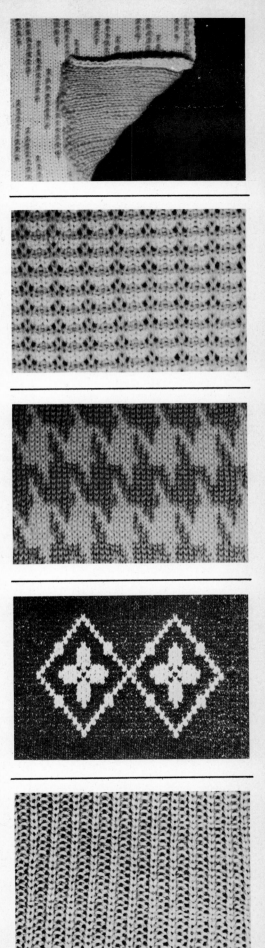

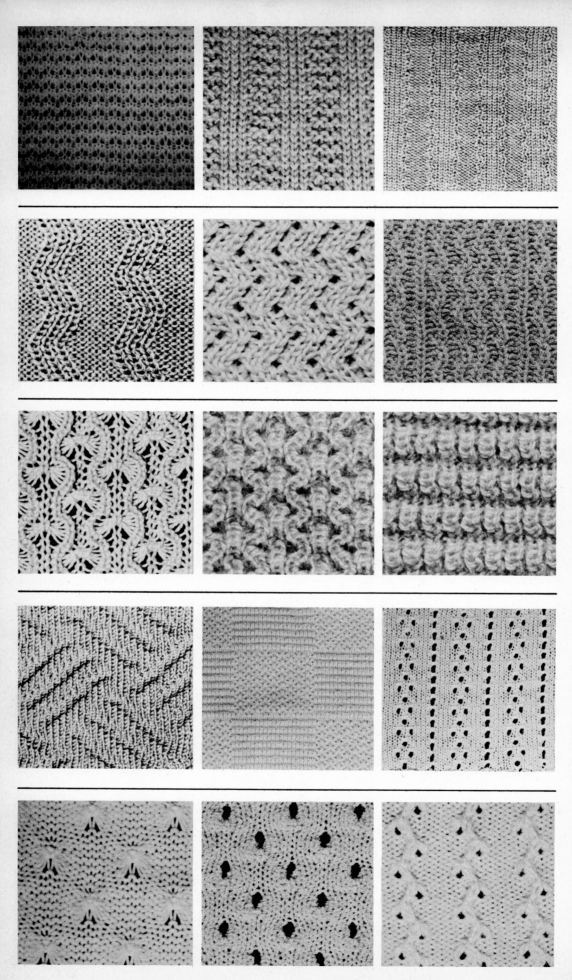

FINISHING

Professional finishing is the most important step to master when knitting a garment. The beautiful design and stitches, even tension, and hours of knitting are all lost if the garment is poorly assembled. This is when "homemade" becomes "handmade."

PRESSING AND BLOCKING

Step 1 Check the band or label on the ball of yarn to see if it can be pressed. If there is a picture of an iron with a slash or an X over it, *do not press this yarn.*

Step 2 If the label indicates that the yarn can be ironed, carefully press each knitted piece, using a damp or dry cloth as required. Take care not to stretch the piece or pull the pattern out of shape. Always press on the wrong side.

Hint: Press both sides of the front of a cardigan together by placing one on top of the other, right sides together. This will ensure that both parts are the exact same length and width. Sleeves should be pressed in the same way.

If the yarn cannot be pressed, carefully pin the pieces to a board, cover with a *damp* cloth, and leave a weight on top until they are dry and flat. This may take a day or two.

ASSEMBLY

Step 1 To join the pieces of a garment, place them together, right sides together.

Step 2 Pin each seam, being careful to match all curves or patterns.

Step 3 Baste the seams by hand.

Step 4 Sew by hand or machine. For hand sewing, use the same yarn used for knitting the garment. To sew by machine, match the thread to the yarn.

Step 5 To crochet the seams, use a matching yarn of lighter weight. With right sides together, work a row of double crochet through both thicknesses along the selvage edges. This technique makes a very neat, invisible seam.

Step 6 If you plan to line the garment, use the blocked pieces as a pattern for the lining. Coats, jackets, and skirts will keep their shape better if lined. Additional warmth will be added to a sweater or jacket by a lining and interlining.

Step 7 Sew on any borders or pockets after the garment is assembled.

Step 8 Sew buttons or zippers (see p. 48) in place last. The edge of the closure will retain a neat appearance if a length of ribbon is sewn to the wrong side at the edge before you add the buttons. The ribbon is also used before adding machine-made buttonholes.

CARE OF KNITTED GARMENTS

WASHING KNITTED GARMENTS

Washing

Any garment that might be damaged by machine washing should be washed by hand in cool water with a soap or detergent specially made for cool-water use.

First put the knitted piece in a net bag. This will help prevent snags. You can wash knits without a bag if you are very careful.

Dip or swirl the bag gently in the water-soap mixture. Carefully squeeze the bag to remove the soiled water. Repeat this procedure several times, until the water remains fairly clear. If the garment is very soiled the water-soap mixture may have to be changed two or three times.

Rinsing

Now rinse the knitted piece several times in clear cool water. Remember to squeeze the bag gently—never wring the garment. The rinse water will have to be changed several times. Remove excess water by rolling the knitted piece, still in the bag, in a soft cotton towel.

Drying

Remove the garment from the bag and place on a fresh towel, supported by a flat surface or, ideally, on a hammock. Do not put a sweater on a hanger. A hanger will not support the weight of the garment and will leave the knitted piece stretched out of shape. *Never* put any wool knit in a dryer, near an open flame, or in direct sunshine. It will shrink, mat, and fade.

Ironing

Woolen knitted garments can be ironed with a damp pressing cloth with the iron set on permanent press. Always press on the wrong side.

Synthetic yarns or mixtures should never be pressed. The heat of an iron can mark some of these fibers with a permanent line or crease. Some synthetic fibers have a low melting point and will melt or fuse together. It is safer to put the synthetic-yarn knit on a flat surface, covered with a dry towel. Secure the garment to the towel with rustproof pins and cover it with a second towel, dampened with cold water. Put a flat board over the second towel and weight it down firmly with some heavy objects or books. Let the garment dry naturally.

Dry Cleaning

Many people prefer to have their knitted garments professionally dry-cleaned. Always check the band from the yarn to be sure that dry cleaning is indicated. It is helpful to take the band from the yarn to the dry cleaner's along with the garment. They can usually determine from the fiber content listed on the band if a special process is needed.

Storage

A knitted garment should never be stored without being washed or cleaned first. Fresh stains are easier to remove. Moths are attracted to the smallest, most invisible stains and can destroy your knits very quickly.

The safest way to store a knitted garment is to put it, neatly folded, on a shelf or in a ventilated plastic bag. Moisture can form in a sealed plastic bag, and the knitted piece can develop mildew. A few holes punched in the bag will allow the proper circulation of air around the knit. Throw in a few moth balls or flakes when a long or seasonal storage is planned.

Some experts have recommended the padded hanger as a safe method of storing knitted garments. Its use is debatable.

INDEX OF STITCHES

BOBBLE STITCHES

SLIP STITCH PATTERNS

CROSSED STITCHES

TUNISIAN KNITTING STITCHES

PULLED LOOP PATTERNS

#7

*With permission, Needlepoint Plaids by Marion Broome Pakula. Published by Crown Publishers, Inc.